Theresa Foy DiGeronimo, M.Ed.

How to **Talk** to **Your Adult Children** About **Really Important Things**

Specific Questions and Answers and Useful Things to Say

JOSSEY-BASS
A Wiley Company
www.josseybass.com

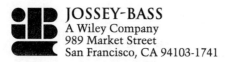

JOSSEY-BASS
A Wiley Company
989 Market Street
San Francisco, CA 94103-1741

www.josseybass.com

Jossey-Bass books and products are available through most bookstores. To contact Jossey-Bass directly, call (888) 378-2537, fax to (800) 605-2665, or visit our website at www.josseybass.com.

Substantial discounts on bulk quantities of Jossey-Bass books are available to corporations, professional associations, and other organizations. For details and discount information, contact the special sales department at Jossey-Bass.

We at Jossey-Bass strive to use the most environmentally sensitive paper stocks available to us. Our publications are printed on acid-free recycled stock whenever possible, and our paper always meets or exceeds minimum GPO and EPA requirements.

Library of Congress Cataloging-in-Publication Data

DiGeronimo, Theresa Foy.
   How to talk to your adult children about really important things : specific questions and answers and useful things to say / Theresa Foy DiGeronimo.—1st ed.
      p. cm.
   Includes bibliographical references.
   ISBN 0–7879–5614–7
   1. Parent and adult child. 2. Communication in the family.
3. Adult children—Psychology. I. Title.
   HQ755.86 .D54 2002
   306.874—dc21   2001003954

FIRST EDITION
PB Printing   10 9 8 7 6 5 4 3 2 1

Contents

Acknowledgments

I would like to thank my editor, Alan Rinzler, for his ongoing support and help. I am also indebted to the professional guidance from editors Amy Scott and Lasell Whipple.

I would like to acknowledge the following people who enthusiastically offered their time and insights to give me their expert point of view:

Robert K. Doyle, CPA, PFS
Spoor, Doyle & Associates
St. Petersburg, Florida

Barbara Ensor, Ph.D.
Baltimore, Maryland

L. Mickey Fenzel, Ph.D.
Loyola College
Baltimore, Maryland

Donald K. Freedheim, Ph.D.
Case Western Reserve University
Cleveland, Ohio

Gail M. Gross, Ph.D.
Houston, Texas

Jeff and Debra Jay
Grosse Pointe Farms, Michigan

Anthony P. Jurich, Ph.D.
Kansas State University
Manhattan, Kansas

Andrea Kay
Cincinnati, Ohio

Noelle C. Nelson, Ph.D.
Malibu, California

Les Parrott, Ph.D.
Seattle Pacific University
Seattle, Washington

Alen J. Salerian, M.D.
Washington, D.C.

Esta Soler
Executive Director, Family Violence Prevention Fund
San Francisco, California

Paula Stanley
Radford University
Radford, Virginia

Catherine Tuerk, M.A., R.N., C.S.
Washington, D.C. 20015

Marion L. Usher, Ph.D.
Washington, D.C.

Patricia E. Wicks, Ph.D., FPPR
Wicks Psychological Services
Omaha, Nebraska

To Matt, my adult child and new best friend, who is always willing to listen, even when he disagrees

Introduction

When our children were young, we parents had all the answers. There were rules, and there were right and wrong ways of doing things. We take turns. We go to bed at a certain hour. We do homework right after dinner. But now things have changed. Our way of doing things may not be their way. Our rules may no longer be the rules they live by. Our viewpoint may be different from theirs. There are now limits on our responsibility and authority, and so we cannot always talk to them as the parent. In fact, that responsibility and authority legally ended when they turned eighteen.

But that doesn't mean we can no longer give our children advice and the benefit of our experience—*if* we are able to change the dynamics of the relationship. To talk to our adult children and still make an impact, we have to remember that our roles have changed. Now we need to learn how to give advice to our children as we would to a friend—as a way to help them see another point of view, mix it with their own, and make their own decisions. We also need to find that place between being controlling and being completely distant where we can hold back and let our children stand on their own two feet and make decisions independent of our input, yet still share in their excitement and concerns.

Once we accept this role change, we'll find that we need to stop and think before instinctively reacting as a parent to an adult child who says something like, "I'm thinking about changing jobs. What do you think?" The challenge here is to resist the urge to jump in with an immediate solution or dictate. We have to think carefully before we use controlling words like *should*, *must*, and *ought* that shift the dynamics of the conversation back to a parent-child exchange.

The goal of this book is to help you talk to your adult children as you would a friend. Ask for the details. Be a good listener. Offer tempered advice like, "If I were in your situation, this is what I would do, but you need to decide what's best for you, not for me." This is how we build a mature relationship with our children and, we hope, become good friends in the end.

The key to making this happen is to show respect for our adult children: respect for their hobbies, talents, career ambitions, significant others, and them as individuals separate from us. Keep the following general guidelines in mind to help you do this when you talk to your adult kids:

- Trust your children. Let them know it.
- Show confidence in their ability to run their own lives.
- Encourage them to set and pursue their own goals.
- Offer emotional support.
- Acknowledge and praise their accomplishments.
- Listen first; advise later.
- Be loving if they stumble, and share with them stories of when you stumbled.

Of course, the way we talk to our adult children and the subjects we talk about are based in large part on the communication patterns we have established over the years. What kind of communication habits have you developed with your adult children? Some families are extremely open; they talk about everything from sex to politics, and there is a strong, respectful give and take of information. Other families are built on a hierarchical system in which the parents are the authorities and they do the talking and their children (no matter how old) do all the listening. Other families drift apart emotionally when the children grow up and move out; they rarely talk about important matters at all.

Whatever your situation, the chapters in this book can help you open up a dialogue that will keep you in touch with your adult children. This is the start of building a new, mature relationship with your adult child based on mutual love and respect. Before long, you'll find that your new best friend is your own child. What a wonderful thing!

Theresa Foy DiGeronimo
Hawthorne, New Jersey

PART ONE

Life Topics

Alternative Lifestyles

"We all have to find our own way in life, but it's hard for parents to allow children the freedom and support to do that if they choose an unfamiliar path."
Paula Stanley, marriage and family counselor

What is an alternative lifestyle? In its simplest terms, it is any lifestyle that's not the same as yours. If you have raised your child in a traditional nuclear family and he decides to remain single and adopt a child, that's alternative. If you have always worked a nine-to-five job and your adult child becomes a freelance photographer who works all hours around the clock on a very unpredictable schedule, that's alternative. If you have lived your life competing in the corporate rat race and your child decides to live in a spiritual commune, that's alternative. Choosing a different political party, a different religion, or a marriage partner of a different race are all alternative lifestyle choices.

When adult children choose alternative lifestyles, it can be very difficult for parents to understand and accept these decisions. It is these decisions that make us stare down the fact that our children are separate from us. They do not exist solely to please us or repay us. They are adults with hopes, dreams, and desires that have nothing to do with us. Coming to grips with these facts is not always easy.

We all have a set of conscious or unconscious expectations and hopes for our children that can get crushed when they choose another path. But it is especially difficult to accept a child's alternative lifestyle if you have been an authoritarian parent. If you have raised your children to give you unquestioning obedience and have attempted to shape their behavior according to precise and absolute standards of conduct, it will be very hard now to back off and watch them make what you may view as a mistake. If your child is a parent pleaser, you may still be able to order him or her to adopt a lifestyle that pleases you, but in that case, you may end up with an unhappy adult who is unable to make important decisions independent of "daddy and mommy." If you attempt to order an adult child who is independent minded to choose a certain lifestyle, you'll have a battle on your hands that no one will win. In the past, you may have been able to make your kids see things your way by using psychological control tactics like domination, persuasion, manipulation, and emotional threats, but now that your child is an adult, these methods can tear a family apart.

To avoid the family battles that can erupt over alternative lifestyle choices, you'll need to ask yourself some hard questions and be honest about the answers. For starters, ask yourself, "What do I want to happen after I talk with my child about his lifestyle decision?" Would you say, "I want him to see he's wrong, and I want him to live the life that I think is good for him"? Of course, when it's phrased that way, you might say, "No, that's not what I mean." But be honest with yourself. What is your real goal? In your heart, you probably know that you cannot tell your grown children how to live, what career path to follow, whom to marry or not marry, how much money to make, or how to nurture their spiritual life. Given those facts, again ask yourself what you want to happen when you talk to your child.

All you can realistically do is express your feelings, encourage your child at to least listen to your point of view, and work hard to keep the lines of communication open. In the end, your adult child needs to know that you care about him and value his ability to make his own choices.

The goal of this chapter is to help you talk with your adult children so you can maintain a relationship that honors and respects them as they are, regardless of their ideological differences or lifestyle choices.

WHY TALK ABOUT ALTERNATIVE LIFESTYLES

When adult children choose a lifestyle that upsets their parents, the subject needs to be talked about in ways that will help everyone live with the decision. *Talking* does not mean yelling, crying, or ridiculing. It does not mean slamming doors, making threats, or falling into a war of silence. *Talking* means creating a safe environment where you can both state your feelings, your hopes, and your fears. It means sharing points of view with an open mind and working to find a point of agreement or understanding so you can both live in peace and maintain family ties.

When you talk to your adult children about their lifestyle choices, you open up the possibility that you may learn something. Of course, you are most comfortable in the lifestyle you have chosen for yourself (and would naturally love your children to choose also), but there are others out there that you might find interesting when you are willing to listen and learn. Talking brings an openness to your relationship with your adult child that allows both of you to learn from each other and grow with one another.

Sometimes you need to talk to your adult children about lifestyle choices because you believe they are dangerous to their mental or physical well-being. In that case, the only way you can help your child more objectively see the problem and perhaps change course is to talk about it.

Whether you want to support a lifestyle or encourage a change in lifestyle, the consequences of not talking can be quite dramatic. It is not unheard of for an adult child who does not "respect" his or her parents by living the life they choose to be totally isolated from the family. Children have moved away and never made contact again. Some keep in touch, but the relationship is forever tense and strained. Some parents who cannot accept their children's lifestyle become strangers to their grandchildren. Without ongoing dialogue, the situation gets worse and worse. Feelings of disappointment turn into anger and rejection. Not talking is painful for everyone. Talking in a rational, adult manner opens up the possibility for a more loving, compassionate, and respectful relationship with your adult child. Learning how to talk to one another about lifestyle differences without argument or criticism, while maintaining an attitude of honor and respect, is the first step toward building a strong and lasting relationship with your adult child. Talking helps you show that you respect the person even when you can't respect the choice.

WHEN TO TALK ABOUT ALTERNATIVE LIFESTYLES

The decision to live an alternative lifestyle is a big one in your adult child's life that does not necessarily call for a one-time, sit-down discussion. Your talks with your adult children should be ongoing throughout various points of the decision-making process and continue throughout a lifetime.

You should talk to your adult children:

- When they are thinking about an alternative lifestyle
- When they announce a decision about a lifestyle choice
- Over the course of your lifetime

Talk When Your Child Is Thinking About an Alternative Lifestyle.
Steve had always been a quiet and introspective kid, so his mother, Clara, wasn't surprised when he told her about his meditation and yoga classes. But as time went on, she realized that he was in the process of making a major lifestyle decision. It seemed that his teacher ran a spiritual community (that sounded like a cult to his mother), and Steve was thinking of subletting his apartment and moving into this community group home. He was no longer going to services at the church where he was a parishioner because "my teacher says there is no god in the heavens—only the god we each create within ourselves." Clara's first reaction was to sit her son down and do whatever she had to do to save his soul and his life. She hoped there was still time to talk some sense into him.

If your child has been dropping hints that maybe he or she will make a lifestyle choice that you might not approve of, you too will probably feel the need to talk some sense into him. Some parents try to "save" their children by doing research and sending them literature, bringing in "experts" to talk them out of their plans, and having siblings and other family and friends call to help the child make the "right" choice. Whoa! If an adult child were not sure of what to do before this barrage, he will surely choose the road less traveled once his family jumps on his back. Don't put your child in the position of having to prove he's right before he's even sure what he thinks.

Instead, you'll have more opportunity to help your child think through the choice and exert some influence if you stay away from the "I know what's best for you" conversation. Instead, this is the time to begin a dialogue in which you can communicate that you are interested in understanding his situation and are willing to help him think this through if he feels comfortable talking about it with you (as explained later in this chapter).

Talk When Your Adult Child Announces a Decision About a Lifestyle Choice. The call came early on a Saturday morning. Trisha began meekly, "Mom, Dad. I'm calling to let you know that I've dropped out of college, and I've joined this really great band. We play every night and are making some really good money already. We're renting an apartment, and I just love it! I know you're not going to be happy about this, but it's what I need to do right now."

How do parents respond to this? Obviously, this is a life decision that they will want to talk about with their daughter—but maybe not right away. If they respond immediately, there's a good chance they will begin to argue, threaten, or criticize. No good will come of that. At this point, the parents' emotional reaction is bound to insult and alienate the adult child. As soon as she realizes that everything she says is going to be met with strong negativity, she will avoid telling her parents anything in the future.

A lifestyle choice that upsets you is best discussed when you are ready to talk without heightened emotions that can get in the way. If you attempt to talk when you are feeling extremely angry or even panicked, for example, it's unlikely that you'll be able to have a rational conversation. A lifestyle is a long-term event. Nothing will change if you wait a few days or even weeks until you feel calm enough to talk about it adult to adult. Your goal is to have a conversation that will allow both of you to share feelings, explain motives, and talk about the future. Wait until you can do that without yelling or crying.

Talk over a Lifetime. Twenty years ago, Kate, whose family is staunchly Roman Catholic, married Josh, a Jewish man. "For the first five years of our marriage," remembers Kate, "my mother would call me before every Catholic holiday and ask if I wanted to go to mass with her. She just couldn't get it that Josh and I were not 'religious.' Then we both joined a local nondenominational church, and slowly, over time, my parents, and Josh's as well, began to accept our choice. They started asking questions about our beliefs and the services we attended. We actually talk a lot about our church now and have even enjoyed the company of our parents at several of our church functions." It has taken a long time, but this family has learned to respect each other and interact as loving adults.

The conversations about alternative lifestyles are not a one-time event that is a big crisis. They are conversations that communicate caring, concern, and love. Over and over again, they say, "I think about you a lot. How are you today?"

WHAT YOU SHOULD TALK ABOUT

If your adult child chooses an alternative lifestyle that you find undesirable, of course this will be upsetting to you. But the way you express this upset has a lot to do with the kind of conversation you can have with your child on the subject and the way your relationship will grow or die. You might be able to engage in a constructive conversation with your adult child by thinking about the conversation you would have if you were talking to a friend who told you he or she was going to make a drastic lifestyle change. In that case, you could probably be less self-centered and emotional and focus instead on your friend's decision and the reasons for it. You would ask questions that would help you better understand rather than blame. You would try to be helpful rather than judgmental. You would be able to keep your own insecurities out of the dialogue (for example, "Did I do something to deserve this?"). You might also feel an obligation to try to persuade your friend out of this decision, doing all you can to help her see all sides but realizing in the end that the decision is her decision.

Doing this isn't easy or simple, and it will not diminish the difficulty of the situation. There's no doubt that it will be difficult to have an adult conversation when your heart tells you that your adult child is acting like a five year old who needs to be sent to his room until he matures. But to have any hope of continuing a sound relationship with your adult children who choose alternative lifestyles, you'll need to try very hard to treat them as the adults they are.

Breaking the Ice

When you strongly disagree with your adult child, the best approach to the initial conversations is one that is the exact opposite of what your gut may tell you. If you immediately go on the attack, or forcefully plead your case, or insist that your children listen to reason before you've heard their point of view, it's likely that they will put up their defenses and the verbal battles begin. And some adult children withdraw and tell you no more of their plans. In this situation, you're in the dark; you have no idea of what's going on and therefore no opportunity to have any influence at all.

Instead of rushing in with your own feelings and opinions, hold back and let your child do most of the talking. Good listening skills can best break the ice on this subject and give you the information you need to have a productive adult-to-adult conversation.

Marion had been a nurse before her marriage, but once her daughter was born, she stopped working outside the home and became a full-time mother. When her daughter grew up and moved out on her own, Marion returned to work at a local hospital, where she had the wonderful experience of being present at the birth of her first grandson. But soon the joy of having her first grandchild was crushed when she learned that her daughter planed to leave the baby in day care when he turned six weeks old so she could return to work. This is breaking Marion's heart. She wants her grandchild to have a full-time mother and can't believe her daughter can hand this infant over to the care of strangers. "After all I sacrificed to give her a good home, how can she be so selfish and deny her daughter the same kind of upbringing that she had?"

The only way Marion will get an honest and open answer to this question is to tell her daughter how she feels, and then sit back and listen. Even when we're sure we know why our children are making certain lifestyle decisions (assumed selfishness, in this case), it's worth the effort to hold back and let the adult child do the talking. This takes listening skills that admittedly are not always easy to use.

It is difficult to be a good listener when your adult children are saying things you don't want to hear. You're anxious to jump in and set them straight. You want them to know how you feel about this before they get the idea that you approve. But one of the most effective communication strategies you can use when talking about alternative lifestyles is one that lets your adult children initially do most of the talking. If you can hold your tongue, you send the message, "I care about what you are saying. I think your words have value. I want to understand you." When your adult children believe you care, they'll be more inclined to open up and share their feelings and beliefs. We in turn are drawn into this honest discussion. Even in this time of differing opinions, this can't help but create better and healthier relationships.

Good listening skills will also improve your ability to persuade, motivate, influence, and connect with your adult children. Every time you go into a conversation about their choice of lifestyle looking to do all the talking and quickly convincing them of your viewpoint, you'll both end up feeling dissatisfied with that conversation. But if you can learn to hold back a bit and work harder at listening to your child and ask questions that will draw him or her out, the conversation will give you the information you're after without resorting to a shouting match.

When you listen to your child's plans, you say loud and clear (without even speaking) that you're interested and you want to understand and know more. This attitude will help the two of you build a relationship of mutual respect that acknowledges an opposing opinion, takes it into consideration, and makes a decision with all facts and feelings in mind.

To be a good listener, you'll need to practice some active listening skills. Following are a few that can get you started:

Be Open-Minded. When you're close-minded, you just can't hear anything that doesn't agree with your beliefs. There's little need to listen when you already know it all or have a strong prejudice or bias toward the subject. But when you allow yourself to be more open and say, "Okay, I might be able to take something useful from this conversation," then you'll be able to listen with interest. This frame of mind allows you to be mentally curious rather than intellectually and emotionally shut down.

Instead of saying, "I know what you're going to say, and I have to tell you that you're wrong about this."
You might say, "If you give me more information, maybe I'll find that I need to rethink my opinion."
You might say, "Teach me. I want to know."
You might say, "That's a good point. I never thought about that."

Be Patient. Active listening means letting another person fully explain a thought, even a negative one, before responding. This isn't easy to do. It's hard to hold back and let another person finish a story or make a point that you emphatically disagree with—but that's exactly what you have to do. Focus on what your child is saying rather than jumping ahead and anticipating what you think is going to be said. Turn yourself down and wait: don't interrupt, don't finish her sentences, and don't push ahead in the direction you want the conversation to go.

Instead of saying, "Wait right there. That just isn't true. I don't know how you can say that."
You might say, "Go on. Tell me more."
You might say, "I want to hear your point of view on this."
You might say, "I'm not sure I agree with you, but tell me more about this."

Be Positive. We seem to be programmed to defend ourselves against even the slightest negative or critical comment. You'll undoubtedly have trouble listening after your adult child says, "You don't know what you're talking about!" or, "You have no idea how I feel." You'll be able to keep the conversation going after you've been "attacked" only if you can put aside the defensive mind-set that makes you want to fire back, "*You're* wrong!" Where can the conversation constructively go from there? Rather than throw out a defensive block, it's far better to ask for clarification and listen some more.

Instead of saying, "You're wrong!"
You might say, "Why do you say that?"
You might say, "Help me to understand better."
You might say, "I'll take what you've said into consideration."

This kind of response doesn't mean you agree with your child; it just means that you acknowledge that you have heard what she said. This is a major accomplishment.

Clarify. A powerful listening skill is the habit of clarifying information by using the techniques of paraphrasing and asking questions. Sometimes before you respond, it's a good idea to make sure that what you're hearing is what is really being said.

You might say, "So what you're saying is . . ."
You might say, "Did you say this is not a cult?"
You might say, "What did you mean when you said . . .?"

Consider the Adult Child's Point of View. When you're conversing, there is a tremendous difference between hearing something from your own point of view and hearing it from the speaker's point of view. What feelings are behind your child's words? What experiences have brought him to choose this lifestyle? When you try to understand from your child's point of view, you are acknowledging that there may be another side of the story, another way of looking at the world. You have to consider that just because something does not support the established family value system does not mean it is wrong.

Instead of saying, "What were you thinking? That's the dumbest thing I ever heard!"
You might say, "Why do you think this is a good idea?"

This response lets your child talk and explain his or her point of view and feelings. You may still disagree, but at least you'll have the information you need to help you see all sides, and you'll have time to formulate a more tempered response.

Use Verbal Prompts. As you listen, your facial expressions and the sounds you make can signal your feelings sometimes better than your words do. If you roll your eyes, exhale heavily, look at the floor, click your tongue, or shake your head while your child is talking, you'll cut short any meaningful conversation that might have taken place. But if you instead use facial expressions and verbal prompts to show you are engaged in the conversation and are following along, you'll encourage your child to keep talking. Try to use good eye contact, and lean forward toward your child. Nod your head to show understanding. Occasionally, use encouragers like, "Really?" "Hmmm," or "Is that so?" These send the message that you are truly interested in what is being said and want to know more. If you can do this, you'll find that your children will be more willing to open up and share their beliefs and feelings with you.

Addressing Specific Issues

You may have a million questions you want to ask your adult child about this alternative lifestyle idea. How will you support yourself? Whose idea was this? Where will you live? What about your job? And so on. But asking these questions right off the bat puts you on unsteady terrain. At first, you will be feeling a mix of negative emotions, and your adult child is going to be defensive right from the start. So before you get into the details, take some time to step back. Use these tactics to diffuse some of the tension so you can have productive conversations:

- Take time to think.
- Identify your emotions and talk in "I" statements.
- Be curious, not demanding.
- Talk about consequences.
- Agree to disagree.

Take Time to Think. When you first hear of your adult child's decision to lead an alternative lifestyle, Rule No. 1 is to bite your tongue. The first words out of your mouth can set the tone for all further conversations, and your first reaction is more than likely to be a negative one: "Have you gone mad?" "You must be out of your mind!" "I knew those friends of yours were no good." In fact, these kinds of reactions are what your child is expecting, and she will have set up her defenses against an authoritarian response that tells her what she should and shouldn't do. Surprise her, and set the stage for an adult conversation where each person can express what's important to him or her but still have room to make personal decisions:

Instead of saying, "I can't believe you're doing this."
You might say, "I'm not sure I understand. Tell me more about it."

Instead of saying, "You're crazy."
You might say, "This is unexpected. I need time to think about this."

Don't even try to give words to your feelings right away. The best thing you can do for your relationship with your child is to say that you need time to mull this over. During this time, you can do some soul searching to find out how you really feel and why. This understanding will help you talk without ranting during your next conversations.

Identify Your Emotions and Talk in "I" Statements. When you talk to your adult children about your feelings, own those feelings. Saying, "I feel concerned," is very different and sets up a different communication dynamic than saying, "You're wrong."

Before you form your "I" statements, take time to think about how you feel. When children choose alternative lifestyles, there is usually a whole mix of feelings involved that need to be identified and talked about. This was certainly the case for Jim.

Jim had spent his life climbing the corporate ladder and amassing great wealth. He sent his son to the best private schools and made sure he went to an Ivy League college. As graduation approached, Jim talked to a few well-placed colleagues about bringing his son into the firm, and he began to gather information about graduate schools. His son, however, had other plans. He skipped his college graduation ceremony and headed south to join an artist's colony and raise herbs. Naturally, Jim was astounded. Sure, he knew his son liked to paint some pictures, and he had planted a great vegetable garden in the back yard every year since he was a little kid, but to make a living out of that? To Jim, this was just a ridiculous, foolish, and immature decision.

Before Jim sits down to talk to his son, he needs to know what it is that bothers him so much. Is he angry? Confused? Worried? Embarrassed? Disappointed? Guilty? Maybe a combination of all of these? Take a look at the possible ways Jim can talk to his son about his feelings by rethinking his gut reactions and turning them into "I" statements. (The son's responses that are given are ideal reactions, but they give you an idea of how "I" statements allow dialogue to continue rather than the slam-the-door-shut style so often used in these situations.)

If Jim feels angry:

Instead of saying, "You're throwing all your education right down the toilet."
He might say, "I feel angry because it seems that all your education is going to waste."

This gives Jim's son a chance to understand his father's point of view and respond in a way that will help his father see another side to the story.

Jim's son may say, "Dad, I have a degree in business that I will need to make this struggling artists' group successful. They need me to set it up as a real business, set achievable business goals, and create a realistic marketing plan. I think I can create an Internet sales and marketing plan that will really get this enterprise off the ground. Thanks to my education, I really think I can do this."

If Jim feels confused:

Instead of saying, "I can't believe you can turn your back on the opportunity to work for a reputable company with a great future!"
He might say, "I feel confused by your decision to work in an area with an uncertain future instead of with my firm, where you know for sure that you can make a very good living."

This response tells Jim's son that his father needs more information about his sense of ambition and achievement.

Jim's son may say, "It's exactly because this is a business challenge that I want to do it. I want to know that I can take a struggling business that I love and turn it into something successful."

If Jim feels worried:

Instead of saying, "You'll never be able to make a living out of this."
He might say, "I'm concerned that you won't have enough money to live on."

This response tells Jim's son that he cares about him and wants the best for him.

The son may say, "I'm concerned about that too, but I'm willing to take that risk. I'm going to apply for a small business loan to get us off the ground, and then I'm going to work hard to make sure we don't default on the loan. If it fails, at least I tried, and that's what's important to me right now. I know I have my degree to fall back on and can get a corporate job if I need to, but first I need to give this a try."

If Jim feels embarrassed:

Instead of saying, "You're such an embarrassment! What will I tell my colleagues?"
He might say, "I have to admit that I feel embarrassed about telling my colleagues you're not going to work for the firm."

This response tells Jim's son that his father is being honest about his feelings and admits that the problem is his own, not his son's.

The son may say, "I'm sorry if I've caused you embarrassment. Why don't you just say that I've decided I'd like to make my own way in the business world?"

If Jim feels disappointment:

Instead of saying, "I had such high hopes for you. Now you're nothing but a big disappointment to me."

He might say, "I can't help but feel disappointed. I know you would be an asset to our company, and I guess I had my heart set on helping you establish yourself in the business."
The son may say, "I'm glad that you think so highly of me, and I'm sorry if I've let you down. But I plan to make you proud by turning this venture into a business success."

This is the power of "I" statements. They share your own feelings without putting the person you're talking to on the defensive. Before you talk, take time to find the reason behind your feelings, and then consider how you can explain that to your adult child in an honest and calm way.

Be Curious, Not Demanding. One important goal of having conversations with your adult child about lifestyle is to gain information. But if you begin with the third-degree style of questioning, you'll find yourself quickly shut out of the conversation. Instead, show your adult children that you want to understand by presenting an attitude of curiosity.

Instead of saying, "Are you going to be able to pay your bills?"
You might say, "Can you explain to me how this works financially."

Instead of saying, "This is an immature and just plain stupid decision."
You might say, "I'm not sure I understand what's in this for you. Can you explain to me the upside of this?"

Instead of saying, "I think you're making a mistake."
You might say, "I'm not sure I agree with you, but I'd like to understand you. Can you tell me more?"

When it comes to your adult child's thoughts, feelings, and needs, you really don't know it all. Be open and curious so you can get all the facts.

Talk About Consequences. When you've listened to your adult children's point of view and have a good idea of how they feel and why they've made this decision, then it's time to talk about the consequences of this decision and how you will relate to each other if, in the end, you don't share the same opinion.

Your adult children are going to live their lives the way that makes the most sense to them, but that doesn't mean they can't use some help. Your conversations with them can help them think things through and explore possible outcomes. In the excitement of a new venture, we all need an objective voice to help us see the reality of our plans. The key is to do this without being judgmental. One way is to avoid close-ended questions that require only yes or no answers. Instead, use a series of open-ended questions that ask your child to think and explain:

Instead of saying, "Have you thought this through?"
You might say, "Where do you see yourself a year from now?"

Instead of saying, "Do you know what you're getting in to?"
You might say, "Have you talked to others who have done this? What is their experience?"

Instead of saying, "Can you understand why I would think this isn't going to work?"
You might say, "I don't understand how this is going to work out. Can you explain how this decision is good for you?"

Instead of saying, "Do you expect to come crawling back to me when this whole thing falls apart?"
You might say, "What will you do if you find that this isn't exactly what you thought it would be?"

These kinds of questions help another person think out loud. They bring up points for consideration and exploration without being judgmental or accusatory. These kinds of questions will help you talk to your adult children without telling them what to do.

Agree to Disagree. It is possible that you will never understand or approve of your adult child's lifestyle choice. How will you handle that? Again, this depends on your goal. If it is very important to you that your adult child does what you say, then you may break off all communication until he does what you want. If it is very important to you that your adult child learn this life lesson the hard way, then you may withdraw all help and support until she falls on her face. Or it may be important to you that your child knows you disapprove of the lifestyle but still love him. If this is the case, then all you need to do is say so.

You might say, "I don't agree with the way you're living your life, but I still respect you as a person and respect your right to make your own decisions."

The important thing at this juncture is to focus on your child's positive qualities and on the love that you feel for her. This is a way of supporting your adult child without supporting her ideas and opinions:

You might say, "You are a very spiritual and creative person, and I have always admired that in you."
You might say, "You are an intelligent person. I'm sure you've thought this through and feel this is best for you."
You might say, "You have a lot of enthusiasm and energy to offer the world. I love you for that."

When you agree to disagree, you put this subject behind you. You are then free to talk about other topics and other aspects of your lives. You both respect the decision that has been made and move on to building a strong parent-child relationship that does not hinge on this one aspect of life. You can finally recognize that just because something is different, that doesn't make it bad—unless, of course, your child has fallen into a clearly dangerous situation.

Dangerous Situations

Some alternative lifestyles can be viewed as dangerous to one's health and well-being, especially so-called cults. If you suspect your adult child has joined a cult, naturally you worry that he has joined a group similar to the most infamous cults—the Heaven's Gate extraterrestrial cult (which in 1997 ordered the mass suicide of thirty-nine of its members), the People's Temple group led by Jim Jones (which staged the notorious mass murder-suicides), and David Koresh's Branch Davidians (who met a fiery death in Waco, Texas)—that grab headlines and shock us. But the majority of "cults" are harmless groups focused on an appealing life philosophy. There are neo-Christian religious cults; Hindu and Eastern religious cults; occult witchcraft and satanic cults; mystical cults; Zen and other Sino-Japanese philosophical-mystical cults; racial cults; flying saucer and outer space cults; psychological or psychotherapeutic cults; political cults; and self-help, self-improvement, and lifestyle systems cults. If your adult child decides to join such a group, you will need to meet this challenge to your own beliefs with lots of patience, active listening, love—and the ability to gauge when the group poses a real danger and intervention is required.

Like most other lifestyle choices adult children make, it is unlikely that a parent can force his or her own morals and beliefs on the adult child. Experts have found that it is usually far better to find out about this lifestyle in a way that communicates respect for his right to choose his own life. This will have a direct influence on the quality of information you receive. Be direct and clear about

your interest. Explain that you'd feel much better if you had a better understanding of the life he wants to lead. Ask him to tell you
about some of the other members of the group. Ask him to explain
the group's philosophy and how he feels about that philosophy. Ask
about his health and his general satisfaction with his life path. If you
can ask without showing signs of subtle criticism or anger, you'll find
that your adult child is anxious to help you understand his choice.

In *When Sons and Daughters Choose Alternative Lifestyles*,
Marianna Caplan reminds us, "When going through the sometimes
painful cycle of adjusting to new circumstances, which your adult
child's choices are demanding of you, it is easy to feel victimized by
the onslaught of feelings and reactions you may be experiencing at
this time. It is important to remember that your son's or daughter's
choice to lead an alternative lifestyle is not about you, it is about
him or her. This choice is his attempt to find a way of life that
expresses his need for meaning and fulfillment, not an attempt to
bring unnecessary pain to your life."

When you talk to your adult child about her lifestyle, keep
these tips in mind. They will help you have meaningful conversations that do not dissolve into screaming matches in which no
one wins:

- Do not attack the group. Avoid name calling and emphasis on
  the word *cult*. This approach can be counterproductive if your
  child is just beginning to be swayed by the group's propaganda,
  which can include impressive, high-sounding philosophies and
  goals.
- Remain open-minded, and avoid rigid positions. Views that
  may sound heretical are not necessarily destructive.
- Discuss the situation in a sincere, respectful, nonjudgmental,
  and consistent manner. If you cry or attack, your child will

shut down, and you'll have no chance of staying involved in her life.

- Without being deceitful or underhanded, find out as much as you can about the group so that you can discuss it intelligently. See if you can get the group's own literature to learn from, or call the American Family Foundation listed in the Resources section at the end of this chapter. It has information on some specific groups.

Although you may not like the fact that your adult child has taken up with some kind of religious, psychotherapeutic, or lifestyle group, in most cases the choice is not dangerous to your child's well-being. But in some cases, there is reason for real concern and sometimes more forceful action. You should consider intervention if your child's group matches the following description of dangerous cults:

- The cult is a group that violates the rights of its members, harms them through abusive techniques of mind control, and distinguishes itself from a normal social or religious group by subjecting its members to physical, mental, or financial deprivation or deception to keep them in the group.
- The cult members have banded together under a charismatic leader.
- The group leaders use deceptive tactics in their indoctrination process, including trance induction, prolonged chanting, detailed interrogations, long lectures, long sermons, or exhausting work routines, in order to suppress doubts and enforce compliance.
- The cult wants its members to give money, work for free, beg, and recruit new members.
- The cult requires mindless devotion that severs ties with family and friends, creates total dependence on the group for

identity, and imposes high exit costs by creating phobias of harm, failure, and personal isolation.

If your adult child has joined this kind of cult, you may choose to step in and try to "save" her, but you will need professional help. Your child needs a therapist who is trained in the process of mind control and brainwashing and has knowledge of the specific content of the group to which your child belongs so as to identify the language system, buzzwords, philosophical teachings, specific types of behavioral control used, and the demands to which your adult child has been subjected.

If you cannot convince your child to meet with a trained therapist, you might consider a process called deprogramming. Deprogrammers are agents of force hired by parents to rescue their children. The deprogrammer will "kidnap" the child and isolate him or her in order to deprogram the effects of brainwashing. This is a highly controversial method and has landed many families in court on legal charges, but it is an option. Even after deprogramming, it may be difficult to keep your child from returning to the cult. Your words of love and encouragement are no match for the cult's psychological tactics. Get professional help by calling the American Family Foundation. Staff will refer you to a therapist in your area trained in exit counseling.

IN THE END

When your children choose an alternative lifestyle, you have choices to make. You can create a relationship that is filled with resentment and tension; you can completely alienate your child; or you can keep an open mind, respect his or her adulthood, and emerge with a deeper understanding and stronger relationship as a result. The choice you make will be conveyed in the way you talk to your adult children.

RESOURCES

American Family Foundation
(914) 533-5420; www.csj.org.

EXPERT HELP

This chapter has been written with the expert help of marriage and family therapist Paula Stanley, Ph.D., an associate professor in the Counselor Education Department at Radford University in Virginia. She has written numerous articles in professional journals, including "The Tie That Blinds: Understanding Intergenerational Conflict Within a Moral Development Framework," *Family Journal: Counseling and Therapy for Couples and Families* (1998). She is the coauthor, with William Watson Purkey, of *The Inviting School Treasury: 1001 Ways to Invite School Success* (Brookfield Printing, 1997) and *Invitational Teaching, Learning, and Living* (National Education Association, 1991).

Careers

"No one has a magic wand to help an adult child find the perfect career path. The real answers to career problems lie within our children. All we can do is give them support and guidance when they're open to it. But ultimately this is their life, and they must find their own answers."

Andrea Kay, career consultant and author

Career choice is a common subject of family conversations. There's so much to talk about! What's a good career? How do you find the job that's right for you? How do you deal with an incompetent boss? How do you balance work and family life? When should you ask for a raise? What's more important: high salary or good benefits? The topics for discussion are countless and can fill many dinner conversations.

Talking to an adult child about the one career path that will lead to fulfillment and happiness for a lifetime is a more sensitive issue that requires much tact, patience, and understanding. From early on in life, some parents steer their sons and daughters toward the family business. Others instill in them pride in the legacy of five generations of police officers (or teachers, or politicians, or something else). Some are determined to make sure their offspring do not repeat their own mistakes. Many believe that all life's miseries will be spared the child who goes to college. Others worry that the family name will be marred if a child chooses a job without social status. For these and many, many other reasons, it's very difficult to separate our own needs and desires from those of our adult children when we talk about their future in the work world.

This chapter takes a close look at these conversations. It will help you consider why it is, and sometimes it is not, appropriate to talk about the subject of careers. It will highlight the times when this subject is most likely to come up. And it will give you some tips about how to talk to your adult children about their careers without being judgmental, critical, or dictatorial.

WHY TALK ABOUT CAREERS

Career choice can be a delicate subject. How your adult children choose to make a living is their choice as adults, not your choice. But unfortunately, the world is full of examples of major family battles that erupt over an adult child's career choice. We've all heard the stories about the young man who was disowned when he refused to join his father in the family business. We've heard about the family who pressures their children to choose occupations in fields like law, medicine, or business. We all also know stories about young people who bend to the pressure to please their parents and then live with regret and personal disappointment for the rest of their lives. Some young adults do both: they earn the college degree their parents insist on and then turn away and follow their heart into another field. In all of these situations, feelings are hurt, misunderstandings abound, and mistakes are made over and over again.

Talking to our adult children about their careers in an open, nonjudgmental, and noncritical fashion can avoid these pitfalls of career selection. You should talk to your adult children from a giving, helpful place that encourages them to look inside themselves to find the right direction. If you can do this, your children will stay open to your advice and may even find that you have information that can help them. They'll understand that you are an important member of their support group. And they'll realize that you love them and may be able to help them answer some difficult questions.

This doesn't mean you necessarily know best or that you have the right to insist on any career choice, but it does mean that you can play a vital support role by listening, asking thoughtful questions, and steering your children in the direction where they are most likely to find their own answers.

WHEN TO TALK ABOUT CAREERS

As informal conversation, the subject of careers is something you can talk about any time at all. Talk about your own job. Talk about your friends' jobs. Talk about the economy and its effect on the job market. These small-talk conversations open the door to more personal conversations about your adult child's career. But there are also specific moments in time when it's a good idea to explore the subject on a deeper level. You can talk about your adult child's career:

- When your adult children ask for advice
- When it's time to choose a career
- When you see signs of trouble
- When their job troubles affect your life

Talk When Your Adult Children Ask for Advice. Talking about the work world in general is one thing. Talking about your adult child's field of work is another; this is a private matter. How much your children earn and when they become eligible for a promotion or bonus are pieces of information that they may or may not want to share with you. This is why the best time to talk about our adult children's career is when they bring up the subject. But keep in mind that this is not an invitation to lecture, dictate, judge, or criticize. You will have much more impact if you use empathic communication skills to listen and understand your child's point of view before you offer your own.

Talk When It's Time to Choose a Career. It is appropriate for you to bring up the subject at a time when your children are choosing career paths. This might be when they are graduating from high school, college, or graduate school; choosing a college major; or leaving one job and looking for another. These life experiences make the timing right for a sit-down conversation about options, risks, and benefits, but keep in mind that your adult children always have the right to make these decisions without your input if they choose. You can offer your opinion. You can give advice based on your own experiences. And you can offer help and support. But that doesn't mean your adult child will listen. Do you remember the old saying: "You can lead a horse to water, but you can't make him drink"? Keep this in mind when you try to steer your adult child to a certain career: you can't make her choose that path.

Talk When You See Signs of Trouble. Because you are your child's parent, you will naturally want to talk to him when you feel that he is not doing what he should be or could be doing. For example, you will have a lot to say when you feel your child is underemployed as a waiter when he has a degree in computer science. You'll want to help when she is frequently fired or regularly job hopping. You may feel the need to step in when you see him repeating the same mistakes. In these kinds of circumstances, there is a parental need to solve the problem. But there is a very fine line here between helping and meddling. You have to use well-sharpened communication tools to offer help without dictating what to do.

Talk When Their Job Troubles Affect Your Life. An adult child's career circumstances can sometimes affect parents' lives as well. If this happens, those parents certainly have a right to speak up. If your underemployed child, for example, continues to be financially dependent on you, you have a right talk to him about finding a better-paying job. If your unemployed child moves into your home and you are now supporting him, you have every right to talk about his plans for future employment. When career problems cause family tension, everyone needs to sit down and explain his or her feelings, expectations, and needs. In these situations, open and honest communication is the first step toward a solution.

WHAT YOU SHOULD TALK ABOUT

There are many topics surrounding the subject of careers that you might talk to your adult children about. The details of these conversations depend on your child's problems, questions, and needs. But the key to having any conversation on this subject is the ability to put aside your "I know best" hat and keep an open mind that respects your child's adulthood.

Breaking the Ice
Your child's career is a subject that can be discussed anytime in casual conversation. If you can avoid being critical or judgmental, you can always ask, "How's work?" This makes work a subject you can both easily talk about without your necessarily offering advice.

When you know you'll be spending some time with your adult child, think of some open-ended questions you can ask to start the conversation. Open-ended questions are the kind that ask for information and cannot be answered with a quick yes or no or other one-word answer. Avoid close-ended questions that stop a conversation dead and leave you little room to continue the discussion. Notice that the first example of each of the following dialogue starters asks a close-end question (requiring only a yes or no answer). A simple rephrasing of the same idea opens the door to conversation.

Instead of saying, "Do you like your job?"
You might say, "What is one thing you especially like about your job?"

Instead of saying, "Do you get along with your boss?"
You might say, "What's your boss like?"

Instead of saying, "Do you think you'll stay with this company?"
You might say, "What are your future plans with this company?"

Instead of saying, "Are you happy with the career you chose?"
You might say, "How have your expectations matched up with the reality of your job?"

Instead of saying, "Is your job some kind of management job?"
You might say, "Tell me what you do on your job."

Instead of saying, "Do you think it's good for your career to stay at home three days a week?"
You might say, "Tell me about your job. I don't understand how telecommuting works."

Get the idea? Open-ended questions are a good communication tool that can help you get a conversation going.

Addressing Specific Issues

It is frustrating when your children won't listen to you, even when you're *sure* you know best. It can be infuriating when you can see why your children are having a hard time in their career, but they don't want to talk about it. You may inevitably throw up your hands and say, "He doesn't want to hear what I have to say. He thinks he knows it all."

If you find that your adult child won't listen to you, you might be able to bridge that communication gap by talking less and listening more. If you can do this, you'll be able to understand the problem better. You'll know if your own experiences are similar, and therefore appropriate to talk about, or if your perspective is very different. You'll also better know if your advice will be considered helpful or intrusive.

The following sample dialogue starters will give you an idea of how you can get a conversation going that will open the doors of communication so you can offer your help and guidance if your child wants it. You might want to talk about:

- The "right" career
- Personal strengths and weaknesses
- Your observations
- Following in your footsteps
- What they "might" do, not what they "should" do
- The definition of success

Talk About the "Right" Career. The fact is that your idea of the "right" career may not be the same as your child's. Your job then isn't to make him see that you're right and he's wrong; your job is to have a conversation that offers your point of view as something to think about—and nothing more. You may feel that the amount of the paycheck is the most important thing to consider. Or you may feel that the opportunity for advancement within the company is vital. You may think that job security or benefits are what matter most. There's nothing right or wrong about these beliefs; they are simply your point of view. State any career-related information you like, as long as you don't make it sound that there's no other sane alternate view:

Instead of saying, "This job would be perfect for you."
You might say, "Do you think you'd like this job?"

Instead of saying, "Don't choose that career; it's too hard to make a good living."
You might say, "I have a good friend who is a stockbroker. He says that on-line trading is killing his business, and he doesn't think young brokers coming into the business have a chance of surviving. That's something you should think about. Would you like to talk to my friend about it?"

Instead of saying, "You don't want to take that job; you're qualified for other jobs that pay much more."
You might say, "Why do you think that's the best job for you?"

Talk About Personal Strengths and Weaknesses.   Patty was miserable in her career as a computer programmer. "Honey," said her mom, "do you know what it is about your job that you don't like?"

"It's so boring," complained Patty. "I just sit there all day long; sometimes I just can't stand the thought of going to work. But I guess that's why they call it 'work.'"

"Well," began her mom, "there's really no reason to be stuck in a job that doesn't fit you. With your outgoing personality and your love of challenges, this may not be the right place for you. There's nothing wrong with changing career direction and finding work that is more suited to you. Maybe there's even something in the computer field where you would be able to work more directly with other people."

"I think you're right," said Patty. "I hadn't thought about it before, but I really would rather work with people. And I need to feel challenged. I'm going to start looking around. Thanks. I guess I just needed someone to point out the obvious!"

If, like Patty, your child seems to be unhappy on the job, or is having trouble choosing a profession, or seems to be job hopping looking for just the right job, you can help him or her identify the personal strengths and characteristics that fit certain careers and make for a good and lasting fit. In fact, one of the goals of a good job counselor is to find a match between a person's individual characteristics and skills and the job. Asking your child to think about how his or her personality matches certain career options and isn't appropriate for others (without being critical or judgmental) is very helpful:

Instead of saying, "You always totally overreact when someone criticizes your work. You just can't work for anyone."
You might say, "I've noticed that you sometimes react poorly to authority and being told what to do. Why do you think that is?"

Instead of saying, "I could have told you that you would never be able to get along with all those complaining customers."
You might say, "Maybe this job just doesn't suit your temperament. Have you thought about what kind of position you would feel happier in?"

Instead of saying, "You shouldn't work with computers. You'll go crazy if you have to sit down all day."

You might say, "Would you say you'd be happier in a job where you can move around and interact with people, or would you rather be in a quiet environment working with computers and files?"

Instead of saying, "You're very stubborn. It's going to be hard to find a job where you can fit in."

You might say, "If someone were to describe your personality, what would that person say? What job would be a good match for your personality?"

Talk About Your Observations. William was completely out of ideas about how to help his twenty-eight-year-old son, Randy. Although he was very smart and had a degree in economics from a good university, Randy was fired from one job after another. But, he said, it was never his fault, and his list of excuses was extensive: the boss was unreasonable; the company was going under; his coworkers were stupid; the hours were too long.

Finally, against his better judgment, Randy's father gave him a job in his own company. But Randy was not effective there either. His supervisors complained that he was always late to work, never finished a project, and made excuses for everything. William had tried lecturing Randy on the qualities of a good employee, but Randy would just roll his eyes and walk out of the room. This situation was frustrating to William because he knew his son was a responsible person and his work habits had always been much better than this. Something was very wrong, but William just couldn't put his finger on what it was.

Finally, William changed tactics. He took his son out to dinner and asked him to do the talking. "Tell me," William said, "what you want to do with your life and what you think you'll need to do to accomplish that. In the past, I think I've done too much of the talking about your career. I'd be very interested in hearing your side of the story." Randy was stunned. His father had never asked his opinion before. After a hesitant start, he confessed to his dad that he had a small business on the side creating and selling acrylic artwork, but it often interfered with his ability to work in the corporate world. "You're right Dad," smiled Randy. "I just don't fit in your company. Would you be terribly disappointed if I quit and opened up my own art studio?"

William's gut feeling that Randy was not living up to his potential was right. But he just couldn't put the facts together until he gave his son the opportunity to open up and talk about what was important to him. This conversation changed Randy's life and made both him and his dad much happier.

It's true that you know your child perhaps better than he knows himself. You may be well aware of his personal habits or characteristics that make it difficult for him to keep a job. You may be aware that she has trouble getting along with people. You may feel sure that his inability to take direction or criticism is the reason he quits so many jobs. Or you may understand why her obsessive-compulsive or perfectionist personality makes it very difficult for her to tolerate incompetent people and ineffective or nonproductive work environments. However, if you point out these shortcomings, you may sound overly critical, and that would end any possibility of a constructive conversation.

When you share these kinds of observations with your adult child, be direct about your concern, and leave the door open for further conversation. You don't have to solve the problem, just put the subject on the table for consideration.

Instead of saying, "What's the matter with you? Why can't you just keep your mouth shut and do your job so you don't get fired all the time?"

You might say, "I've noticed that you seem to be having trouble staying in one job for very long. If you ever want to talk about that, I'm here to listen."

Instead of saying, "You're driving me crazy. Why are you always complaining about your job? If you think you're underemployed, why don't you do something about it?"

You might say, "I'm really concerned about what's happening to you and your career. You seem so unhappy. I'm open to talking about what's going on. Are you?"

Instead of saying, "You just don't get it. You can't start at the top. You have to pay some dues."

You might say, "Many young people want to use their talents where they are most valued: at the top. But in my experience, it seems that most people have to work their way up to that position. Do you think you can do this?"

Instead of saying, "You're in bad shape. You need professional help!"

You might say, "I'm concerned about you. I'd like to offer to pay for some career consulting to help you find your way. Would you like to give that a try?"

Talk About Following in Your Footsteps.   Claire was a pediatric nurse. She enjoyed her work and was thrilled when her four-year-old daughter, Kim, said she wanted to be a nurse too. Every birthday and holiday, Kim received another nurse doll and pretend nursing kit. She wrapped all her stuffed animals in bandages and regularly checked their temperature and blood pressure. She dressed up as a nurse almost every Halloween. She always told her teachers she was going to be a nurse like her mother.

Claire didn't push her daughter in this direction; she didn't insist that she become a nurse. It was just something that everyone assumed over the years. No one ever sat down and talked about what nurses do all day and the kind of training, skills, aptitudes, and even personality required for the job. It was something Kim said she wanted when she was a preschooler, and it stuck.

Finally, Kim went off to college to study nursing. What a shock! As she skimmed through her first-semester math, science, and anatomy textbooks, it dawned on her for the first time that she was headed in the wrong direction. "I have always hated the math and sciences," she now recalls. "I struggled through these classes in high school and never wanted to do another dissection again in my life." Although Kim worried that her mother would be disappointed, she felt a stronger obligation to herself and switched her major to elementary education. "I feel like that move saved me from a major mistake. My mom was really understanding and said she just wanted me to be happy. I wish we had talked about this sooner."

Whether the plan to follow in a parent's footsteps is spoken or implied, it is a subject that should be talked about in a way that lets the adult child express feelings and opinions. It should never be assumed or dictated that an adult child will fall in line with a family career.

Instead of saying, "I'm printing up the business cards with your name on them. They'll be ready for you as soon as you graduate."
You might say, "Would you like to join the family business when you graduate?"

Instead of saying, "For three generations, the men in our family have all been doctors. I'm looking forward to adding your name to this proud family list."
You might say, "What career do you want to pursue?"

Instead of saying, "I've contacted my friends at the admissions office. You're certain to be accepted at the law school there."
You might say, "I have friends at the admissions office I can contact if you'd like to go to law school. Let me know if you'd like me to make a few calls."

Instead of saying, "I'm counting on you to take over the family business."
You might say, "You know this business means a lot to me, and I would be very proud to hand it over to you. But I want you to follow your own dreams. So think about what you want to do, and let me know if I should add your name to the door. Either way, I will be proud of you."

Talk About What They "Might" Do, Not What They "Should" Do.
Hank entered college to major in journalism, but after his freshman year, he was unsure what exactly he wanted to do in this field of study. His dad reminded Hank that in high school, he had been very good at doing special events for the student council and at getting people to work together to make things happen. He reminded his son about the time he worked so hard to put together a video highlighting the need for a new soccer field that he presented with great enthusiasm to the administration. "Have you thought," asked his father, "about staying in journalism but putting your emphasis on public relations?" Hank's dad wasn't telling him what he *should* do; he was offering some insights and a course that he *might* follow. Hank thought it was a great idea and went back to school eager to try this new direction.

This is a conversation that gave Hank an idea without a dictate. Hank's father knows his son's strengths and knows what has made him feel accomplished in the past. He used this information to talk with his son without telling him what he *should* do.

Like any career counselor would do, it's best to help your child figure out where her strengths lie and to think about her own interests and desires. As the parent who knows this person very well, you have the opportunity to share insights (like, "You have always liked to do things that help other people," or, "You're a very good problem solver"). You can offer these insights without telling your child what she *should* do.

Instead of saying, "With your personality, you should be a salesperson."
You might say, "I think you're a very outgoing person who loves to be with people. Let's think of jobs that let you do that."

Instead of saying, "You've been sewing your own clothes for years. You should be a fashion designer."
You might say, "With your talent for sewing and great fashion sense, you might find fashion design very interesting."

Instead of saying, "You're good at math and science; you should be an engineer."
You might say, "You're good at math and science. Have you ever thought about being an engineer?"

Instead of saying, "This is what you should do."
You might say, "I can't tell you what to do, but I can tell you how I see the situation. I'd like you to listen, think about what I say, and then tell me what you think."

Instead of saying, "I've been in the business world all my life, and I know a thing or two more than you do. You should be applying to M.B.A. programs right now."

You might say, "If you can take my perspective and mix it with your own feelings, maybe you'll come out with a pretty solid feeling for what you want to do. I've seen many young people with an M.B.A. degree get ahead much faster than those without that degree. Have you ever thought of going back to school?"

Instead of saying, "You should ask for a raise."
You might say, "Does your company offer opportunities for promotion? Are you interested in moving to a different position?"

Talk About the Definition of Success. We all want our children to be "successful." But we frequently stumble over the meaning of this word. Does *successful* mean having a corner office, a spouse, two kids, and a house in the suburbs? Does *successful* mean living a life that you can brag to your friends about? Does *successful* mean doing what you think is productive and worthwhile? When you talk to your adult children about their career success, it's important to recognize that you may be talking about two very different definitions of success.

Barry is a good example of this confusion over what constitutes a "successful" career. Barry went to college to study sociology. His father thought that this was an unusual major for someone who was planning to go to medical school, but he didn't push the issue at the time. He figured that good grades in any field could get him into medical school. But upon graduation, Barry shocked his father by announcing that he had taken a job with the state welfare department. "You've got to be kidding!" yelled his father. "You can't seriously think you want to spend the rest of your life earning hardly any money taking care of poor people who don't even want you involved in their lives. I'm telling you, you'll regret this if you don't get smart right now and apply to medical school."

Barry's father defined *success* as having money and status. Barry defined *success* as personal fulfillment. These two may never see eye to eye, but if they can at least sit down and talk, they may discover that they both feel helping others is a valuable career goal. Barry has simply chosen a way to do this that is different from the one his father had in mind.

We want our children to be stable and secure. We want them to be settled and happy. When we don't feel that our kids have a job that meets our definition of *stable* and *secure*, we want to jump in and turn them in the "right" direction. But be careful about how much you focus on what "I want." Start to listen to find out what they want.

Instead of saying, "I want you to be successful."
You might say, "What does *success* mean to you?"

Instead of saying, "I want you to be financially secure."
You might say, "Is financial security an important issue for you?"

Instead of saying, "I want you to be happy."
You might say, "Are you open to talking about what it is that would make you happy in your career?"

IN THE END

When you talk to your adult children about their careers, try not to slip into a judgmental or critical role. It won't help your child find the right career path when you accuse, blame, or point out faults and shortcomings—quick ways to end the conversation. Your children are adults now. If you start to treat them like children, they won't respect what you're saying—even when you're right!

RESOURCES

If your child is having trouble finding the right career and your conversations are not proving helpful, the objective help of a career counselor might be useful. To find a career counselor, you can look in the telephone book. You can also search the Internet using the term *career counselor*. Or you can contact the National Career Development Association for a referral to a local career counselor:

National Career Development Association
c/o Creative Management Alliance
10820 East Forty-Fifth Street, Suite 210
Tulsa, OK 74146
(918) 663–7060; toll-free: (866) 367–6232; fax: (918) 663–7058

EXPERT CONSULTANT

Andrea Kay is a career consultant, executive coach, and syndicated columnist and author who advises seasoned professionals, as well as those just starting careers, on workplace and career dilemmas. Among her books on career and workplace issues are *Greener Pastures: How to Find a Job in Another Place* (St. Martin's Press, 1999), *Resumés That Will Get You the Job You Want* (Betterway Books, 1997), and *Interview Strategies That Will Get You the Job You Want* (Betterway Books, 1996). As host of a live radio talk show, "Ask Andrea," she answers questions from listeners with career dilemmas. You can read more about her work on her Web site, www.andreakay.com.

Your Adult Child's Homosexuality

"It's up to you to educate yourself about homosexuality and the gay community. This is an ongoing process of personal growth that you can share with your children. Show them that you are interested in their lives and care about the joys and difficulties they experience. Being gay may not be a person's first choice, but it is not second best."

Catherine Tuerk, counselor and psychotherapist

M y thirty-year-old son is gay, and he and his partner have adopted two absolutely precious little boys," says Mariam very proudly. "I just couldn't be happier for him and his family, but when I think back over his childhood, I'm filled with shame. My husband, Isaac, and I are liberal, intelligent people who with the best of intentions made his life miserable because we just couldn't stand the thought that he might become a homosexual. We foolishly equated being gay with being unhappy.

"We noticed from the very beginning that Jacob was different. He was very gentle, very timid, and had lots of separation problems. As time went on, we noticed that he preferred 'girl' toys. This made us uncomfortable, but we didn't do anything about it until he went to nursery school. His teacher called us in to tell us that Jacob was not playing with the trucks and balls but instead wanted to spend all his time in the dress-up area.

"This frightened us so much that we consulted a child psychiatrist, who said he had an aggression problem and needed to be pushed into 'boy' play. This is when we became gender cops, censoring all of his play and interests. We signed him up for soccer, and my husband even became the soccer coach so he could more directly get Jacob into the action. Although my son was a good athlete, he hated this game with all the physical bumping and kicking, so no matter how much we pushed him, he just hung back and watched.

"This didn't do anything to change Jacob's preference for 'girl' activities, so after two years of soccer, the psychiatrist suggested he try karate to toughen him up. This so-called expert actually told us that if we didn't help Jacob get over his anxiety and learn to be more aggressive, he might become gay. Well, Jacob went on to win an award in karate, but it was in the form division—the dance part. We laugh about it now, but I feel so awful when I think of how hard my son tried to be tough to please us. This gentle soul found no joy in punching and kicking, but he kept trying.

"When karate failed to change him, we subjected this eight-year-old boy to psychoanalysis four times a week for four years so that he would not be gay. That's how afraid we were of this possibility. It was at this time that Jacob wrote in his journal, 'I hate myself; I think I'm a fag.' He didn't know what that meant, but he did know it was bad. Then when Jacob was twelve, I heard of a therapist who believed that people are born with their sexual orientation. Hearing this was like an epiphany for me. Finally, something that made sense!

"This therapist's theory was called the 'sissy boy syndrome'; at that time it claimed that 80 percent of sissy boys grow up to be gay [today the number is believed to be much higher]. So although being born gay made more sense to us and offered some degree of comfort, we were also comforted by the hope that our son would be one of the 20 percent who would *not* become gay. Later, during his teens, Jacob went back to his therapist on his own, and unbeknown to us, the therapist tried to scare him out of being gay by telling him horrifying stories about gay men and their sexual habits. It was an awful time for all of us. Looking back, we are extremely lucky that our child did not attempt suicide, which is thought to be two to three times higher for gay teens than for the general teen population.

"But at first we thought it worked. When Jacob was going off to college, he told us that he knew we had been very worried about his being gay, and there was a time when he did have some confusion about his sexual orientation. 'But you don't have to worry anymore,' he said. 'I don't want to be gay. I'm not gay. I'll never be gay.' Well, we were thrilled to hear this, but still we said, 'Whether you're gay or not, we will always love you.'

"During his junior year of college, Jacob came home and tested the truth of that statement. I confess that my husband and I were heartbroken when Jacob said, 'I now know for sure what I guess we all suspected for years. I'm gay. You always taught me to be honest, and I want to lead a truthful life.' It was as if someone called us up and said, 'Your son is dead.' I didn't get out of my pajamas for three days. It took me about a year to come back to life. At some point in that year, I reached a turning point when I called a support group called Parents, Family and Friends of Lesbians and Gays, and the woman on the other end of the line sounded happy. It hadn't occurred to me that people who have homosexual children could be happy—and I certainly was surprised to learn that gay and lesbian people can be happy too. After this year of learning and sharing, I began to realize that there is absolutely nothing wrong with my child—but there is something very wrong with the way our society views him.

"I still look back over Jacob's life and feel great sorrow. Because of our own fear and the ignorance of the mental health providers at that time, we abused our child and made his childhood miserable. For that, I will always be sorry. But I'm very glad that we have been able to talk this over and move forward to build a loving and supportive relationship."

Mariam's story is, sadly, a common one. It is often a long struggle through years of denial and false hopes before homosexual children arrive at a place where they can talk to their parents about their same-sex orientation. In fact, sexual orientation is not a subject that anyone wants to talk about. Heterosexual parents expect that their children will grow up, date members of the opposite sex, eventually become engaged, marry, and have children. But if your child is a homosexual, if he or she deviates from the expected pattern of sexual development, this expectation is shattered. In this case, silence often becomes a shield for shame, embarrassment, and denial.

Some parents may be absolutely unable to accept a homosexual child and will imagine him or her dead rather than deal with this change in the life they imagined. But if you want to keep your child in your life and want to continue to build a relationship with him or her, then it's a subject that can't be denied or ignored. Only when you make an effort to talk, listen, and understand will your child feel affirmed as a person and accepted as a member of the family.

This often is not easy. You will need to bring all the love, forbearance, courtesy, and patience you can muster to these discussions. You may need to hold your temper, watch your tongue, and think carefully before you speak, because this is an emotionally charged issue, and it's easy to say hurtful, cruel things that you don't really mean or that you will come to regret. You may not escape from these early discussions without pain. But you will find that you have a choice about whether that pain will destroy your relationship with your child, or whether you will use it to broaden and deepen the way you experience the joy of having a loving child. You may not believe it at first, but the challenge of talking to your child about his or her homosexuality is a valuable opportunity for growth in your life.

This chapter will help you understand why this is a subject you need to feel free to talk about, no matter what has happened in the past. It will help you see when the subject needs your attention. And it will help you know what to say to your adult children about being lesbian or gay.

WHY TALK ABOUT YOUR CHILD'S HOMOSEXUALITY

Barbara and her dad, Henry, were an inseparable team during her childhood. He loved his "little tomboy" and took her everywhere with him. He bragged to everyone who would listen about his only child's strong athletic abilities. Barbara was a standout three-sport high school athlete who had her dad's support every step of the way to earning a college softball scholarship. He didn't worry that Barbara never dated during high school, because he wanted her to focus on her studies and her sports anyway. He assumed that she kept her hair very short because it was easier to manage for sports; he never worried that she wouldn't wear dresses because he knew she had hated dressing up since she was little. Barbara could do no wrong in her dad's eyes. She meant everything to him.

While away at college, Barbara continued to make Henry proud. She excelled both in the classroom and on the field. But during this time, Barbara admitted something to herself that she wasn't sure her dad would approve of, something she had long suspected: she was a lesbian. This acknowledgment was good for Barbara, because it freed her from the uncertainty and anxiety that had plagued her high school years. She now had a loving partner; she was happy, relaxed, and fulfilled. But she worried about how this would affect her relationship with her father.

Over the semester break in her sophomore year, Barbara brought her friend home to meet her parents and to tell them of her sexual orientation. "Mom and Dad," said Barbara, "I know this will surprise you, but Kate and I love each other. We're lesbians, and we're hoping you'll be able to accept that."

After a few seconds of excruciating silence, Henry said, "You don't know what you're talking about. This is just a phase you're going through." He walked out of the room and refused to discuss the subject any further.

"That was five years ago," says Barbara. "My dad still won't talk about my sexual orientation. He'll talk about the weather and about the Yankees, but he won't talk about me, and I know he's uncomfortable even being in the same room with me. I've hurt him deeply because I've killed off the daughter he thought he had. So mostly I just stay away and I cry a lot because I miss his friendship and because I love him and I know he can no longer love me back."

This is an example of a wonderful parent-child relationship that has died because the parent won't, or can't, talk about the child's sexual orientation. This denial of his daughter's identity steals Henry's ability to enjoy her life *and* his own. Parents need to talk to their children about this sensitive and sometimes painful subject so that neither of them has to live with this incredible loss.

Sexual orientation is a very important issue. It has to do with who your child is. It is a major aspect of how we all identify ourselves. We are men or women, black or white, gay or straight. How can you love your child if you don't know who he or she is? It is likely that your child has been hiding his real self for years. Now that he is out, you can take this as an opportunity to get to know him as he really is. After all, if you do not know who your child is, you will not be able to share in the joy of his life.

You also need to talk to your child because she can be your teacher. Most parents of gay people are heterosexual, so they need the help of their children to understand this culture that is different from their own. When you listen and learn and explore the world of homosexuality together, you can then support your child's efforts to have a good life, and you can be an advocate to help other people understand. When you talk about homosexuality and learn about the culture, you can look at your child and see a wonderful human being rather than a second-class citizen. You'll be able to understand her and love her for herself. You will also learn that gay people have normal lives; they desire and find life partners and increasingly become parents.

Talking about your child's sexual identity can also strengthen your relationship with her. Pretending year after year that she is someone she is not creates an invisible wall between the two of you. It also reinforces the notion that homosexual unions are shameful. *There is nothing wrong or unnatural about being gay.* In fact, all of the mainstream professional organizations, representing more than 477,000 health and mental health professionals, have taken the position that homosexuality is not a mental disorder and there is no need for a "cure." If you cannot accept this, you unnecessarily deprive yourself of the great source of joy that your child could bring to your life.

Talking about this subject also strengthens your child's own sense of self-worth. Your child has taken a risk by revealing this side of himself to you. He has entrusted you with the knowledge of who he really is. Your effort to understand gives him a new sense of freedom and self-respect because now he no longer has to hide his real self.

Talking about your child's homosexuality can also help you grow as a person. This life experience is an opportunity for you to accept the fact that differences are not something to be afraid of, but rather something that can be enriching if you let down your guard and show a willingness to learn and grow. Talking openly about your adult child's same-sex orientation can be a vehicle for greater self-understanding. No doubt, the parents of homosexuals are presented with a personal challenge, but also with an opportunity to grow.

WHEN TO TALK ABOUT YOUR CHILD'S HOMOSEXUALITY

Sometimes the topic of your child's homosexuality drops out of the sky unexpectedly, and other times you have the opportunity to plan a sit-down conversation. Sometimes you will talk about same-sex orientation because your child brings up the subject; other times you may have issues or questions you want to broach with your child. This section looks at three common occasions for conversation:

- When you suspect that your child might be gay or lesbian
- When your gay or lesbian child comes out
- When it's about time to talk

Talk When You Suspect That Your Child Might Be Gay or Lesbian. "I have a strong feeling that my son is gay," Julie confided to her best friend. "You know how he's always been a little bit different from other boys, and now he's living in San Francisco and he is being very secretive about his male roommate. I've worried that he might be gay since he was about five years old; now I just feel that I'd like to get this out in the open, but I don't know if I should say anything. It breaks my heart to think that he might be afraid to tell me about his life, but I don't think I can bring up the subject without crying. I just don't know what to do."

If you are in Julie's situation, now is a good time to talk to your adult child about her sexual orientation. Most homosexuals believe that their parents were aware to some degree of gender variance, interests, and behaviors during their childhood. Girls who are "boy-like" are encouraged and even admired for their athletic and assertive traits, so their homosexuality is often a true surprise to the parents. But boys who are "girl-like" are of great concern to their parents for many years.

Some parents see that from an early age, their sons are gentler than other boys; they have interests that are not typically masculine; they avoid rough play and contact athletics; they have female friends. (Certainly it is not true that all gay men are effeminate, but some boys show these interests, and these are the ones who worry their parents.) About one-third of gay men remember their childhood as typically masculine, one-third remember being very gentle, and one-third remember being very gentle and having strong feminine interests. (Interestingly, one-fourth of straight men remember their childhood as being very gentle also.)

Many parents notice early signs of same-sex orientation in their children but deny it and put it out of their mind. Others worry excessively about it. Others rationalize and say, "Johnny acts like that because he has two sisters," or, "Johnny has an artistic personality."

When these kids become teens, they begin to label their differences as gay. Although some teens with same-sex orientation accept themselves and come out at this time, many others try to deny and hide their true self. They date people of the opposite sex; they act more like they're "supposed" to; they may even become homophobic and put down and ridicule homosexuals. Their parents at this point feel much better.

But then when these kids leave home for college or to set up their own households, the parents' worst fears become more evident. They'll notice that they don't date members of the opposite sex anymore. They dress "funny." Their friends all seem "gay" or "butch." They probably move far away and don't invite their parents to visit. How long can the family keep this secret going?

Parents who have these suspicions based on the evidence of their children's lives are usually afraid to say anything. Many want to protect themselves from the truth for as long as possible, while others feel they should wait until their children say something to them before they talk about the subject. However, experts agree that a parent who can broach this subject offers a great gift of love. Adult children are usually terrified to tell their parents about their sexual orientation. They often drop hints for years hoping their parents will catch on and say something. When they do, it's a great relief.

When Your Gay or Lesbian Child Comes Out. "I consider myself a pretty liberal and open-minded person," says Kimberly. "But I didn't make it easy for my son to tell me he was gay. When he came out to me, he was terrified. He was pure white, he was shaking, and he was choking back tears. It was awful for him. I guess the need for a parent's love and blessing and the need to avoid disappointing the parent is so strong at any age that making this 'confession' and risking that love and approval is a terribly difficult thing to do. I could see he was struggling, but at the same time, so was I. I just didn't know what to say."

The news that a child is a homosexual often lands like a bomb, no matter how much a parent may have suspected the possibility. The finality of this announcement makes it something that cannot be ignored with silence any longer. Some parents refuse to face the fact and continue to deny who their child is (and may do this for the rest of their lives), but most often when a gay child comes out to a parent, it's time to talk.

When It's About Time to Talk. "Derek told his mom and me about two years ago that he was gay," remembers Derek's dad, George. "We both took it very hard, but eventually we got on with life, and neither of us has ever brought up the subject again. I just don't know what to say, and so after we talk about the weather, it gets very awkward. I guess that's why we don't see Derek that often, and when we do we're all kind of tongue-tied."

It's time to talk to your adult child about his or her homosexuality if you've been avoiding the subject since the day you got the news. On some level, you may have accepted your child's sexual orientation, but if you can't talk about his or her life as a homosexual, this acceptance is similar to the way we accept things like taxes and floods. It's probably apparent to your child that you know you can't change it but you don't like it. If you don't know anything about your child's life, friends, social activities, and hopes and plans for the future, it's time to talk.

WHAT YOU SHOULD TALK ABOUT

The details of your conversations with your gay son or lesbian daughter are personal and private. This section looks at some large issues that most families grapple with, and it gives you some dialogue suggestions to help you get started. After that, your heart will lead the way.

Breaking the Ice

If you have heard from dependable people or have your own strong suspicions about your child's same-sex orientation, you might bring up the subject yourself. "But why," you might ask, "would anyone broach the subject of homosexuality if the child doesn't bring up the subject first?" The answer to this question is that if you don't, you will continue to live the lie of who your own child really is. If you don't, you will see the silences between you grow louder and longer. If you don't, you will have to continue to live in that twilight area between suspicion and knowledge. For the sake of their parent-child relationship and their own peace of mind, some parents take the risk to talk to their children about their suspicions.

You might say, "I saw a TV show last week about a woman who was a homosexual who couldn't talk to her parents about her sexual identity. So she lived a lie to save them the pain of this reality for forty years. I think this must have been so hard for her. This got me thinking that I wanted to tell you that I hope you understand that you can talk to me about anything at all. I may not like what you have to say sometimes, but I'd rather have things out in the open where we can try to understand them than have important secrets from each other."

You might say, "There's something that's been on my mind for a long time, and I need to talk to you about it. I have felt for a long time now that you might be living with a secret about your sexual orientation. I think this must be very hard for you to do, and so I just want you to know that you can talk to me about this any time. I also want you to know that I love you." (If your child, in fact, is not homosexual, he or she will either be amused or furious at your suggestion. Either way, you can state that you simply want your child to know that your love is unconditional.)

If talking about private matters has never been easy in your family, it might be easier to talk with your adult child about your concerns in a letter. A carefully worded letter with lots of reassurance and love is a wonderful way to express your feelings. The letter has to be humble; you need to acknowledge: "I don't know very much about this, but I love you and I'm willing to learn."

After you broach this subject, you need to give your son or daughter time to decide how to react. Remember that by adulthood, homosexuals are so conditioned to deny who they are to those closest to them that they may automatically say, "No! I'm not gay! Why would you say such a thing?" They may feel very ashamed of who they are and have internalized all of the negative stereotypes about being gay. Your words and your patience can help them overcome feelings of shame.

You might say, "I'm not accusing you of anything. I'm just saying that if that should be true, it's something that I hope you would feel you could talk to me about."

In a week or two, your child may come back and ask to have that conversation.

Addressing Specific Issues
The specific issues that you'll want to address really depend on your child and your family situation and your feelings. This chapter offers these conversation starters for some of the most common conversations:

- What to say when your child comes out
- What to say when you've calmed down
- What to say about your feelings
- What to say when you're sorry
- What to say before you shut the door

What to Say When Your Child Comes Out. It takes a great deal of courage for adult children to tell their parents about their same-sex orientation. They know that once the words are out, life changes for everyone in the family. Ideally they'd like us to say, "We're glad you told us. This information doesn't change our feelings for you, except perhaps to make us love you even more because we realize you went through some tough times alone when you discovered you were lesbian [gay]."

But that's rarely the reaction because parents have so many issues of their own to deal with. When your adult child first tells you, "I'm gay," this one brief statement can unnecessarily dash all your hopes and dreams for your child and future grandchildren. You will probably experience a wide range of feelings, including shock, confusion, and pain. This person you raised is suddenly a stranger.

That's why this is not the best time to talk. At that moment, it's very likely you will say things out of ignorance or shock that you don't mean. Your child has been thinking about this conversation for years; you need time to prepare yourself also.

Instead of saying, "Get out of my house. I can't even look at you."
Or, "What are you talking about? That's not true!" Or, "How could
you do this to me?"

You might say, "I need time to think this over. It's quite a shock to
me. We'll talk some more about this another time."

You might say, "I need some time to process this. I'm not going to say
anything right now for fear I'll say something I don't really mean.
What I need from you is some time, some resources, and some help."

What to Say When You've Calmed Down. When you've recov-
ered from the shock as much as you can (perhaps in a week or two),
contact your child and arrange to sit down and talk (if that's not
possible, set aside a quiet period for a long telephone conversation).
You don't have to memorize a speech or worry about what you're
going to say. This is your child's story; all you really need to do at
this point is listen. He or she has held this inside for so long that it
may be a great relief to give the experience words.

You might say, "I've been thinking a lot about what you told me, and
I have some questions. The answers might help me better understand you. What has it been like for you? When did you know you
were homosexual? How do you feel about this now?"

Homosexuality is a difficult subject to talk about because sex
is inherent in the topic, and that's private territory for anyone. So
don't push into personal issues. Questions like "When did you have
your first homosexual experience? With whom? How many partners
have you had? How do homosexuals have sex?" are intrusive and
rude. They violate privacy boundaries that we probably would not
violate with our heterosexual children.

You might say, "I have a lot of questions because I want to understand your life better. But if I should ask something that you feel is private, please say so."

What to Say About Your Feelings.   Your child may be so caught up in his feelings about this subject that he may forget that it arouses many feelings in you too. But you may need time to go through the typical stages of grief: (1) denial and isolation, (2) anger, (3) bargaining, (4) depression, and finally (5) acceptance and, hopefully, affirmation. This process will be easier on everyone if you work through your grief as a family facing, acknowledging, and sharing your true feelings and dealing with them realistically. Your child can't solve your emotional problems, but just talking about your feelings may help you put them in perspective. These conversations will also give your child the opportunity to talk about his or her own feelings. Some rather typical concerns and fears can be introduced with the following dialogue starters.

You might say, "I'm worried that you will have an unhappy life. But I'm learning that the only reason gay people sometimes lead a difficult life is because of the stigma that society has attached to that sexual orientation. Maybe, with your help, I can learn more about your culture and help other people to understand it as well."

You might say, "I want you to be surrounded with people who love you when you get older and I'm not around anymore. I guess I thought that that could happen only if you were married and had children. And so the thought of your being lonely worries me. I guess gay [lesbian] people have lifetime partners and families too."

You might say, "There are so many people who are prejudiced against homosexuals that I worry about your safety. Have you ever had to defend yourself against this kind of bias?"

You might say, "I know that male homosexuality is linked to AIDS, so of course this worries me. How do you feel about that?"

You might say, "I've heard that homosexuals are very promiscuous. I guess that's a stereotype, but I wonder if this is true. What do you think about that belief?"

You might say, "You know our religious faith doesn't accept homosexuality, and so I'm very concerned about that. How are you handling your spiritual life?"

If you are upset over your child's sexual identity for religious reasons, it may be especially hard for you to be understanding and accepting. Tell your child your concerns, and explain your beliefs. But remember that almost all religious denominations are rethinking their position on homosexuality, especially because it is now evident that homosexuality is biological in nature, much the same way as right- or left-handedness is. There are many subgroups of people among most religions who are totally affirming of homosexuals. These groups can help you and your child continue on as a valued member of that religious community—if he or she wants to do that.

Keep in mind that your religious despair is not necessarily your child's. Choosing a religious belief is a private matter for all adults. Many straight adult children turn away from the religious faith of their parents. Certainly, this upsets their parents, but in time they may come to understand and accept each other's point of view. This is no different for the parents of a homosexual child.

What to Say When You're Sorry. Like Mariam and Isaac, whose story was told at the opening of this chapter, many parents have forced their children into painful situations, hoping to mask their own fears of homosexuality. Others have said and done things that they later regret. Others have turned away from their children completely. With time, many of these parents find peace when they apologize for the hurt they have caused their children.

If you feel badly about the way you've handled things, the first thing you should do is let yourself off the hook; you are not a bad parent. Anger, denial, and tears are all very common reactions to loss and grief—the very emotions you are dealing with. So you don't have to beat yourself up about it. Give yourself time to adjust, to change your view of your child, to alter your dreams with a set of new dreams, and to learn more about homosexuality. While you're working on these things, you might think about using some of the following apologies.

You might say, "I know that most homosexuals struggle with their sexual identity for a long time before saying anything. I'm sure you have felt very alone in your life, and for that, I am very sorry."

You might say, "I am sorry for the way I reacted to your announcement. I still haven't learned exactly everything I need to know. But I do know that my initial reaction was painful to you, and for that I am sorry."

You might say, "I've been doing some reading, and I've come to realize that the world we live in is a better place because of the work of many same-sex-oriented people. I didn't realize that such accomplished people as Walt Whitman, Leonardo da Vinci, Michelangelo, Willa Cather, Edith Hamilton, and Tchaikovsky were all homosexuals. I realize too that you have a lot to offer the world, and I hope that I can support you in your efforts."

You might say, "I realize that many of my worries are unfounded. I see now that both homosexuals and heterosexuals can enjoy constructive and rewarding lives with full family-oriented lives. I'm sorry I didn't realize this at first."

What to Say Before You Shut the Door. It may happen that no matter how much you try, no matter how much you want to, you just can't talk openly with your child about his or her homosexuality. If this is the case, at least be honest about it and keep the door open. Ask yourself: What *can* I say? How far will I extend myself?

You might say, "For now, I do not want to talk about your homosexuality, but I do want to keep in touch with you. Can we do that?"

You might say, "I'd like to know about your job and your apartment and your vacations and things like that; I'm just not ready to talk about relationship issues. Is that okay with you for now?"

WHAT YOU SHOULD NOT TALK ABOUT

Talking to your adult child about his or her homosexuality is positive most of the time. But there are some conversations that can do more harm than good. Be careful how you talk about your own losses and negative feelings.

Many parents feel a sense of loss when they discover that their child is gay or lesbian. You may feel the loss of your plans for your child to marry and live a life much like your own. You may feel the loss of control over his or her life, the loss of potential grandchildren, the loss of traditional and religious values of home and family life. But keep in mind that all parents suffer losses that force them to adjust their dreams.

If a parent wanted his child to be a rocket scientist, but he grew up to be a newspaper journalist, he would have to adjust his dream. If another parent wanted her daughter to live nearby so she could see her often, but the daughter moved across the country, she would have to adjust. You may have wanted your child to be straight, get married, and have children; now you too have to adjust your dream. (Maybe your child will find a loving partner and adopt children.) Life presents all of us with many situations that interrupt our plans, but life is still wonderful if we adjust and accept and enjoy to the fullest what we do have. You may come to realize that the losses are few; gay people can and do have perfectly fine lives.

Although it's good to share your feelings with a spouse, a friend, or a therapist to help you accept your losses, this degree of honesty with your child can be very hurtful and make it even more difficult for the two of you to move on and build a supportive relationship. The following are examples of the kinds of feelings and statements that you should censor out of your conversations with your adult children because they serve no constructive purpose at all:

Blame: "How could you do this to us?"

Guilt: "Where did we go wrong?"

Bargaining: "If you seek counseling . . ."

Rejection: "I don't want to see you again until you're over this nonsense."

Denial: "Don't say that. You just need time to find the right person."

Parents in denial may be tempted to give their children literature published by groups that promise help in changing from a same-sex orientation to a heterosexual orientation. All mainstream psychological organizations agree that sexual orientation is not changeable. Programs that purport to change sexual orientation can actually be dangerous in that they cause depression and lead some to suicide.

Many experts in the fields of family therapy and psychology advise parents that if they reject or disown their child, the reason is rooted within them, not their child. If you loved your child before you learned of his or her sexual orientation and do not love that child now, your own insecurities and fragile sense of self-esteem are getting in the way of a loving relationship. It is not your child's "fault" any more than it is your fault.

IN THE END

We all have dreams for our children's lives. We all want them to be happy, healthy, and fulfilled. We want to look back on our lives and know that we have given the world the gift of our child. We want to know the joy of loving our offspring. The parents of homosexuals may have to change the details of their dreams, but with honest, open communication, they can still see all these dreams fulfilled.

RESOURCES

When you first learn of your child's same-sex orientation, you may feel isolated and cut off from your familiar world. You will find comfort in knowing that millions of parents have fully affirmed their same-sex-oriented children. You are not alone.

Parents, Family and Friends of Lesbians and Gays (PFLAG) promotes the health and well-being of lesbian, gay, bisexual, and transgendered persons and their families and friends through support, education, and advocacy. Serving more than eighty thousand members and supporters, PFLAG's 450 chapters and affiliates are located in communities across the United States. This organization can help you better understand your own feelings and the needs of your adult child.

Parents, Family and Friends of Lesbians and Gays
1726 M Street NW, W. 400
Washington, DC 20036
(202) 467–8180; info@pflag.org; www.pflag.org

Suggested Reading
In the Family.
This is a magazine for lesbians, gays, and bisexuals and their families. For subscription information: lmarkowitz@aol.com or (301) 270–4771.

Aarons, L. *Prayers for Bobby: A Mother's Coming to Terms with the Suicide of Her Gay Son.* San Francisco: HarperSanFrancisco, 1996.

Bernstein, R. A. *Straight Parents, Gay Children: Inspiring Families to Live Honestly with Greater Understanding.* New York: Thunder's Mouth Press, 1999.

Griffin, C. W., Wirth, M. J., Wirth, A. G., and McNaught, B. *Beyond Acceptance: Parents of Lesbians and Gays Talk About Their Experiences.* New York: St. Martin's Press, 1997.

EXPERT CONSULTANT

Catherine Tuerk is a clinical specialist in adult psychiatric and mental health nursing with a private practice in psychotherapy in the metropolitan Washington, D.C., area. She is a member of a professional group that provides assessment, treatment, and support for children with gender-variant behavior and their parents. Since 1992, she has been a volunteer therapist at the Whitman Walker clinic, a community-based clinic serving the gay, lesbian, bisexual, transgender, and HIV/AIDS population. She is also immediate past president of the Metro D.C. Parents, Families and Friends of Lesbians and Gays (PFLAG). In 2000, she received the Adele Starr Award, PFLAG's highest national award for an outstanding parent. Tuerk is married and has two adult children: a gay son, who has two adopted daughters, and a straight daughter.

Cohabitation: Yours and Theirs

"Treating your adult child in the same way you would treat a friend in an equal adult relationship is a very affirming event for your son or daughter."

Anthony P. Jurich, professor of marriage and family therapy, Kansas State University

Today, 10.7 million unmarried sweethearts live together, and more than half of first marriages are preceded by cohabitation, according to the U.S. Census Bureau. So with literally millions of people doing it, why is this subject so hard to talk about? Maybe for parents like Tammy, it's because we're just not ready to acknowledge our children's sexuality so openly and publicly.

Tammy called her daughter, Karin, at 2 A.M. to tell her that her dad was in the hospital suffering from a kidney stone. The telephone rang a few times, and then Tammy heard Karin's boyfriend mumble a sleepy hello. Tammy froze. She didn't know what to say, and so she hung up. "I felt like I had just walked in and found the two of them in bed together. What could I say? I didn't want to embarrass either of them, and I didn't want to get into a discussion about it, but I did have to talk to Karin. So I dialed again, and this time Karin answered. I rather abruptly gave her the message and hung up. It was very awkward for both of us."

When Karin met her mother at the hospital, she tried to explain why she hadn't told her that she was living with her boyfriend.

She was afraid. She was afraid her mother wouldn't understand, that her mother would think less of her. Tammy did disapprove and she didn't understand, but that wasn't what made her feel so hurt and angry. She had suspected for several weeks that Karin was living with her boyfriend but didn't say anything, assuming Karin would tell her when she was ready. But now this secrecy felt like a betrayal. It's very hard being the last to know something so important.

Even a personal and sensitive subject like cohabitation needs to be open for family discussion because, as Tammy and Karin found out, not talking about it affects the quality of your relationship.

This chapter will help you find the words you need to broach this subject, talk it through, and find a mutually agreeable way to live with this situation. It will also take a look at how to talk to your adult children if *you* decide to move in with an intimate partner.

WHY TALK ABOUT COHABITATION

Sometimes not talking is deafening. If you don't talk about your adult child's decision to move in with an intimate friend, the silence will be so loud you won't be able to talk over it about anything else.

Think back to your parent-child interactions years ago. Let's say your child knocked over a treasured vase and stood over it as you entered the room. He would expect you to say something, do something, yell, cry, and punish him. But what if instead you said nothing? What if you acted as if nothing had happened and calmly walked out of the room? That silence would be much worse than any punishment you could think of. It's like waiting for the bomb to go off and never knowing when that will happen. The waiting is torture. That's the same dynamic you set up if you think or know your adult child is cohabiting with someone, but no one says anything about it.

A few general reasons discussed in this section include talking because:

- Silence causes misunderstandings.
- Secrecy can hurt you.
- Cohabitation is a major life event.
- You should be honest.

Talk Because Silence Causes Misunderstandings. In many cases, the message the silence delivers may be different from the one you intend. Even if your silence is meant to convey acceptance and noninterference, your child is likely to interpret it as condemnation. Obviously, this isn't good for your family relationship. Even if you don't like the idea of cohabitation, it's possible that you won't communicate the degree of condemnation that your kids think you feel. If you don't talk about this, there will always be a barrier between you based on what you want to say and what your adult children think you want to say. Their imaginary scenario is probably far worse than what would actually happen if your feelings were out in the open.

Talk Because Secrecy Can Hurt You. Cohabitation is a life decision that is open to societal ridicule in some corners. For this reason, your children may be afraid to bring up the subject. Should they risk opening themselves to a lecture? To criticism? To guilt? It's a tough call that many will sidestep through secrecy; they will not say anything and hope no one ever finds out. Living a secret life is very difficult for the adult child and for his or her family—and it never works for long. Would you rather find out from your nosy neighbor or from your child? Would you rather have an open discussion or a wall of secrecy between you? Whether you approve or do not approve, when the information is out in the open, you can both deal with this life circumstance; when it is hidden, it is completely unmanageable.

Talk Because Cohabitation Is a Major Life Event. As a family, we need to talk about all major life events. Can you imagine not saying a word when your child takes a new job? Or decides to marry? Or graduates school? Of course not. So why would you both try to turn this important decision into a nonevent?

How can you have any kind of relationship if you both pretend this isn't happening? After you talk about the weather, what can you say? You probably can't even ask, "How's Susie?" without both you and your child feeling as if you really asked, "Did you and Susie have sex last night?"

Talk to Be Honest. If you don't talk about this lifestyle choice, you cannot have an honest relationship with your adult child. You'll both spend much energy on keeping this secret, pretending nothing out of the ordinary is happening, and lying. There's no way this can be good in the long run. The most valuable thing we can possess in our relationship with our adult children is mutual respect and trust. Silence about such a life-altering move makes that impossible.

Let adult children know that you can talk about this. You don't need to be protected; you don't need to be spared the details. You are open to trying to understand this decision, but can't do that if you both can't talk about it. This will create a model for all future adult-to-adult conversations.

WHEN TO TALK ABOUT COHABITATION

Mark was on his way to work when he noticed that his son, James, had left his golf shoes in the back of his car. With a few minutes to spare that morning, Mark decided to stop by his son's apartment and drop them off. He rang the bell and was shocked when James's girlfriend, Sarah, answered the door. They both stared at each other in surprise; neither was able to recover fast enough to avoid the awkward silence. Finally, finding his voice, Mark mumbled an apology, handed the shoes to Sarah, and hurried away. Neither one of them mentioned this incident again, and Mark never told his wife. But from that time on, Mark, James, and Sarah always felt very uncomfortable when they were together. The silence was killing their relationship.

The longer this charade went on, the more awkward everyone felt. Finally, Sarah pushed James to tell his father that they were living together. "Why didn't you tell me sooner?" asked Mark. "Why didn't you ask?" replied James.

In some families, cohabitation is no big deal. The subject is easy to talk about, and everyone feels comfortable discussing the details. In that case, there is no need to search for "just the right time" to talk and there's no big concern about saying "just the right thing." But in families like Mark's, this subject is not easily talked about. It's embarrassing, it's personal, and it's often hidden or ignored. If that's the case in your family, it is important that you take the lead in bringing the subject out in the open. That's the only way to avoid the confusion and tension that happen when you wait for your adult child to say something and your adult child waits for you to say something.

Ideally, your adult child will come to you and tell you his or her plans to move in with an intimate partner. This is a good time to talk. But in many cases, you'll bring the subject to your child based on a gut feeling or because somebody else let the news slip. In these cases, the best thing to do is to make the covert overt. This means taking something that is being hidden and bringing it right out into the open so it can be dealt with.

Talk to your adult child about your suspicions as soon as you have reason to suspect. If you wait until you have more evidence, the whole situation can get away from you, and the silence will become too loud to talk over. If you notice men's clothing in your daughter's closet, that's a good time to talk. If you see women's toiletries in your son's bathroom, talk about it. This isn't being nosy; this is your child, and this is an important part of his or her life. This is something you should both be able to discuss as adults.

WHAT YOU SHOULD TALK ABOUT

The only time you'll be at a loss for words about the subject of cohabitation is if you disapprove. But remember that you don't have veto power in your adult child's life anymore. You can't say, "I forbid you," or "You're not allowed to," or "If you do this, I don't want to see you again." These kinds of statements can quickly ruin a good relationship. You have to ask yourself if you feel strongly enough about this to cut off all ties with your adult child. Some parents do; that is their choice. But if you want to keep your relationship alive and healthy, then you'll need to find the words that honestly express your feelings and encourage your children to do the same, even if in the end you have to agree to disagree.

Breaking the Ice

If you hear through the grapevine that your child has moved in with his or her partner, you may feel betrayed that you have been kept in the dark. But the longer you allow the silence and suspicion to continue, the harder it will be to have a constructive conversation. Without anger or condemnation, ask your questions, and get some answers.

You might say, "I get the feeling that Mike is living with you. If that's true, this is an important part of your life that I'd like you to share with me. Can we talk about that?"

You might say, "Your life is important to me. I'd like to know what's going on."

You might say, "If you and Eileen are living together, tell me. At least I'll know what the reality is, and basing my feelings on reality is a lot better than basing them on my imagination or on rumors."

Addressing Specific Issues

When your children cohabit and you don't like this arrangement, you need to learn how to talk about your feelings adult to adult. This is a subject that may bring out the protective parent in you, but your child is no longer a child. Talk in the same way you would to a friend who told you this same news. You may not agree with your friend's decision and you may be concerned for her welfare, but you would probably not argue, yell, or condemn. Don't do this in your conversations with your child either. Instead, talk to your adult child adult to adult.

When you do this, you might talk about:

- Your feelings
- The practical details
- The future

Talk About Your Feelings. Your disapproval really comes from deep feelings; don't be afraid to say so. If you put too much emphasis on logic only, you'll risk sounding condemning, and your child will totally turn off what you have to say. Your strong disapproval can also cement your child's conviction to stay in the relationship even if it should turn bad just to avoid hearing an "I told you so."

You might say, "I have some strong feelings about this that you may not agree with. If you will hear me out, I will then listen to your side too. Okay?"

Instead of saying, "This isn't wise; you'll probably end up paying most of the rent and doing all the housework."
You might say, "I'm scared that this may be a bad financial decision for you. Have you talked about how you will be dividing up the household bills?"

Instead of saying, "You're not thinking straight because you're in love. He's just looking to mooch off you. He doesn't have any ambition of his own that I can see."
You might say, "I worry that you'll be taken advantage of. I'd like to talk with you about ways you can keep that from happening."

Instead of saying, "You're crazy to do this."
You might say, "I may have an opinion on this that you won't like, but it's because I love you and I can see this situation a bit more objectively than you can. I'm hoping we can talk about this and both share our feelings."

Talk About the Practical Details. Once you show that the subject is not taboo and you're open to talking about it, your adult child may be more willing to hear your point of view. Then you can talk to him about the day-to-day considerations of this arrangement. It's most likely that your child will not agree with you or admit that you have a good point when you note the possible pitfall of this arrangement, but at least you have the opportunity to give him food for thought.

You might say, "You're entering into a financial contract that is new to you. I've had some experience with this, and so I might have some information that might be useful to you. Would you mind my asking what the financial arrangements are? Do you feel they are fair?"

You might say, "If you're going to do this, at least let me help you avoid some problems. Because you're not married, you may not be able to have both your names on the lease. If his name alone is on the lease, he can pack up and leave, and you have no claim on the apartment. If your name alone is on the lease, you are totally responsible for paying the rent no matter what happens. Have you thought about what will be best for you?"

Your adult child may say, "I'm not worried about that. We're going to split the rent and I trust him."

Then you can say, "That's fine. This is just an issue I think you need to think about."

You might say, "Have you two talked over the details of this arrangement? Who will buy the food? How you will divide up your money? What kind of banking account—joint or individual—you will use? Who will do what housework? If you get these things straight right in the beginning, you can probably avoid trouble down the road. These are the kinds of things many couples, married or not, argue about."

Talk About the Future. If you're right, and this decision turns out to be big mistake, what do you hope your adult child will do? Let's say that in a worse-case scenario, she ends up alone, broke, and pregnant. If you have been very verbal in your condemnation of the living arrangement, she may not be able to come to you. She may be too proud to let you hit her with a gloating *I told you so!* She may have the child without telling you. She may go out and fend for herself because she doesn't think the two of you can talk about it.

So if you want your adult children to rely on you for support, no matter what happens, don't close the door to future communication. When your child tells you that he or she is going to live with a partner, express your feelings and viewpoint, but then end with a positive, supportive statement.

You might say, "I don't agree with your decision, but I want you to know that I still love you. If you should ever need me for anything, don't think that now you can't come to me. If this is a bad decision and you end up learning from your mistakes the hard way, that's not such a bad thing either. I'm always here to support you."

Talking about your child's decision to cohabit brings the subject out in the open. There are no secrets, no sneaking around, no lying. Honest conversation, even when you disagree with the point of view, is far better than silence.

WHEN YOU YOURSELF COHABIT

In the Williams's household, the tables are reversed on the cohabitation issue. Forty-seven-year-old Jennifer is about to move in with her boyfriend, and she is afraid to tell her twenty-five-year-old daughter. She has been dropping hints for weeks, but her daughter just won't take the bait. Neither of them wants to be the one to broach the subject, but as moving day draws near, Jennifer is going to have to say something.

In a circumstance like this, the tables may be turned, but the rules are the same. You should talk to your adult children about this living arrangement as soon as you decide to make this life change. They do not have the right to tell you not to do this; you do not have to ask for their permission. But because this move will change something about your life, your children have a right and a need to know what's going on.

Consider how you would handle this information with a good friend. Would you hide the news? Would you pretend no one else is living with you? This would be very bad for the friendship. What would you say when your friend finds out that you've been lying to her? How would you defend your decision to keep her in the dark about something so important? How would your friend feel about this lie?

Your adult children should be given the same consideration you give your friends. As adults, they will have many of the same reactions as your friends: some may feel happy for you, others may feel anxious or cautious, and others may insist you're making a mistake. Whatever the reaction is, your right to do what you want as an adult remains the same.

This may be a more complicated situation if your adult children are not married. You may worry that your decision to live with your partner will give them permission to do the same with their intimate partners. If you don't want your children to cohabit, you'll have to come up with a reason that it's okay for you but not for them. This is not easy to do, but if you don't address this issue, your children will quickly label you a hypocrite.

If you can't think of a reason that it's okay for you to cohabit but not okay for your children to do the same, then you need to change the rules for either yourself or your children. If you're absolutely dead set against your children cohabiting, then maybe it's not the best thing for you either. If, on the other hand, you are sure cohabiting is good for you, then maybe you'll have to accept it as a lifestyle for your children also. This is something to think about.

A study done back in 1962 by researchers Bell and Burkel asked daughters in college and their mothers this question: Is it okay to have premarital sex? It was no surprise to find that the mothers were more likely than their daughters to answer no to this question. But then the researchers asked the college-age daughters: If you were your mother's age and you had a college-age daughter, would it be okay for your daughter to have premarital sex? This question received a very high number of no responses. These girls were as protective of their hypothetical daughters as their own mothers were of them. The point is that we are often more willing to put ourselves into precarious situations (based on the assumption that we can take care of ourselves) than we are willing to allow those we love to do the same (fearing that they may not be able to take care of themselves). If you do not want your children to follow your example and cohabit, you need to think carefully about your reasons. Again, this is an issue that shouldn't be avoided; you're both thinking about it, so get it out in the open.

You may have very logical reasons for cohabiting; if this is the case simply say so.

You might say, "For me, this is really an economic decision. I don't want to mix our finances and confuse the inheritance issue. I also don't want to risk losing my pension survivor benefits. Do you see why this makes my circumstance very different from yours?"

On the other hand, you might have no logical reason at all, but just feel strongly that you would not like your child to model your own actions. Be honest about this also.

You might say, "I'm fifty-two years old, and I'm mature enough to make this decision. My life right now is very different from yours."
Your adult child might say, "I'm just as mature as you are. And I can make this decision too."
Then you might say, "I agree that this sounds like a double standard. But I think there is a good reason for it. I think it's okay for me because I'm more experienced in knowing what I need and what will work best for me. I would still prefer it if you did not do the same—at least until you're older and can make a more informed decision."

Your child will not agree with that logic at all. But at least you have talked about your decision and your feelings. You have acknowledged that this may appear to be a hypocritical move, and you have opened up the subject for further discussion. This is far better than saying nothing and letting feelings go unsaid.

IN THE END

Whether you're talking about your child's cohabitation or your own, the bottom line is the same: be honest, be open, and talk about your differences. Then, even if don't see eye to eye, you can agree to disagree and keep your relationship strong and alive.

EXPERT CONSULTANT

Anthony P. Jurich, Ph.D., is a professor of marriage and family therapy at Kansas State University, Manhattan, Kansas. He has done research on premarital sexual attitudes and the process of marriage and family therapy. Jurich is also a therapist at the Kansas State University Marriage and Family Therapy Clinic. He is a member of the American Psychological Association, the National Council on Family Relations, and a past president of the American Association for Marriage and Family Therapy.

PART TWO

Family Issues

Sibling Relationships

"You can be a tremendous resource for guidance, support, and advice when dealing with issues between siblings, but you don't have to be a major player in their relationship. Far better to be a consultant than the one in charge."

Donald K. Freedheim, family counselor and founding director, Schubert Center for Child Development at Case Western Reserve University, Cleveland, Ohio

If you have more than one child, then you know all about siblings. They have a bond like no other in life with shared history and memories. And as they grow, many turn this special relationship into a lifelong friendship. Others, sadly, lose track of each other, and unfortunately, some become completely estranged. Whatever type of adult relationship your siblings have developed, your role as their parent, mediator, peacemaker, and counselor continues long after they leave home—but in a very different way than when you all lived under the same roof. Talking to your adult children about their siblings can be very tricky business because it's hard to know where the line is between meddling and helping. Imagine this scenario:

MOM: Honey, your sister says she needs a little breathing room. She says that she thinks you spend too much time at her apartment and you're eating most of your meals there. You know she doesn't make that much, and it's hard for her to pay her grocery bills. And I think she needs a little more privacy.

DAUGHTER: WHAT??!! You have to be kidding me! She said that about me? Mom, she is such a liar! I do not go over there much at all, and I even bring her food sometimes. I can't believe she'd run to you to complain about me! She's a big baby, and you always take her side.

There's no way this is going to have a happy ending. Although your children are now adults, your relationship with each one can easily slip back into the parent-child dynamic, putting you in the position of having to solve problems and stroke egos—not a healthy position to be in between mature and independent adults.

Of course, what you say to siblings depends on the type of relationship you have with each one, the seriousness of the issue at hand, the maturity level of the adult child, and your own view of your role in their lives. You have to keep in mind (something you're probably keenly aware of) that no two siblings are alike. What you can say to one, you might not be able even to hint at to another. Their personalities, vulnerabilities, and sensitivities have been formed throughout their lifetime and in many respects may be a direct reflection of their sibling position or birth order. The effect of birth order has been studied and debated for many years. There is now a strong feeling that people who are the oldest, or in the middle, or the youngest share certain general characteristics.

Oldest children are often perfectionists who are reliable, serious, critical, and well organized. They tend to buy into the family values and to be more parental. They are the ones who have to break the ice for younger siblings. Middle children have a little more trouble finding their place, but they often have lots of friends and do well in life because they are born negotiators. Youngest children tend to experience their parents as more relaxed, but they often feel they are not taken seriously. They might be manipulative, but they are outgoing and can become the clowns of the family. Of course, like all other generalizations, this theory will not fit all families, but it's interesting to consider the role of birth order in the way your children develop their personalities and relate to each other.

You also have to respect the relationship between the siblings as it exists, not as you wish it would be. Not all siblings are going to be close; not all are even going to be friends. The bonds they formed in childhood are influenced by many factors, some of which you have had no control over. A study of siblings in England in the early 1980s found dramatic differences between same-sex and different-sex sibling pairs in all measured interactions. The researchers found that these differences were most striking for the families with firstborn boys. Elder boys with a younger brother were far more frequently friendly and less negative toward their sibling than the boys with a younger sister. But whether boys or girls, same-sex siblings were found to be much friendlier and closer than opposite-sex siblings.

Whatever kind of relationship your siblings have—whether they are close, estranged, or somewhere in between—when you talk to them about each other, watch out for that thin line that separates the meddling parent from the helpful one. This chapter can help you do that. It will take a close look at why it's important to keep a dialogue going among all siblings, and to know when our children might appreciate our input and when it's best to stay out of the way.

WHY TALK ABOUT SIBLING RELATIONSHIPS

Asking why we should talk to our adult children about their siblings is like asking why we breathe air; we just do. We talk to our grown children about their siblings as a common point of conversation and to share feelings about the events of their lives. It's natural to say,

"Have you seen Linda's new puppy?" Or, "Did you hear that Bobby got a promotion?" Or, "Ned got a new job I think he's really going to like." These everyday conversations about the life and times of your children's siblings are the meat of most family interactions. But if you think about the conversations you have with your children about their siblings, you'll see that sometimes they serve a larger purpose.

In many families, the parents serve as a clearinghouse of sibling information. Assuming you're in touch with all your children on a regular basis, all big news may be sent to you first for dissemination to the other family members. "Margaret broke her toe." "Ken is going to Europe this summer." "Steve is writing a book." Talking to your children about their siblings keeps them in touch even when they don't have the time or inclination to do it themselves.

We also talk to our children about their siblings as we have always done: to help them solve squabbles, see the other's viewpoint, and keep the family together. When Paula stops talking to Carrie because she stole her boyfriend, you can invite them both over for dinner to work things out. When you notice that your children are drifting apart and aren't making an effort to keep in touch, you can drop little hints and reminders like, "Why don't you give Michele a call and see how's she doing?" And when two of your children aren't even speaking, you can offer to be a *neutral* go-between by asking, "Is there anything you'd like me to tell your sister when I talk to her?"

We can also enlist one sibling to help another. Sometimes when you know your grown child will not listen to your advice but you can see him heading for the edge of the cliff, you can call in the troops to help.

This was the tactic Fred and his wife, Rosemary, used when they heard from their daughter-in-law that their youngest son, Jason, was spending more and more time in the local bar with his buddies and less time at home with his wife and children. Fred called their other son, Tim, whom he knew had a close relationship with Jason. He asked Tim to invite Jason out for dinner and see if there was something on his mind that he needed help with. Sometimes a favored sibling can offer help that no one else in the family can.

As explained later in this chapter, these kinds of interventions work best when they are not intrusive or meddling. In the example, Tim can start a family war if he says to Jason, "Your wife called Mom and Dad and told them you're drinking too much. They called me and asked me to find out why."

WHEN TO TALK ABOUT SIBLING RELATIONSHIPS

Of course, you will talk to your children about their siblings in almost every conversation you have. That's part of all "How's the weather?" conversations. But when it comes to more serious life issues, like finances, romances, and health, what is said between you and your child may be confidential and not for family sharing. Be careful what you bring up during a holiday dinner. If you ask your son how his friend with HIV is doing, he may become furious that you betrayed this confidence that he didn't want his siblings to know about. If you announce to the family at cousin Julie's wedding that your daughter too is getting married (before she has officially made that announcement), you'll find yourself in big trouble. Be very careful about what you say about one sibling in front of the others.

What goes on between siblings when they are adults is also very often their own business and not open for just any family discussion. It is not always best to get things out in the open at family gatherings, for example. If your two sons are waging a silent war, it might not be appropriate to talk about that in the middle of Thanksgiving dinner. If you know your roommate daughters are quarreling over who didn't pay last month's rent on time, this would not be a good subject of conversation in a public restaurant. When bringing up a volatile subject, try to be sensitive to your children's right to privacy.

The best time to talk about sensitive issues between siblings is when they initiate the conversation. If they open the subject to discussion at a family gathering, in a restaurant, or during a holiday meal, then you can follow their lead. Also, if one of them privately asks for your advice, this is obviously a good time to talk, whether on the telephone or in person. The guiding principle when talking about siblings and sensitive issues is to find a time when they will not be publicly embarrassed and when they indicate they are open to discussing that subject.

WHAT YOU SHOULD TALK ABOUT

The topics of conversation about siblings are as endless as the number of possible sibling issues and personalities. This section is not intended to cover this range of topics, but rather to give examples of conversations about typical sibling issues that require caution on your part as a parent. You'll find you need to tread carefully and use restraint in conversations in which you:

- Use one child as a sounding board about the other
- Compare one to the other
- Share personal information
- Mediate sibling arguments

- Find yourself in the middle
- See one sibling taking advantage of the other
- Want to bring estranged siblings together

Avoid Using One Child as a Sounding Board About the Other. Be very cautious when talking to one sibling about the other. In most cases, after the children have moved out of the house, you will talk to each one when the other isn't present. That's how rumors and misunderstandings start. Even if you innocently say to one daughter something as simple as, "Have you seen Judy lately? I haven't heard from her this week," the conversation may take on a different tone when relayed to the other daughter: "Boy, is Mom mad at you! She said you never call her." If you know that private conversations in your family tend to get turned around and twisted, think twice before you say anything that may be construed as critical by an absent sibling.

Knowing how you can innocently hurt a sibling's feelings, imagine the damage you can do to your relationship with one child if you *do* complain about him or her to siblings. You might feel that Johnny shouldn't spend so much money on vacations, or that Stephanie shouldn't date men who are so much older than she is, or that Mike shouldn't propose to Janie. But if you share these feelings with their siblings, you risk the pitfall of common gossip that causes bad feelings all around. If the child who is the object of your concern finds out that you've been talking about him behind his back (as he surely will), he may feel ridiculed or betrayed. And even if the siblings listen with interest and contribute their own views on the subject, it puts them in the awkward situation of having to defend a sibling or side with you and betray the sibling.

When you feel tempted to complain about the actions of one of your children to another one of your children, try to restrain yourself. Save that conversation for your spouse and close friends, but leave the siblings out of it. Instead, turn your complaint around to an observation or a simple nonemotional piece of daily conversation.

Instead of saying, "There's no way Mike should marry Janie."
You might say, "I wonder if Mike will propose to Janie."

Instead of saying, "I don't know why Stephanie always dates such older men."
You might say, "Have you met Stephanie's new boyfriend? Do you like him?"

Instead of saying, "I can't believe Johnny spends so much money on vacations."
You might say, "I hear Johnny had a good time on his vacation. I'm eager to see the pictures."

Comparing One Child to the Other: A Real Danger Zone. "Why can't you be more like your brother?" is an age-old, stereotypical comment by parents who pit one sibling against the other. We have learned over the years that blatant comparisons like this are psychologically damaging to both siblings. One is made to feel inferior and the other, the "golden child," becomes the unwilling target of sibling rivalry.

Although it is generally known that these overt comparisons are damaging, there's also reason to beware the more subtle comparisons that damage self-esteem and sibling relationships.

Betty had no idea that her conversations about her youngest daughter, Kristen, were excruciatingly painful for her eldest daughter, Maria, to listen to. Betty loved to talk about Kristen's lovely home with the big backyard and the marble foyer. She could wax on for hours about Kristen's two children who were just the cutest angels and who looked just like Kristen. Maria endured hours of hearing about Kristen's domestic bliss, feeling all the time that every word was meant to show her how shallow and unfulfilled her own single lifestyle in a studio apartment in the city was in comparison. There's a possibility that Betty secretly hoped that her stories about Kristen would encourage Maria to seek wedded bliss in the suburbs, but whether consciously or not, Betty was driving a wedge of resentment between the sisters.

Instead of saying, "Kristen's home is so lovely."
Betty might say, "Have you seen Kristen's new kitchen cabinets? Do you like them?"

Instead of saying, "I'm so glad your brother has given me such beautiful grandchildren."
Betty might say, "Have you seen your niece and nephew lately? They're growing so fast."

Instead of saying, "Did you know that Joe came over to paint my porch? Isn't he such a good son?"
You might say, "When Joe came over to paint the porch last week, I showed him the vacation pictures you sent me. I'm so lucky to have two thoughtful sons."

Be Careful When Sharing Personal Information. It's a slippery slope you tread when you reveal a confidence of one child to another. Your children are adults now. If they want their siblings to know about personal issues such as finances, health, marital problems, and so on, they have to be the one to tell them, not you.

Jim learned this lesson the hard way. He listened intently as his son, Kyle, explained his plans to send his emotionally troubled son to a private boarding school out of state. The decision was a heart-breaking one that Kyle needed to talk about with someone he trusted. Jim was very happy that Kyle felt he could open up his heart to him to explain his decision as well as his fears. Jim had always been a good listener, and Kyle felt comfortable sharing his emotional burden with him. Unfortunately, what could have been a tender father-son experience blew up into anger, resentment, and embarrassment when Kyle's sister called him the next day to talk about his "problem." It never occurred to Jim that this wasn't family business. The family was close, and so he assumed that everyone would know all the details of everyone else's business. Maybe when the kids were young, this was true, but now as an adult, Kyle needed his father to respect the confidentiality of such a personal matter.

Before you assume that your adult child wants to share information with siblings, ask how he feels about doing that.

Instead of saying, "I'll call your sister and see what she thinks."
You might say, "Is this something you've shared with your sister, or would you rather keep it between the two of us?"

Instead of saying, "Your brother's a lawyer; let's call him and see what he advises."
You might say, "Do you want to ask your brother for help, or would you rather find a neutral lawyer and keep your brother out of this?"

How to Mediate Sibling Arguments. Sibling rivalry can be alive and well even in adulthood. This is especially true when the family gets back together over the holidays. Through the very common process of regression, your children may fall back into old roles in which you can watch the whining and arguing pick up right where it left off: "Mommmmm, tell Jack to give me a break and get off my back." "Daaaaad, you said I could borrow the car tonight, but Kathy says she's taking it." The same fights and disagreements come up over and over.

Your first reaction when this happens may be the conditioned response of years gone by. When your kids were, well, kids, did you always jump in and resolve the problem? Did you let them work it out themselves unless it looked as if someone was going to get hurt? Did you act as the mediator helping them come to agreement? Whatever your style then is likely to be your style now—but it may not be the best way or an appropriate way. As your children become adults, it's important to know when to stay out of sibling fights and when to offer some help. In many cases, you'll find it's best to ignore the problem and let the siblings work it out themselves.

This is true for a very good reason. By their very definition, mediators and negotiators have to be neutral and objective, with no prior interest in the parties involved. This automatically disqualifies all parents from this role between adult siblings. When they were children, we could say, "Do this because I'm your mother." We could dictate, "Stop your fighting right now." We could step in the middle and break it up. But now that they are adults, if they complain to you and expect you to resolve the conflict, you have to be very careful about how you respond. As a parent, it's important to listen, empathize, help them do some problem solving, and point them in the right direction without getting smack in the middle yourself.

Getting caught between two siblings is a situation fraught with possible drawbacks. If one daughter tells you disturbing news about another daughter, what can you do? If you call the troubled child and say, "Your sister said . . .," you're bound to hear, "She's such a tattletale. Why does she have to tell everybody my business?" If at all possible, this is a situation in which you can encourage mature action by the "tattler" without getting involved yourself.

When you want to stay out of it, you might say, "I'm sorry to hear that. Please keep in touch with your sister, try to help her, and let me know what happens."

If your daughter says, "But aren't you going to call her and talk to her about this?"

You might say, "No. I don't want her to think that you and I are ganging up on her. I'm sure that you two can handle this yourselves."

In some situations, a sibling may come to you with a complaint about the other sibling and expect you to solve the problem. If, for example, one sibling tells you that his brother borrowed fifty dollars and never paid it back, you may feel that you must get involved. But if you do, you'll take away the siblings' ability to work these things out for themselves and you'll put yourself in the middle of a no-win situation.

Instead of saying, "Brian says you owe him fifty dollars. I want you to pay him back immediately."

When you want to stay out of it, you might say, "If your brother never pays you back even after you remind him, I guess you've just learned something about loaning him money."

When you can't resist doing some parenting, you might say, "Have you thought of what you might say to remind your brother of this loan?"

You might call the borrowing child and say, "Have you seen Brian lately? He seems to be a little stressed for money lately; do you know anything about that?" This puts out cues that might lead the one child to repay the loan, but it doesn't put you in the middle.

In another case, Susie says, "Dad, you have to talk to Mary. She's just driving me crazy. She's always borrowing stuff from me and she never returns it."

When you want to stay out of it, you might say, "I'm going to let you and your sister work this out for yourselves. This is between the two of you, and you don't need your father to get in the middle. Nothing good can come of that. So I encourage you to talk to her and find a way to settle your differences, but there's nothing I can do for you."

When you can't resist doing some parenting, you might say, "Let's talk about ways the two of you might resolve this problem. Have you talked to Mary directly about this problem? What can you say to her to let her know how you feel?"

Of course, if one sibling tells you something about another sibling that is life threatening (regarding excessive substance abuse or spousal or child abuse, for example), you will immediately get involved to offer help and support as you would for any other friend. You will find you still can't make an adult child do things your way, but you can stay close by as long as they need you. (See additional information on talking about substance abuse and on spousal or child abuse in the corresponding chapters in Part Three.)

When You See One Sibling Taking Advantage of the Other. From her objective vantage point, May could see that her youngest son, Dave, was taking advantage of her middle son, Ryan. Dave was what his friends would call a moocher: he borrowed money from Ryan that he never paid back. He used Ryan's house whenever he felt like grabbing a quick meal or washing up after work. He let Ryan's wife do his laundry and often borrowed her car when his was once again in the shop. Ryan didn't seem to mind being his brother's keeper, but May worried that Ryan's love for his brother was enabling Dave to avoid being responsible for himself and would eventually do irreparable damage to the relationship when Ryan realized he was being used.

What can a parent say in this situation? Because the relationship between two grown brothers is their own business, it's difficult for the parent to step in and point out the flaws. But it's also difficult to watch this happen and remain silent. In most cases, it's best to settle for the middle road, where you objectively raise issues and see if you can bring some awareness to both siblings.

Instead of saying, "You're being taken advantage of. Don't let him do this to you."
You might say, "How do you feel about your brother using your house as his own?"

Instead of saying, "You're a fool to let your brother use you like this."
You might say, "Has your wife ever complained about doing your brother's laundry? How do you feel about that?"

Instead of saying, "You're helping your brother be an irresponsible loafer."
You might say, "How do you think you can help your brother learn to be more independent?"

All you can do is raise the issues, and then let your children take it from there. Be an active listener who gives full attention and asks questions that help the other person think things through without jumping in to dominate the discussion with your own opinion and directives.

When You Want to Bring Estranged Siblings Together. It's heartbreaking for a parent to watch siblings become estranged from each other. Ideally, they should love each other, and they should be best friends. So it seems unnatural when they're not. But it happens. In fact, some siblings do not speak to each other during their entire adult lives. If you'd like to help your warring siblings, it's going to be difficult to find the magic words that will push them to make up. Keep in mind that there's probably more going on than you know about, and your role in their personal struggle may be very limited.

Although you feel desperate to say something that will bring them back together, getting involved is risky. One wrong word, and you can make matters worse and damage your own relationship with one or both of your children. So when you broach the subject of estranged siblings, be aware that the topic may be explosive. You should do it like you would if you were walking across a minefield. To do it safely:

- You have to know the territory. Do you know all the details? Do you know both sides? Are you making any assumptions that may not be true?
- You should bring to the conversation verbal detectors so you know what to expect. Ask questions to test feelings like, "Have you talked to your brother lately?" Or, "Will you be joining the family at your brother's house for the barbecue on Sunday?"

The response to these questions will let you know if you can probe a little further. If your son says, "I don't want to talk about my brother," you'll know he's not ready to discuss the problem with you. But if he says something like, "No, you know we're not talking. I don't think he would want me there," he's opened the topic for further discussion. Then you can ask, "I know you're both angry with each other, but I'm not really sure why. Is it something you can talk about to me?" This conveys the message that you're not looking to preach or argue but that you're concerned.

If one sibling wants to make amends with the other and comes to you for help, you may have a more helpful role to play. Without taking sides, you may be able to arrange for both of them to come to dinner to talk about the problem. Or you may be the neutral go-between who relays messages. But be careful here. This will work only if you can stay completely neutral and resist telling your children what to do. As a facilitator of peace, you can encourage them to work this out for themselves; you can't make them kiss and make up.

Instead of saying, "You know, your sister wants you two to be friends, and she says you won't even talk to her. What's the matter with you? I want you to call her and work this out."

You might say, "Your sister says she feels badly that the two of you aren't talking. Do you think there's anything the two of you might do to work this out?"

You might say, "It is so important for cousins to have good relationships. Is there any way that you and your sister could try to heal things for the sake of the children?"

You might say, "If you want to patch things up with your sister, maybe talking to a counselor would give you some ideas about how to approach her."

You might say, "I understand that there are counselors who can really be of help in situations where siblings are having difficulties. If the two of you sit down with an objective listener, you might be able to work things out."

If neither of the squabbling siblings asks your advice and neither seems to have any interest in making amends, your role is very limited. You can test the waters occasionally by bringing up the sibling's name in conversation and drawing each child out to talk about the other. You can invite them over to your house just to get them talking. But you can't insist that they do as you say and make up and be friends. You can't insist that they tell you what's going on. This is between two adults, and they have a right to keep their disagreement between themselves.

If you are agonizing over a situation between your children and don't know how to approach it or what to say, it may be helpful to talk to a family counselor. This would give you an opportunity to explain your anguish and your uncertainty and learn how to deal with your feelings and your role as the parent of adult siblings.

EXPERT HELP

This chapter was written with the expert help of Donald K. Freedheim, Ph.D., professor emeritus of psychology at Case Western Reserve University, Cleveland, Ohio.

Moving Out

"When you talk about moving out, be authentic and speak from your heart. Let your children know that because you love them, you want them to become self-actualized adults."

Gail M. Gross, *developmental expert*

Robert graduated from college with a degree in English in May; he was immediately hired as an editorial assistant by a major book publisher in a nearby city. Although at first Robert couldn't wait to find an apartment and move out of his parents' home, he soon found that his salary would not cover the rent and the cost of living in the city. That was two years ago, and Robert is still living in his childhood bedroom. Robert's parents are concerned that it will be years before their son will be able to afford city rents; they feel he should compromise and find a small apartment in the suburbs and commute to work. But they don't know if it's their business to tell him this.

Gina's parents were happy to pay her tuition and have her live at home while she commuted to a nearby college. Then after she earned a degree in art history, Gina signed up for and completed a graduate program in art education. Now, eight years after graduating high school, Gina is studying for an undergraduate degree in teaching. Her parents are going broke and wondering if Gina has decided to be a professional student all her life.

Thirty-two-year-old Jake moved back in with his parents a year ago after he was laid off from his job as a landscaper. He isn't really looking for work right now because he says he's pretty worn out and just needs a break. His parents feel they need a break too—but how can they tell their only son that they want their privacy back and that they're tired of cooking, cleaning, and picking up after him?

Samantha returned home last year with her two toddlers in tow after she separated from her husband. Her parents offered the little family a place of refuge and financial support during this time of crisis. But now they are wondering how long this arrangement will continue. Although they love their daughter and their grandchildren, they just don't have the patience to live with the constant noise and chaos anymore. But their daughter has not mentioned moving out. What should they say?

If you have an adult child living in your home, you are part of a growing trend. According to the U.S. Census Bureau, a whopping 18 million adult offspring (age eighteen and older) were living in their parents' home in 1990. That number jumped to 21.5 million in 1998. That's a lot of adult children living at home! In some families, the multigeneration arrangement works out fine for everyone. But if you've been thinking that you'd like your adult child to move in the near future, you've probably been looking for just the right words to carefully and lovingly convey the message: "Move out!"

This chapter will help you find those words. It will help you explore why it's okay to expect your children to move out, when is the best time to broach the subject, and exactly what you can say in specific circumstances. When you find a way to explain your feelings, communicate that you value your child's feelings, and then find the compromise that fulfills both your needs, you'll see how this sensitive situation can actually strengthen family bonds.

WHY TALK ABOUT MOVING OUT

In many circumstances, having an adult child live in your home is not a problem for you or your child, and so there is no need to have conversations about moving out. Some people of certain cultures and ethnic backgrounds are comfortable having several generations of one family living under one roof. In some homes, the adult child offers a needed financial or physical support system for the parents. There are also multigeneration households where the parents and adult children are happy to be living together; for them, the situation is tension free and agreeable to all. If your adult child lives with you in these kinds of circumstances, no one can tell you it's wrong. Ignore neighbors, friends, and relatives who say your adult child is taking advantage of you and that you should make him or her move out. If you're happy with the arrangement, that's what's best for you.

On the other hand, if you are unhappy or uncomfortable with your adult child living in your home, then you have the right (and the responsibility) to talk about that. There are many sound reasons you may feel your adult child needs to move out of your home. His continued reliance on you may be a financial drain. Ongoing arguments may fill your home with tension. Disagreements may be putting a strain on your own marriage. You may feel that your adult child has become a lazy leech who needs a push into adulthood. Or you may simply want to have your house to yourself after all your years of unselfish parenting. The point is this: if you are uncomfortable with having your adult child living in your home, you have a very good reason to do something about that.

You may also want your child to move out so he can move on to the next step of development: adulthood. Part of healthy human development is the process of separation that usually begins in adolescence. However, in recent years we have seen that the maturation process is being delayed. One reason is the strong economy that has allowed parents to give their children more and more, and without asking for anything in return. But the fact remains that the whole idea behind raising children is to help them become whole people who can separate from their parents and live an independent, self-sustaining life. Therefore, you may want your child to move into his own place when you realize that as long as he lives under your roof, he has no reason to grow up. You may notice that he tends to act childish, immature, and unmotivated as long as all his earthly needs are taken care of at home. You may want to help your child become a capable and responsible individual and feel that you can't do that as long as he is tied to your apron strings.

The place to start moving your child out of the family home is with honest, open, and genuine conversation.

WHEN TO TALK ABOUT MOVING OUT

This is not a one-time conversation that you should have when you reach the boiling point and shout, "It's time for you to move out!" You cannot send your child out on a limb by allowing her to live at home without any responsibilities and then one day saw off that limb by sending her out on her own. Growing into an independent person is a gradual process. Talking to your children about how you can help them complete that developmental step is also a gradual process.

If your adult child has never moved out of your home and shows no inclination to do so in the near future, you should initiate periodic conversations that move him step by step toward responsible behavior and independent living. One day you may talk about new family rules. Another day you may talk about responsibilities you want him to take on. Another time you'll talk about future plans. Each of these conversations gives both of you a chance to share your feelings and move closer to a living arrangement that suits both of you.

If your adult child moves out but then moves back in, the best time to begin your dialogue is immediately on her return (or even better, if you have advance warning, long before she plops down on her old bed). Talking right from the start about expectations and boundaries will avoid conflicts and misunderstandings.

You will also need to talk to your adult children about moving out when you realize that your relationship is no longer productive, tension free, or happy. But don't talk in a time of emotional upset. If your adult child takes your bottle of scotch whiskey and invites his girlfriend to stay the night after you have specifically said this is not okay with you, this gives you a good reason for a sit-down talk—but not at that moment. This kind of situation guarantees a shouting match, misunderstandings, and a hurtful outcome. Wait until you're sure you can talk calmly and relate the message that you value your child and want to help him to become a strong, independent adult, but you also have a right to expect him to respect your feelings.

Many parents put off this conversation because they're hoping that their child will grow up and move out without any interference on their part. Eventually, this may happen. But if you don't see your child packing his bags today, it's likely that a change won't happen tomorrow. We get into the wait-and-see situation because we want our children to love us and to view our home as their home. So we lovingly (albeit sometimes begrudgingly) open our doors and make them comfortable. But being a good parent is always about hard choices. What do you have to do to help your children learn how to survive without you? A good place to start is to talk about the situation and together look for a solution.

WHAT YOU SHOULD TALK ABOUT

Moving out can be a difficult subject to talk to adult children about because in many cases, they are acting like dependent children (for example, letting you wash their laundry and serve them food) but insisting that you treat them like adults (by allowing them to come and go without explanation, for instance). You have a right to tell them they can't have it both ways. Say it, and then allow for negotiations. The goal of your conversations should be to foster an environment in which your grown children can and want to separate. This creates the right atmosphere for building a strong relationship.

How you deliver this message will make all the difference in the outcome. Empathic conversation is your best communication tool. It will help you better understand your child's point of view, recognize why he or she is living at home, and help you both find a solution that supports your needs.

In an empathic conversation, you will both have an opportunity to explain your feelings and point of view and then find mutually agreeable ground to stand on. This is a far better type of conversation than one in which you do all the talking. If you blame, ridicule, or dictate to your adult child by saying something like, "I'm tired of picking up after you. You're an adult now; it's time you started acting like one," you push your child into a defensive position where he can't back down to consider your point of view and you haven't left the door open to negotiations so you can't help him take the next step toward maturation.

When you talk to your child about moving out, try not to put her in the position of having to defend her position. Instead, give her space in which to negotiate and yet have room to maintain your own integrity based on the fact that this is your house and these are your house rules. This allows you to make it clear that you value yourself and your children. It encourages you to listen from an open and respectful position, and it leaves room for compromise and negotiation.

Breaking the Ice

There is no one correct way to talk to your adult children about moving out, but it is never a good idea to do it suddenly, without warning, and without giving your child a chance to be in on the discussion. You're bound to stir up an argument and cause lasting resentment if you announce over morning coffee: "Your mother and I have talked it over, and we've decided it's time for you to move out." Your goal is to help your child move to the next step of development, not push him off a cliff.

In the following sections you will see how you can use empathic conversation skills to:

- Look for the cause.
- Explain your feelings.
- Explore their point of view.
- Find the middle ground.

Look for the Cause. Humor columnist Erma Bombeck said it best: "One night my husband and I sat down and tried to figure out what the attractions of living at home are—other than free laundry, free rent, free toiletries, security, love, a permanent address for mail, unlimited storage, financing and loans, convention rooms for private parties and entertaining, and guest privileges." Why do your children like to live in your home?

You'll be able to have a more productive conversation about moving out if you have a good idea of why your children are staying at home. In addition to the appeal of having all the comforts of home, maybe they can't afford to set up their own household because of expensive rents and utility bills. Maybe the payment of exorbitant credit card bills and car loans eats up their paycheck. Maybe they're saving money to buy their own place. Maybe they need short-term emotional support following a separation or divorce. Maybe unemployment or a minimum-wage job makes it too difficult to pay the bills. And just maybe they like living with you and see no reason to give up the lifestyle you offer.

You might say, "Do any of your friends still live in their parents' home? Why do you think they choose to stay at home?"

You might say, "Is there any one thing that keeps you living at home now that you're an adult and could be living in your own place if you wanted to?"

You might say, "I was wondering why you like to live at home when so many of your friends have moved out of their parents' homes."

You might say, "Part of growing into adulthood is becoming financially and emotionally secure. Do you think you have reached that point yet?"

Put the subject of living at home on the table as something you can both talk about freely. You can't begin to understand why your kids won't move out until you can get them to tell you why they stay.

Explain Your Feelings. After you give your adult child a chance to talk about why he or she has decided to live in your home, share your own feelings about the arrangement.

You might say, "The job of a parent is to raise children to be independent human beings. Sometimes I wonder if I've given you what you need to be an independent adult."

You might say, "If you need to be dependent on me to have a good life, then I feel that I have failed you. My job is to help you separate from me and become a self-sustaining adult. Let's talk about how you can take a step toward that goal."

You might say, "Of course, as your mother [father], I would always like to have you nearby, but I also want to help you move on to the next step of your life."

You might say, "I would like to move on to the next step of my life. Your father [mother] and I have put in a lot of time and effort raising you and think we did a pretty good job. Now that you're an adult, we'd like to spend more time and attention on ourselves: travel more, entertain more, and have the time and space to just relax in our home. We'd like to help you find a way to have your own place so we can all move on and live as adults."

You might say, "The easier thing is to let you live here forever. But it is a parent's responsibility to help bridge the sometimes very difficult leap from childhood to adulthood. By giving you too much and allowing you to completely avoid responsibility, I feel that I'm unfairly making that jump more difficult than it should be."

You might say, "I respect and value your position. Now I want you to know how I feel. I'm not comfortable with our living arrangement, and here are the reasons . . ."

You might say, "I'll help and support you in any way that I can. But this is not working out, and I want us to come up with a plan that will help you get on your feet and will also help me maintain my integrity. So I'm going to support you in the next stage of your development. I'm going to help you find a way to live independently, and I'll stay nearby to help make that work. I'm not abandoning you. I love you, and I'm staying with you to help you become a whole adult."

Explore Their Point of View. After you have made your feelings clear, give your child a chance to explain how she feels. At first, she may feel insulted (how could you, her parents, not want her!?); she may feel angry or embarrassed. Whatever her reaction, let her know that you respect and value her position.

You might say, "How do you feel about this?"

You might say, "I've been thinking about how you must feel living at home as a grown adult. How does living at home rather than moving out help you?"

You might say, "What do you like the most about living at home?"

You might say, "What do you find most difficult about living at home?"

You might say, "Do you ever think about what kind of place you'd like to live in when you move out on your own?"

The key is to stay engaged and connected. Don't let strong feelings shut the door. Whether you agree with your child's viewpoint or not, you can always give it validity by saying, "I respect how you feel."

Find the Middle Ground.   You want your kids to move out; they want to stay. This situation doesn't have to be a stalemate. There's plenty of room for compromise on both sides. You might agree to allow your child to stay, but give up the intensive parenting jobs of cooking, cleaning, and picking up after the adult child. Your child might agree to a timetable to start looking for a new place. You might start charging rent at an ever-increasing rate, or maybe you can give your child an apartment within your house that has its own entrance and separates his life from yours. Maybe you can finance the cost of moving out. There's lots of middle ground if you and your adult children are willing to sit down and talk about it.

Addressing Specific Issues
Clearing the air about feelings is a good way to open a dialogue on the subject of moving out. Once your adult child knows how you feel and you understand the situation from his perspective, you can address specific topics of discussion that will help your child move closer to independent living. You might talk about:

- House rules and boundaries
- Time lines
- Finances

Talk About House Rules and Boundaries.   After he separated from his wife, Jeff moved back in with his widowed father. "This was a tough time for both of us," remembers his father. "Jeff was really depressed and angry and not very good company. I didn't want to upset him more by laying down a bunch of house rules, but after a few months, things were really out of hand. I guess the thing that bothered me most was that Jeff is a smoker and I'm not. My house just stunk of cigarette smoke. He had ashtrays filled with filthy butts all over the house. He also smoked in bed late at night, and I worried he'd fall asleep and burn the house down. His friends were no better; they'd all sit around watching my TV, drinking my beer, and smoking. I felt as if I was running a saloon."

Jaclyn was upset about the way her life had changed since her daughter returned home after college. "At first, I was so happy to have her back that I fell right into my old parenting role," remembers Jaclyn. "I cooked her breakfast every morning and dinner every night. I did all her laundry. I'd buy whatever toiletries or special foods she wanted from a list she would give me each week. She did nothing: no chores, no dishes, no shopping. Now that we've set up this pattern, it's going to be hard to change it, but I'm worn out. I'd like to have back the life I had while she was away."

These two parents found out the hard way that it's better to set up house rules and boundaries right from the start for peaceful coexistence. This helps define the relationship and the expectations for everyone. These things allow adult children to separate slowly, and they allow us to maintain our own sense of self and well-being. They also help your child wean from you in a healthy way. Remember that you cannot help your adult child move toward the goal of independent, self-sustaining adulthood if you take over all adult responsibilities for him or her. You have a right and a responsibility to expect your child to take on household responsibilities that reflect adult behavior. Grown children should be expected to clean up after themselves, shop for themselves, and do their own laundry. It is your right to establish the house rules. It is your house! And it's your right to say what you need to feel peaceful and happy in your own home and to avoid the feeling that you're being walked on.

Your adult child has rights too. He has the right to voice his opinion. He has a right to have input in the creation of the rules. He has the right to privacy and personal space. He has the right to stay for an agreed-on period of time if he follows the rules and the right to leave if he can't live with them. This is your house, so you do have an edge here. Although you may understand and sympathize with your child's situation, you have the right, in your own home, to do what is best for you.

Like all other conversations with your adult children, talking about the house rules should be a two-way conversation that encourages give-and-take. To begin, sit down in a neutral space (not the bedroom or personal den, but the kitchen or living room) and, looking eye to eye, share your thoughts and feelings. Show your child that you value what he has to say and that you also have to respect your own need to complete the job of parenting that moves a child from dependence to adulthood. It's your responsibility to do this. Your child isn't going to do it.

You have to decide what kind of boundaries to set. You may be comfortable with general rules like: "Hold down a job, stay off drugs, stop smoking in the house, and pay your own car insurance." Or you may feel your child needs more specific rules: "Create a budget to pay rent and save money, respect other members of the family by keeping the TV and radio volume low, no sex under my roof, do your own laundry, wash your own dishes, and keep your living area clean." Whatever the case, you need to make your expectations clear. You can't assume that because your child is an adult, she will automatically understand that you want her to help pay the grocery bill or ask you before she invites her friends over to spend the evening. If you talk about these matters in advance, you can avoid hurt feelings, misunderstandings, and angry confrontations down the line.

You might say, "Here's the situation . . . Here's what will work for me . . . Here are the house rules . . . How does that work for you?"

You might say, "I value how you feel, and I respect who you are. I need you to do the same for me. Let's set up some household rules that we can both live with."

If your child agrees to the rules but then does not feel any need to follow them, it's time to talk again. Sit down, and ask your child to share his reasons for breaking the house rules. Maybe he feels they are inappropriate to his situation. Maybe he feels they are too strict for his status as an adult. Maybe a lot of things. Listen, show respect, and then calmly state how you feel. Maybe there is room for negotiation. Maybe the rules can be adjusted so you are both happy. But maybe you'll find that your child simply plans to come and go as he pleases without having to report to you. In this case, it's time to write the rules down as a contract: a binding agreement that must be followed, or consequences must be paid (just like in the real world).

You might say, "If you want to live in my house, you have to follow the rules we create together and that you agree to. Can you do that?"

You might say, "These rules are important to me. If you can follow them, you're welcome to stay."

Talk About Time Lines. Some adult children need to move toward independence in carefully planned steps. You can help them make the transition from living at home to living on their own by establishing some agreed-on time lines.

You might say, "I'd like to help you set up a budget that will put aside money each month to save for the day you move into your own place. I know you'll be wanting to move out into your own place soon, and the cost of moving can be expensive. Besides the cost of rent, you'll need money for the security deposit, moving costs, household items like towels, curtains, and so on. If you start this month, you should have plenty saved to move out in style one year from today. What do you think?"

You might say, "As we've talked about, it's a good idea for you to start thinking about moving out into a place of your own. How long do you think you'll need to get ready to move?"

You might say, "It seems as if you're stuck and can't move forward. Let's put together a time line to help you get organized. I'm sure that in the next thirty days, you can find yourself a job. Thirty days after that, you should know how much you can afford to pay in rent and where you can find that kind of apartment. Thirty days after that, I'll chip in and pay for the movers. So on this schedule, you'll be in your own place three months from now. Agreed?"

You might say, "Here is the support I'm willing to give you for the next six months: I will let you live here rent free while you save money to cover the cost of moving into your own place. After six months, you will move out, or you will pay me three hundred dollars per month rent. Agreed?"

Talk About Finances. Katy moved back home at the age of twenty-five because the income from her entry-level job as a computer programmer wasn't enough to allow her to set up an independent household. After a long talk, both Katy and her parents agreed that moving home temporarily until she earned a promotion was a reasonable solution to this problem. But it wasn't long before Katy's parents began to worry if it was a wise decision. They noticed that Katy was spending extravagantly on luxury items like a late-model car and expensive vacations. She bought only the most expensive top-line fashions, and she often asked to borrow money from them. No longer worried about the responsibility of monthly bills, Katy felt free to buy herself a lavish lifestyle. Her parents soon realized that their daughter would never be able to move out and pay her monthly bills. But, they wondered, was it their place to tell their daughter how to spend the money she earned?

If your child is living at home for financial reasons, you have a right to talk about her use of money. If it's clear that your child doesn't know how to budget the money she earns and this situation is affecting your life, you have the right to talk about it.

You might say, "We understand that you are not making enough money to set up your own household. But in order to live independently eventually, all adults need to learn how to budget and save their money. We've noticed that you are spending more than you earn, and so we'd like to help you set some economic goals so you can become more financially secure. We feel it will be fair to both of us if you pay us fifty dollars per week rent and ten dollars per week for food. You would help yourself prepare for your future if you also put one-third of every paycheck into a savings account. How do you feel about this idea?"

Don't back down if your child argues that you're being cheap, that you don't need that money, and that she can't afford it. Acknowledge her feelings, and calmly restate your own. Ask her if she would like to suggest a budget that she feels would be fair. You can also offer to put the money she pays you in an interest-bearing account that you will return to her when she moves out on her own. Allow for give-and-take discussion that will give both of you what you need to live together comfortably.

If your child is living at home and unemployed, you obviously won't be asking for rent payments, but that doesn't let him off the hook completely.

You might say, "I know you can't contribute to the household expenses while you're unemployed, but it would be very helpful to us if while you're looking for work, you would take over the yard work. This would be a great help to us. Is that agreeable to you?"

Nothing is final. All rules can be renegotiated; if something is not working, talk about it again. Make time to sit down and reassess the living arrangements. Talk about problems, and work on solutions. Open communication, honest sharing of feelings, and realistic expectations on both sides will enhance your relationship with your adult child and pave the way for him or her to move out into the world.

EXPERT CONSULTANT

Gail M. Gross, Ph.D., is a nationally recognized expert on developmental issues. She is the host of her Houston, Texas, radio show, "Let's Talk," on which she helps parents who call in with a wide range of parenting dilemmas. Visit her Web site at www.drgailgross.com.

Marriage

"Giving advice about marriage is like garlic: a little bit goes a long way."

Les Parrott, professor of clinical psychology and codirector of the Center for Relationship Development, Seattle Pacific University

Robert watched tall, beautiful Robin wrap his son around her little finger. She bossed him around. She belittled him in public. She broke dates without warning. And still he loved her and was planning to ask her to marry him. Robert didn't know what to say. Should he keep his mouth shut or tell his son that this was not the woman he should marry?

Sandy's heart ached as she held her daughter's hands across the table and tried to comfort her as she sobbed. Her daughter had just had her first major fight with her new husband: he did not call her to say he was going to be late coming home. Her daughter was sure this was the end of the marriage and the end of the world. What could Sandy say to help her daughter get past this crisis?

Maria listened as her son rattled off all the reasons he was furious with his wife. "She doesn't make the bed in the morning. She leaves her dirty clothes on the bathroom floor. She talks to her girlfriends on the phone all night. And instead of cooking a meal, she orders take-out every night. She's driving me crazy!" Maria tended to agree with her son, and there were a few things about his wife that bothered her too. But she struggled to keep quiet. "Should I agree," she pondered, "and say that I don't like her either?"

"I just don't feel that really wonderful, intense kind of love for Jennie that I used to," Jake told his dad. "I'm really worried that I made a mistake. I'm thinking of leaving her—just for a while so I can sort this out." Jake's dad remembered when he felt the same way about his wife about five years after they married. Should he tell his son about his experience or keep quiet and let him find his own way?

These four stories are typical of the kinds of marital circumstances our married adult children might want to talk about and the uncertainty we might feel when we think about offering advice. The fact is that most marriages start out pretty well, but almost every marriage eventually trips over something unexpected. This may be communication problems, bad decisions, addictions, sexual unfulfillment, financial debt, constant conflict, boredom, or something else. The bottom line is that every good marriage at some time will trip over something, and when that happens, your adult children may look to you for help. But when talking to adult children about marriage, it's often difficult to know what to say, how much to say, and when to say it.

This chapter gives you some guidelines that will help you talk to your children in ways that will encourage them to build a strong and resilient marriage. (If your child is not in a good marriage and has decided to leave his or her spouse, see the chapter called "Your Adult Child's Divorce," starting on page 185.)

WHY TALK ABOUT MARRIAGE

Marriage is one of the most important decisions anyone makes in a lifetime. If the decision is a good one, the marriage will prove to be the number one source of satisfaction and fulfillment. Because marriage—the decision to marry and the decisions made during marriage—is so important to a person's lifetime well-being, it makes sense to talk about it. You love your children. You care about them and want the best for them. Putting the subject of marriage on the table and talking about it openly and honestly while respecting your child's right to personal privacy is a gift that will allow you to share your own experiences and beliefs, see things from your child's perspective, and strengthen the parent-child bond between you.

WHEN TO TALK ABOUT MARRIAGE

Would you talk about marriage problems in the middle of a happy family celebration? At his own twenty-fifty wedding anniversary, Peter thought it was a great time to tell his sons and daughter about some of the problems and conflicts that he and their mother had faced over the years and how they managed to keep their marriage intact. It was a wise and insightful way for Peter to teach his children an important lesson about marriage.

"Remember that time," he asked his wife, "when you didn't make dinner for three days because I insulted your cooking?"

"You said the meat tasted like an old shoe!" laughed his wife. "So I figured if it was that bad, you'd be glad if I stopped cooking for you. But you came back and apologized. Didn't you?"

"Sure. I should never have said that. You're a great cook. I must have been in a really bad mood about something else."

"That's typical of your father. Instead of telling me that something was bothering him, he'd insult me, and I'd have to figure out what was going on. You still do that!"

"Yes, I do, and I thank you for being so understanding all these years," said Peter.

This simple dinnertime conversation is teaching Peter's children many lessons about marriage. It is saying more to them about how people fight and make up, communicate and learn to understand each other over the years, than any lecture or sit-down discussion about marriage ever could.

You should talk about your own marriage all the time and anywhere. Through casual conversations, you can let your children know how marriage works—or doesn't work. You can share your hopes and disappointments and convey valuable lessons through example, all without lecturing.

Talking about your child's marriage is a different story. Anytime you bring up this subject, there is a risk that you will be perceived as intrusive, nosy, and meddling. So tread carefully when you want to discuss your child's marriage. You may decide to offer your help or support when you see clues that all is not well—when there are major problems like drunkenness or an absent spouse or simply when you notice tension between the couple or when the grandchildren are telling tales.

Be sensitive to how your input is being received. If you're getting a stiff arm from your son or daughter, back off. If you say something that he or she doesn't appreciate and interprets as meddlesome, apologize. Your adult child's marriage is a private affair.

If she wants to open up, be there to listen, but don't insist that she confide all.

WHAT YOU SHOULD TALK ABOUT

When talking about your adult child's marriage, it's very tempting to point out things your children are doing wrong, to criticize the spouse, or to try to run the show. But all of these things are destructive to another person's marriage. Step back before you speak, and ask yourself if what you're about to say will support and strengthen your child's marriage. If it will not, don't say it.

Breaking the Ice
You can ease yourself into a conversation about your child's marriage by talking about other marriages. Start with your own and add interest by referring to magazine articles you've read.

Talk About Yourself. Anytime you can tell your own story, you are able to give advice without appearing to give advice. Tell stories that illustrate what has worked for you and what hasn't worked. Even if you are a divorced parent, you still have an opportunity to talk about what went wrong for you. Be honest here. You can't help your child understand the realities of marriage if you try to hide your own failures, disappointments, and vulnerabilities and talk only about the joys, successes, and strengths. If you hold your marriage up as an example of perfection, your child is bound to feel let down when his or her own marriage fails to meet that high standard. Instead, tell your child stories from your own life that show how you stumbled occasionally in your marriage but were able to recover. Your kids need to know that your marriage may not be perfect (and they should know that no one's is) but that it's still a good one. You don't need to pass on intimate details, just the general message.

You might say, "The details aren't important, but I remember when your dad and I went through a tough time in our marriage. We struggled for a while, but were able to recover, and I think we became even closer after that."

You might say, "I remember the first time after we were married that Dad and I had a major fight. I was more upset by the fact that we were fighting when we were supposed to be blissful newlyweds than I was about whatever it was we were fighting about. I couldn't believe that he could love me and still storm out of the house and slam the door behind him. It took me a long while to understand that even people in love can get really angry with each other, and that's okay."

You might say, "I regret that my marriage ended in divorce, but I can see now that I didn't understand what marriage was really all about when I married your father. We both still had a lot of growing to do before we could commit to another person, but we didn't think about that. It would have been much better for both of us if we had taken our time, gotten to know each other better, and thought about what we wanted in a marriage before we got swept away by the *idea* of being happily married."

Talk About Marriage in the Media. Our world is full of articles, new stories, and TV and radio shows that give advice on love and marriage. You can use this information to help open the door on the subject and see if your child wants to walk through and offer any personal information.

Instead of saying, "Doesn't it drive you crazy that Tom is away on business so often?"
You might say, "I just read this article about husbands who travel. It said that being apart could either make a marriage stronger or tear it apart, depending on the expectations of the couple. What do you think about that?"

Instead of saying, "Are you as happy with Barbara as you thought you would be?"
You might say, "I heard a marriage counselor on a radio show the other day who was talking about how a young couple's expectations of what marriage would be like can affect the way they rate their happiness. Do you think that's true?"

Instead of saying, "I heard a rumor that Kevin is cheating on you."
You might say, "I saw a woman on a talk show the other day who was talking about how she felt when she found out that her husband was unfaithful. It was so sad to hear how alone and vulnerable she felt. That must be an awful feeling."

Instead of saying, "You are too quick to talk about divorce every time something goes wrong."
You might say, "Did you read about those two celebrities who are getting divorced? They just got married! Do you think a couple should split up as soon as the going gets tough?"

Addressing Specific Issues

Because it's best to talk to your adult children about their marriage problems when they broach the subject to you or when you see signs of upset, what you talk about will depend on their specific needs and problems. This section will give you an idea of how to talk about some general marriage topics that you can adapt to your own situation. It discusses how to talk about:

- Choosing a mate
- Marriage myths
- The evil spouse
- Marriage skills
- Serious problems

Talk About Choosing a Marriage Partner. This is a good topic for general conversation any time. The qualities of a good mate and what to look for in a marriage partner are the kinds of topics you can explore in conversation while your children are still dating casually.

Without targeting your comments directly at your children's girlfriends or boyfriends, you can talk in general terms to give them something to think about. If, for example, you are concerned because your son is dating a woman who loves to spend money, you might say, "I had a friend who was just like Rita; she was a good person, but she loved to spend money. It was a real shock for her when she got married and found out that they couldn't afford everything she wanted to buy. In fact, she and her husband had a lot of fights over it. I wonder what happened to them?" That's all: make an observation, tell a story, and let your child think about it.

If you feel that your child's boyfriend or girlfriend is too controlling, or seems unkind, or is very self-centered, it's best not to say so directly. If you say, "Kate seems awfully possessive, don't you think?" your son will be forced to defend her. Instead, make general observations about these kinds of traits and how they affect relationships.

You might say, "I've always thought it was very important to find someone who would love me for who I am, not for who he wanted me to be. It must be very difficult to be married to someone who tries to control your life and dictate where you can and can't go and who you can and can't see. I just don't understand that kind of relationship."

You might say, "I remember a short time before my grandmother died, we were sitting on the front porch and out of the blue, she said to me, 'Is your husband kind to you?' When I assured her that I thought Dad was a very kind man, she smiled and said, 'If he is kind, you'll have a good marriage.' At the time, it seemed like a rather simplistic view of marriage, but I've learned over the years that she was right. Every once in a while, I think about that. My grandmother was a very wise woman."

You might say, "I was reading a woman's magazine, and it had one of those quizzes on choosing a marriage partner. I took the test and found out that Dad and I are completely incompatible! Isn't that funny. They were asking silly questions like, 'What color do you like? What color does he like?' If you ask me, I think it's more important to be compatible in areas like values, life goals, parenting styles, and cultural attitudes. What do you think?"

Once your son or daughter makes the decision to marry, you may want to put in your two cents about whether this choice is good or bad. If she chooses to marry someone you absolutely love, you need no instructions about what to say. But if your child chooses someone you do not like, that becomes a sensitive subject that can make family conversations quite volatile if you're not careful.

Once the decision has been made, the proposal has been accepted, and the plans are in motion for the wedding, you must then make a serious effort to bite your tongue rather than say anything negative. It's important to give your blessing to your adult child's choice of marriage partner. Of course, it's tempting to be judgmental and feel that no one is good enough for your child, but as a mature, healthy parent, you need to set those feelings aside and realize that you will create a gap between you and your child if you don't accept his fiancée. It's his choice. Don't make him choose between you and the person he wants to marry because you'll lose. It serves no constructive purpose to pick on all the faults and weakness of the chosen mate. Doing everything you can to prove yourself right is not going to help your child have a good marriage or help you to have a good relationship with your child. This is a time to be supportive, not critical.

Instead of saying, "I hope you know what you're doing."
You might say, "I hope you two will be very happy."

Instead of saying, "You're making a big mistake."
You might say, "I wish you both every happiness."

Instead of saying, "You'll see I'm right. You're going to regret this."
You might say, "I trust your judgment and pray that your marriage will be a happy and fulfilling one."

Instead of saying, "How can you be so blind?"
You might say, "I can see you really love him."

Instead of saying, "I can't let you do this."
You might say, "You're an adult now, so I'm not going to tell you whom you should or shouldn't marry. I love you and wish you a very happy marriage."

Talk About Marriage Myths. There are certain myths about marriage that many people buy into and then face serious disappointments when reality kicks in. If you see that your child is hung up on unrealistic expectations, you can gently try to show him that love and marriage are not like what he sees in the movies or may have imagined in his head—and that's okay.

Here are some of the common marriage myths to be wary of:

- This person I'm marrying has the same expectations about marriage as I do.
- Everything will get better for me once I get married.
- Everything bad in my life will disappear once I get married.
- We will always feel this kind of love.

Although while wearing your "parent" hat you may be tempted to state the myth and then begin a lecture, that's not the best way to debunk a myth. You don't even need to offer a solution or advice about what to do. Simply helping your child be aware of common myths is great communication.

You might say, "One of the things that I wish I had realized before I got married was that just because you're married doesn't mean you will be blissfully happy ever after. I've learned since then that all marriages hit rough spots."

You might say, "I wish love and marriage were like we see it in the movies, but it's not. If even Romeo and Juliet had lived and got married, they'd end up fighting about something sooner or later. That's just part of being human."

You might say, "I had a friend once who thought that if she got married, all her problems would be solved. She was so sure that she'd never be unhappy again. Boy, was she in for a big surprise! Marriage just doesn't have that kind of magical power."

You might say, "Marriage is not about satisfying all your needs or about how the other person can solve all your problems and make you feel good all the time. It's a partnership, a lifelong commitment to an institution that is both personal and public. It requires devotion, loyalty, selflessness, compromise, and dedication. It's not always easy, but it has its rewards that make the effort worthwhile."

The most pervasive myth of all is the one that says, "We will always feel this kind of love." Certainly, love is the catalyst for commitment, and it is what ensures that every marriage starts out good. But sooner or later, your children will find out that that kind of love alone, no matter how strong, is not enough to make a marriage work. They'll learn that the intense, overwhelming love they feel on their wedding day does not last. Will they be prepared when that happens? Will they understand how longer-lasting, deeper love can grow over years of partnership, devotion, and commitment?

You can help your children understand that love is fluid, not static. It changes, it bends, it ebbs, and it flows. It is not all or nothing. Imagine how comforting it would be for a young married husband or wife to know that it's okay not to always feel the passionate, yearning kind of love he or she felt on the wedding day and that a more mature love can emerge from a lifelong partnership.

You might say, "I think one of the hardest things for married couples to accept is that the kind of love they feel on their wedding day does not last. It's very normal to have high and low times—to be madly in love sometimes and rather bored with love other times. The key is to have other things, like common interests, genuine concern, and respect, to keep the marriage strong when love cycles into a low period."

Talk About the Evil Spouse. When talking about marriage, always remember that there are really three people in the conversation: you, your adult child, and his or her spouse (although the spouse may not be present). If your son comes to you and complains about a marital problem, keep the spouse's feelings in mind. Listen to the problem, reflect back feelings, and offer encouragement to work it out. If you can be a sounding board in a circumstance like this, you give your child some objectivity to see the problem more clearly and without taking sides.

Never get into a "dump on the spouse" conversation. It contributes to the destruction of a strong marriage by adding your fuel to the fire. That may not be your intent, but you can seriously hurt both the relationship between your child and his or her spouse and the one between you and your child. If you take sides with your son against his wife, what will happen when your son and his wife make up (as you no doubt hope they will)? You are now in the very awkward position of having to take back the things you said, and you will probably have difficulty getting your child to open up to you about other aspects of his life or marriage. Now you will probably hear, "I know you don't like her; you said so yourself."

If your adult child says, "Ellen is driving me crazy. Every time I sit down, she thinks of something I should be doing. She makes these lists of things for me to do every weekend. I can't stand it any more."

Instead of saying, "That's so unfair. Ellen only thinks of herself. You deserve time to rest and enjoy life too."

You might say, "I can see why this would really bother you. What do you think you should do?"

You might say, "Have you explained how you feel to Ellen?"

You might say, "Why do you think Ellen needs you to do these things? Do you think she should do them herself? Are they things that really need to be done?"

If your adult child says, "My husband wants to borrow money against our house to put in the stock market."

Instead of saying, "What the hell is he doing? He should never borrow on your house to buy stocks. You could easily lose your house. Then what would you do?! I'm going to have a talk with him."
You might say, "Do you think this is a good idea? Have you told him you don't want to do that? How can you make him see your point of view?"

Siding with your child against his spouse may feel to you like a supportive sympathetic response, but when you do this, you are unintentionally pulling your child away from his spouse. You are saying that he is justified in having his angry feelings because that person really is unreasonable or beastly. It is best to stay neutral and help your child strategize ways to deal with the problem himself.

Talk About Marriage Skills. When the honeymoon period is over and life returns to a normal routine, your children may begin to feel the sense of loss that comes along with marriage. There are new limits on one's independence. The carefree single lifestyle is gone. There is an invasion of privacy—a constant witness to life activities. Soon there is the death of idealized, romantic fantasies. Misunderstandings, disappointments, and dashed expectations are inevitable. Suddenly, the complaints begin: "He just doesn't understand me." "She never listens to how I feel." "I just can't talk to him."

When this happens to your children, there are three things you might talk about that can help them adjust and build a stronger marriage:

- Talk about how normal these things are (assuming these are normal happen-to-everybody events).
- Encourage them to consider what the situation, problem, or event feels like from their partner's perspective.
- Help them learn to communicate better.

Karen daydreamed about how married life would be for years. She imagined how she would feel when her husband sent her flowers for no reason. She giggled at the idea of finding love notes for her hidden around the house. She fantasized about romantic nights spent making love and talking until dawn. But what Karen didn't take into account was the fact that she was marrying a very practical man. Fred would never throw money away on flowers that die after a day; he was a man who worked hard and went to bed early, and he never said, "I love you," because he figured his wife already knew that. "He doesn't love me!" Karen cried to her mother. "He's so self-centered; he never thinks about me."

What can Karen's mother say? If she comforts her daughter by agreeing with her, she supports an emotional separation in her daughter's marriage. If she offers advice, she risks meddling in a private issue that she really knows little about. The best route here is to help Karen talk about her feelings and expectations, and encourage her to use the marriage skills that will help her deal with this "crisis."

MOTHER: Why do you think he doesn't love you?

KAREN: He never says it, and he never sends me flowers.

MOTHER: Have you told him how you feel?

KAREN: Of course not. It's not love if I have to tell him to send me flowers or if I insist he say, "I love you."

MOTHER: Before you decide that he really doesn't love you, why don't you sit down and tell him how you're feeling? To make a marriage work, you have to be willing to talk about your expectations and your feelings [*communicate*].

I remember the time I was convinced Daddy didn't love me. It was our second wedding anniversary, and I had prepared a wonderful meal, chilled the champagne, lit the candles, and waited for him to arrive home from work. Then he called to say he was working late and wouldn't be home for dinner. Not a word about our anniversary! He completely forgot! But when we sat down to talk about what happened, I found out that he had taken on extra work so he could buy me a better car because he was worried that the old one I was driving wasn't safe. To me, that wasn't the same as sending flowers, but it was his way of saying "I love you" [*normalcy*]. It's very difficult to get along if you each expect the other to be a mind reader. Tonight, talk to Fred, and let him tell you how he expresses love [*the other perspective*].

Karen's mother gave her daughter support without supporting her complaint. She asked Karen questions to help her think about her feelings. She shared her own story to help her daughter see that her feelings are shared by other married couples. And then without lecturing, she suggested that Fred might see the situation very differently. This kind of guidance is not intrusive; it is not controlling. It offers information that an adult child can use to learn how to deal with marital conflicts.

Talk About Serious Problems. If you see something in your child's marriage that is unhealthy or destructive but she isn't talking about it, you're faced with a tough decision. Let's say you notice that every time you visit with your daughter and her husband, he gets drunk. Or what if you know that your daughter's husband has been laid off again and is no longer really looking for a job? Of course, these situations must be difficult for your daughter to live with, but what can you say? If you confront your daughter with your belief that she is married to an alcoholic and in for a very rough marriage, you will push her away at a time when she needs your support. Instead, approach the topic sensitively, and show that you are genuinely interested in her well-being. You don't need to solve the problem right away. You don't need to tell your child what to do. You need to help her get information she needs and let her know that you are there if she needs you.

You might say, "This may be none of my business and you can tell me to leave you alone, but I can't help but notice that Tim is very often drunk when we visit. If you'd ever like to talk about it, I'm here to listen. If I can be of any help, just let me know."

You might also try to guide your child to a professional or a support organization that can help. (See the chapters in Part Three: Problem Areas that deal with that subject and offer resources.) Offer a telephone number, a book, or a pamphlet that addresses the problem with a simple, "I thought this might be of interest to you."

BE CAUTIOUS

When you talk to your adult children about marriage, think twice before you say anything. Marriage is a private relationship between two people. You are by definition the outsider: you don't know all the details, you don't know both sides, and you don't really know what's in your child's heart. Offer an empathic ear and offer to help and support, but beware of some conversation killers:

Don't be judgmental: "You're wrong."
Don't use blame: "This is all your wife's fault," or, "You have only yourself to blame for this."
Don't be dramatic: "Well, you've just ruined your life."
Don't be negative: "I knew this would never work out."
Don't be invasive: "How's your sex life?"

If, on the other hand, you are upset because your child has not married and you have none of these conversation problems to worry about, don't say so! If your child is not married, it is inappropriate, insensitive, and rude to ask her why. Obviously, she has not found someone she wants to make a life commitment to, or maybe she is choosing a single lifestyle (many very fulfilled people remain single all their lives). If you ask adult children, "When are you going to get married?" they have a right to shut down and shut you out.

IN THE END

Marriage is a private relationship between two people. When you're talking about your adult child's marriage, you are not one of those two people. So be sensitive, respectful, and careful when you search for information.

EXPERT CONSULTANT

This chapter was written with the expert help of Les Parrott, Ph.D., a professor of clinical psychology and the codirector of the Center for Relationship Development on the campus of Seattle Pacific University (SPU). This is a groundbreaking program dedicated to teaching the basics of good relationships through classroom education, seminars, research, and marriage mentoring. Along with his wife, Leslie (a marriage and family therapist at SPU), he has been featured on many national radio and television programs such as "Oprah," "NBC Nightly News with Tom Brokaw," "CBS This Morning," "The View,"

"Good Morning America Sunday," and CNN. Les and Leslie Parrott are the authors of *When Bad Things Happen to Good Marriages* (Zondervan Publishing House, 2001) and *Saving Your Marriage Before It Starts* (Zondervan Publishing House, 1995). You can read about their work on their Web site: www.RealRelationships.com.

Grandparenting

"The more grandparents can lower their expectations and avoid assuming what's best, the more options they will have for enjoying their grandchildren."

> Marion L. Usher, Ph.D., *clinical professor in the Department of Psychiatry and Behavioral Sciences, George Washington University School of Medicine and Health Sciences*

When Cynthia turned her husband's den into a nursery two years ago, she was ecstatic. She's not so happy now. "My husband hardly ever used his den," Cynthia explains, "so I thought it would be just wonderful to set up a nursery for my new grandchild. I painted the room yellow. I bought a beautiful crib and changing table. I bought a playpen and toys and so many wonderful baby things. I daydreamed about how nice it would be to have a baby back in our house again. I imagined that my daughter and her husband would take long weekend vacations while I babysat, and I envisioned leisurely afternoons sitting on the floor watching him learn to crawl and then walk while my daughter took time off from parenting to go shopping or whatever. But the truth is, in two years, I think my grandson has spent time in his nursery maybe four times—if that. What a waste of time and money—and of a perfectly good den. It just makes me so mad every time I walk by and see that room."

Cynthia is angry because her expectations of her grandparenting role have not matched reality. This is just one of many common problems in three-generation families that are caused by a lack of communication. Now more than ever before, it's important to be open and honest when you talk to your children about your role in your grandchildren's lives. The rules are quickly changing, and roles are being redefined in dual-career families, blended families, step-families, and single-parent families. Yet grandparents remain the family members who hold the family history and therefore are often in the best position to transmit the values, culture, and religion of the family, and so your role is more important than ever before.

This chapter will help you think about how you can best talk about the role and value of grandparents, as well as the concrete details of day-to-day living.

WHY TALK ABOUT GRANDPARENTING

There are many reasons we should talk to our children about our role as grandparents, but sometimes we just don't know what to say.

Helen had preserved her son's christening gown, hoping to pass on the homemade lace dress to a grandchild. But now that her first grandchild is born, her son doesn't want his child to wear "that old thing."

Kevin bought his five-year-old grandson a football for his birthday and couldn't wait to get out and teach him how to throw. But his daughter took the ball away from her son, saying the sport was "too violent and competitive."

Glenn and Madeline took off work so they could lend a hand caring for their two grandchildren when their daughter gave birth to her third child. They were hurt when their son-in-law told them that he had hired a nanny to care for all the children so it wasn't at all necessary for them to come over.

In each of these situations, the grandparents were hurt by their children's attitudes toward their efforts to be good grandparents. Whenever our children reject our plans, we may feel frustrated or even angry and wonder how we can build a meaningful relationship with our grandchildren but still keep the peace with our own children. The only way to make that happen is to open a dialogue that lets both of you explain your point of view.

In most circumstances, it's important to talk openly in order to avoid making incorrect assumptions and find the middle ground of compromise.

Talk to Avoid Making Incorrect Assumptions. It's important to talk about your role as a grandparent so that neither you nor your child makes assumptions about things that will later cause misunderstandings and arguments. Some adult children assume the grandparents will care for the children while they work; some grandparents are too busy with their own lives to do that. Some grandparents assume they have an undeniable right to spoil their grandchildren, but the child's parents may disagree. If subjects like these aren't talked about right from the beginning, family problems will develop that can become a source of long-term tension.

Talk to Find the Middle Ground. Some grandparents jump right in, take charge, and try to take over the raising of the grandchild. In most cases, this is going to cause family problems. At the other extreme, some grandparents hold back and wait for their children to tell them what they want and need. They may not visit for months because they haven't been "invited," while their children are at home wondering why their parents want nothing to do with their grandchildren. If you talk openly and often, you can find the middle ground where you are welcomed and needed but not in charge.

WHEN TO TALK ABOUT GRANDPARENTING

Sarah was in the kitchen preparing foods for Passover with her daughter, Catherine, and her four-year-old granddaughter, Sharon. "Catherine" she said, "watch how I make this dish so you can one day pass the recipe on to Sharon. It would make me feel very happy if I knew that the two of you could keep this family tradition. And while we cook, let's teach Sharon the Passover song that I learned when I was a little girl."

This simple kitchen conversation between Sarah and her daughter Catherine has great meaning because of the timing. If Sarah were to talk to her daughter about the value of family traditions on any other day, it would not have the impact that it did at that moment. Like many other conversations we have with our adult children, timing can be very important when talking about your role as a grandparent.

Talk During the Pregnancy. This is a good time to talk about what role you will play at the time of the birth and shortly after. If you live out of town and will be making plane reservations, don't assume anything. Talk out the details well in advance. Ask when will be the best time for you to visit. Ask what you can do to help. Ask if they would like you to stick around after the baby is born to help around the house. Ask anything you like, and then accept the answers and make your plans around them. This is the time to set up the kind of communication system that will let both you and your adult child talk about your role in your grandchild's life and in their family life from now on.

Talk After the Baby Is Born. The birth of a baby (whether it's the first or the seventh) is a hectic time in any family. Routines are changed, sleep is disrupted, feelings are raw, and uncertainty runs high. This is not the best time to have a sit-down conversation about your needs and expectations as a grandparent. You may be wondering when the parents will schedule the newborn's religious initiation ceremony. You may want to know if it's okay for you to start a bank account for the baby. You may want to advise your daughter-in-law on the advantages of glass bottles over disposable liners. You may have strong feelings for or against breastfeeding. But again, timing is all important. Unless you are directly asked for your opinion, be patient, and wait until your child and grandchild have settled into a more relaxed routine before you try to talk about the details of your relationship with the baby and your parenting beliefs. At this time, the best thing you can say is, "How can I be of help?"

Talk Always. Talking with your adult children about your role as a grandparent should be something you do throughout the childhood of your grandchildren. There are issues that will need to be revisited over the years and agreements that will need to be changed. Let's say that you offer to baby-sit every Monday for your child's first baby. When the second baby comes along, you may need to talk this arrangement over if you feel uncomfortable about watching two young children every week. Or if you host all the family holiday gatherings but find it harder and harder to do this over time, it's time to sit down and talk about starting new holiday traditions.

If you keep a dialogue going, you'll feel free to talk about the many changes that will take place over the years as the baby grows.

WHAT YOU SHOULD TALK ABOUT

Kim's new baby was due in three weeks when she finally found the antique cradle she had been looking for. It needed to be restored, but it was the cradle of her dreams, and she loved just thinking about rocking her infant child in this wonderful wooden bed. As she arrived home with the cradle in the back of her car, she was surprised to see her parents at her door. "Come in, come in," her mother practically squealed. "We have a wonderful surprise for you!" Leading the way to the nursery, Kim's mother unveiled an old plastic cradle that had been her younger brother's. "Look what we fixed up for the baby!" said her mom with joy. "Your dad painted it for you, and I made that nice blanket and pillow. We thought it would be nice to keep this in the family." "Oh, how nice," said Kim weakly.

This is the kind of situation that is going to cause the kind of hard feelings that could easily be avoided if parents and grandparents make a commitment to each other to talk things over before assuming anything.

Breaking the Ice
Rather than jump right into the details of how, when, and at what time you can enjoy your grandchildren, start with general, broad issues. Tell your children that you want to be involved in your grandchild's life but also want to respect his family's needs.

You might say, "Have you thought about how you want us to be in your life now that you are going to have a child?"
Your child may laugh and say, "What do you mean? The same as always."

But after the baby is born, the family dynamic will not be the same as it was, and so this is an important conversation. Showing a willingness to respect your child's desires and his or her family needs will make it easier for the two of you to work out the details.

You might say, "Have you thought about how you want us to be in your baby's life?"
You child may say, "Of course, we want you to be in the baby's life!"

But then you can persist to understand *how* exactly. Your children shouldn't assume that you know when they need help and when they want to be left alone. You can't assume that they want all the help you can give. These assumptions usually lead to hard feelings, misunderstandings, and eventually arguments. Unless you talk, you risk taking over child care activities that your child may want to do herself. You risk backing off when your child needs you to lend a hand. You risk cutting yourself off from your grandchildren unnecessarily.

You might say, "I don't want to interfere with your plans, but I also don't want you to think I'm not available to help. So I need you to be honest about how I can be a good grandparent and respect your life and needs as well."

This open-ended question gives your adult child the opportunity to talk about his or her needs and desires. Some young families want time alone with a new baby without grandparents being there day and night; others are desperate for any help they can get. In either case, it may be hard for the new parents to ask for what they want without sounding selfish and needy. But if you ask them what they want, you give them the opportunity to tell you without risking hurt and misunderstood feelings.

Addressing Specific Issues

Dan is a retired banker who is more than willing to help his daughter in the baby-sitting department occasionally, but unfortunately, when he does help out, they usually end up arguing. "My daughter drives me crazy," says Dan. "I try to help by doing things like picking the kids up after school once in a while if she's busy or delayed, but then she complains about everything I do with them. If I give them a piece of candy, I'm giving them cavities. If I take them to the park, I'm letting them get too dirty. If I give them a few dollars for a good report card, I'm spoiling them. Why can't she just say thank you instead of complaining all the time?"

The way Dan cares for his grandchildren isn't "wrong," and the way his daughter wants them to be cared for isn't "wrong." The way they care for the kids is simply different. The only way Dan and his daughter can make this work out so he can enjoy his grandkids and she can have peace of mind is to talk. They need to have an honest conversation in which they both find a way to compromise and keep a strong, loving relationship intact.

They both need to agree to back off and back down on things that are important to the other person. If they don't, it's very likely that Dan will get tired of his daughter's complaining, and his daughter will get tired of his lack of respect for her wishes, and they'll stop the after-school time shared between this grandparent and his grandkids. Everyone loses in this case, especially the grandchildren.

This kind of everyday situation causes family friction and problems that could easily be avoided if the grandparent and the adult child took time to talk about their feelings and needs. The quality of your relationship is in the details. How you work these out right from the start will set the foundation for your role as a grandparent.

A few topics you might talk about over the years with your adult child include these:

- Control issues
- Family traditions
- Baby-sitting
- Spoiling
- Parenting
- Visitation in a divorce situation

Control Issues. If you have always found it difficult to let your child grow up and away from you, you may find it particularly difficult to let him or her raise the children in any way that is different from your parenting style.

To make the transition from controlling parent to supportive grandparent, you need to move out of the center of this experience. Picture your family as concentric circles. Your child and spouse and your grandchild are at the center of the family circle. You no longer fit right there in the middle of the action. You are now positioned in an outer ring of the circle. You're not completely detached or thrown out. You're just not in the center position where you can dictate the action. You have a different role now.

Sometimes you're going to have to overcome the overwhelming urge to do grandparently things like holding, rocking, looking, and touching; you'll need to step back and get out of the way. And you'll have to learn to take your cues from your own children as they learn how to stand on their own feet without you lurking nearby (albeit with good intentions) to catch their mistakes. You have to back off and have faith in your child's own decision-making abilities (but be near enough to help when you're asked). Sure, your children may make mistakes with your grandchildren, but you will all survive these mistakes. It's far better to be supportive than always right.

Instead of saying, "It's important for the grandchildren to get to know us, so we're going to make the long drive to visit every Sunday." (The truth is, your child and his spouse may not want to sit home every Sunday to entertain you. This is a typical case where talking about the subject will help you find a way to make everybody happy.)
You might say, "We hope that we'll get to see our grandchildren on a regular basis. When is a good time for us to visit this week?"

A good rule of thumb that can help you find the line between helping and controlling is to think before you offer any advice or criticism. Then ask yourself if you would say this same thing to a friend. Would you tell a friend when you'll be visiting and expect that friend to change plans to accommodate you? Unasked, would you tell a friend how to breast-feed better, or what to do about a tantrum, or how to punish back talk? Show your children the same respect you would show a friend, and you'll soon see they may ask for your advice and will actually listen to what you have to say.

Family Traditions. Family traditions are the activities and events that are repeated at the same time and place and give you a sense of continuity and ritual. Maybe your family tradition is to meet for a three-generation family vacation each summer. Maybe you all gather at your house for the Fourth of July picnic every year. Maybe you always bake the birthday cake for your grandchildren's birthdays. There are thousands of ways you and your family may build tradition without even being aware of it. Suddenly you realize that you have been doing it this way for a while, and everyone expects it to continue. Now you have a tradition.

You may find, however, that you need to talk when some members of the family want to break a family tradition. Of course, we all want our grandchildren to grow up with this sense of family tradition, but we also need to be flexible when our children want to try something different. When a member of your family announces that he or she will not be keeping the tradition this year, don't let yourself feel totally crushed by the change. Change is not necessarily bad; it's just different, and sometimes even good.

If your child says, "This year we won't be coming up to the lake for a week; we're going to take the kids to the ocean for vacation." *Instead of saying*, "But you always come to the lake. I look forward all year to spending that time with my grandchildren. Why are you doing this to me? Did something bad happen last year that has made you change your mind?"
You might say, "I'm disappointed, but I understand why you might want to try a different kind of vacation. Is there another time during the summer when I can see you and my grandchildren?"

In the past, you may have been very firm about keeping family traditions. If you now realize that your children aren't enjoying these rituals, talk to them and let them know how you feel.

You might say, "I want you to know that as your family grows, if you ever want to change our family tradition of [doing whatever], you shouldn't feel bound to it. Let me know, and we'll talk about ways to change and adjust. Okay?"

Baby-sitting. Although most grandparents make the best baby-sitters in the world, this is one area of grandparenting that often causes the most misunderstandings. Right from the start, you should talk about your willingness, hesitance, or inability to baby-sit so that your child knows where you stand before assumptions are made and everyone gets hurt. Some parents feel displaced by a very helpful grandparent, and sometimes it's the grandparents who find themselves in demanding circumstances that they never meant to agree to. These kinds of situations are sure to cause family tensions if the feelings aren't brought out in the open and talked about.

   If you can't wait to get your grandchildren to yourself and are perfectly able and willing to baby-sit anytime their parents need you, say so. Tell your children how you feel, and ask how they feel about the offer. But don't assume you will be the only sitter they use. It may be more convenient for them to hire the teenager who lives next door when they're running out for an errand. They may decide to leave the baby at an infant care center during working hours rather than impose on your life. Or if you and your child have a strained relationship, she may not want you back in her life too often. You won't know how your children feel until you talk about it. Make known your willingness to baby-sit, and then wait to see what happens. It's not an insult if your child doesn't take you up on your offer; it's simply a parenting decision. You both have to be able to say what you want and how you feel.

You might say, "I know I've often said that I'd be glad to baby-sit, but I want you to know that it's not an imposition at all. When I baby-sit, I get a chance to get to know Lily, and I just love it—I think Lily likes it too. It's important to me to be able to spend time with her, so please don't hesitate to call me."

Being a grandparent shouldn't automatically make you an on-call baby-sitter. There are many circumstances in which you aren't available for this duty. You may lead your own busy life that leaves little time for baby-sitting. You may have health problems that make it difficult to wrestle with little ones. You may simply not want to. Whatever the reason, it's important to be honest right from the start so your adult child can have realistic expectations.

You have to have the freedom to say, "I can't do this." Don't take on what you can't or don't want to do. Baby-sitting your grandchildren is an enormous responsibility that shouldn't be taken lightly or ever assumed. Barring emergencies when your help might be absolutely required, baby-sitting should always be by the mutual agreement of both you and your adult child.

Instead of saying, "I wish I could but . . . [fill in the excuse]."
You might say, "I know some grandparents are ready, willing, and able to baby-sit all the time, but to be honest, I'm not one of them. I love to see my grandchildren, but I'm just not [ready, willing, or able] to take on the commitment of being a steady baby-sitter."

If your adult children assume you are always available and are always happy to baby-sit because you always say yes, it's understandable that you might become resentful if they begin to show no gratitude or at least have the courtesy to ask you before making their plans.

Instead of saying, "Yes."
You might say, "I'd be glad to, but I want to talk to you about the next time. Although I'm happy to baby-sit, I do need some advance notice, and I need you to know that if I've made other plans, sometimes the answer might be no. Is that okay with you?"

If your adult child says, "I'm going back to work, and I'd like to leave the baby with you, okay?"
You might say, "You know I love Isaac with all my heart, but I can't baby-sit for you full time. I'd be glad to help you occasionally if that would help."

Don't apologize. Don't make excuses. Don't get angry. Don't give in. You should not take on this major responsibility unless you really want to. Your child may end the conversation abruptly and appear upset, but if you stand your ground in an honest and open way, she'll eventually come to understand.

Spoiling. Some grandparents live to spoil their grandchildren. They buy them too many toys, stuff them with too many treats, and let them do absolutely anything they want. This, some say, is the fun part about being a grandparent: all the joy of parenting without any of the responsibility. There is nothing wrong with wanting to give your grandchildren things that will make them happy. Most grandparents are grateful that they are able to give their grandchildren things that they could not afford with their own children. However, if this is your style of grandparenting, you have to understand that your gifts may not be received by your adult child in the spirit with which they are given.

Your generosity may be working against your child's efforts to raise unspoiled children, or your child may be very strong-willed and want things done her way. Or she may even feel threatened by your carefree relationship with her children. Whatever the reasons, spoiling is a subject that can divide a family if it is not openly discussed with the goal of finding a compromise everyone can live with.

You might say, "I do like to spoil Max and Mark, but I agree with you that I don't want to have demanding, rude, or ungrateful grandchildren. How can we compromise?"

You might say, "I would like to buy a special gift for Jackson for his birthday, but I want it to be something that you will appreciate too. Would you like to come with me when I go shopping?" (Or, if you live too far away for a shared shopping trip: "Would you like to suggest an appropriate gift?")

You might say, "When Robin, Harry, and Spencer are in my house, I'd like to feel that I can spoil them. But I agree that I should follow your rules when I'm in your house. Is that compromise agreeable to you?"

You might say, "I know it upsets you when I buy too many toys for Emma. I was thinking that maybe it would be better if I bought fewer toys and put the money that I would have spent in a special bank account for her. Would you like that better?"

Parenting. Your years of experience have certainly taught you many things about parenting. You probably have learned what works and what doesn't. You know how to cool a fever and feed a cold. And you've learned how to discipline and educate for the best results. Too bad that when you finally get it all together, your kids are grown.

The truth is that it is not helpful for grandparents to give out unsolicited advice about parenting or to insist on using a parenting style that is unlike the one used by the child's parents. You have your style of parenting, of course, but this is not your child. You have had your chance; you have tried different kinds of feeding schedules, discipline, health remedies, and so on. Now it's your child's turn.

Granted, it is very hard to keep quiet. Your grandchildren mean the world to you and you want to see them raised "properly." Defining "properly," however, can lead to some brutal family battles. It is especially difficult to keep quiet when you see something happening that you disagree with. Maybe your child is putting her baby in child care. Maybe your child doesn't want to breast-feed. Maybe your child is not going to enroll your grandchild in a private school. Maybe your child is raising your grandchild as a vegetarian. The possibilities for argument are endless. You have to decide if you want to argue endlessly or instead work hard to create a family bond of mutual respect.

If you opt for building a respectful relationship, you'll find many benefits, the most obvious and enjoyable one being that you will see your grandchildren more often. Your child will be much more likely to visit often if she knows that you respect her right to parent her children as she sees fit. It's only natural. Who wants to visit someone if you know you're going to get a lecture about all you're doing wrong?

This is not to say that if you feel you have information to offer your children about parenting that will be of value to them, you have to remain absolutely mute. It's important to pass on your experience and your beliefs to your children. However, here is a tip offered by counselor and psychotherapist Catherine Tuerk that you can use to keep your kids from turning you off and to keep yourself from becoming a nagging parent. Tell your adult children that you would like to feel free telling them your thoughts on parenting, but you don't want to interfere or nag. So you would like the right to voice your opinion on any subject of parenting *one time*. During that one time, you'd like them to agree to listen and take what you say seriously. Then promise that you will never mention it again. Tell them that you will assume they will consider your advice and use it or not as they feel it is best for them. If you should forget (and we all do) and repeat your opinion and advice, invite your child to stop you with the phrase, "This is not new information." This gives you an opportunity to laugh rather than argue.

Visitation in a Divorce Situation. Divorce under any circumstances is devastating to all family members. It is especially difficult for the children of divorce, and this is why grandparents can have a vital role during this difficult time. When the parents are angry, upset, and dealing with their emotional upheaval, the children often are left alone to deal with their own worries and troubles. This is when a supportive and understanding grandparent can be most helpful.

This supportive role is not always an easy one. The battling parents may not make it easy for the grandparents to visit. The children themselves may be so angry or confused that they are not pleasant or enjoyable company. And it is very hard for grandparents to remain neutral in the divorce struggle. But a determined, understanding, and persevering grandparent may be the only person involved who can contribute in a direct way to the child's ultimate adjustment. This is what makes the difficulties worth the effort.

To be a supportive and stable influence on your grandchildren, you will need to stay out of the divorce war itself. Grandparents should not take sides (even when one marriage partner is clearly in the wrong). Grandparents should say only positive things about either parent to the children. And grandparents should not get emotional in front of their grandchildren. This is a tall order, but this kind of family crisis calls for extraordinary actions.

It is the grandparents who can show their grandchildren the unrestrained attention and love they need, especially during this difficult time. Whether in person, on the telephone, or by mail, grandparents in this situation have the opportunity to model how to get on with the good parts of life; they can show how problems can be solved and pain managed; they can give the child a chance to talk out loud about hidden feelings; and they can offer themselves as a stable force in very turbulent times.

You should talk to your adult child and your daughter- or son-in-law about the role you would like to play with your grandchildren during the divorce.

You might say, "I know this is a very difficult time for you and you have a lot on your mind. Because of that, I would like to spend more time [or talk on the telephone more often] with Noah and Kate. I want to take a neutral position and focus on their feelings and needs without taking sides. I think it's important for them to have this support, and I'm hoping you'll let me get more involved in their lives right now."

Unfortunately, divorce can cut off even the most determined grandparents from their grandchildren. If your efforts to make contact by telephone and mail fail, your last recourse might be a legal one. In many states, grandparent visitation is not automatic, and a formal legal visitation request has to be made. This can lead to a long and expensive court battle, so you will need legal advice and support and information. (See the Resources section for helpful organizations.)

KEEP THE DIALOGUE GOING

In the grandparent-parent family dynamic, there are many words and actions over the years that can hurt feelings and cause misunderstandings. When that happens to you, don't brood in silence.

Always talk about your feelings, ask your child to share his or her feelings, and work together to find that middle ground that you can both live with. It will also help if you come to accept that your well-intentioned grandparently advice will not always be heeded. But as long as you're all still talking and sharing feelings, you'll be able to build a close, loving relationship with your grandchildren that will rise above any differences of opinion you may have with your adult children.

RESOURCES

AARP Grandparent Information Center
American Association of Retired Persons
601 E St., N.W.
Washington, D.C. 20049
(202) 434-2296, (202) 434-2108

National Coalition of Grandparents
137 Larkin St.
Madison, WI 53705
(601) 238-8751

Books
Carson, L. *The Essential Grandparent*. Deerfield Beach, Fla.: Health Communications, 1996.
Zullo, K., and Zullo, A. *The Nanas and the Papas: A Boomers' Guide to Grandparenting*. Kansas City, Mo.: Andrews McMeel Publishing 1998.

EXPERT CONSULTANT

This chapter was prepared with the expert help of Marion L. Usher, Ph.D., a clinical professor in the Department of Psychiatry and Behavioral Sciences, George Washington University School of Medicine and Health Sciences, Washington, D.C. Her private practice focuses on working with individuals, couples, and families.

Your Divorce

"The most destructive thing that a parent can do to an adult child during a divorce is blame the other parent. I can't tell you the admiration I have for a divorcing parent who can resist pointing that finger of blame."

Patricia E. Wicks, licensed psychologist

The marriage had never been ideal. Helen and Bob had fought back and forth over everything for years; they rarely did anything together, and the atmosphere in their home was cold and tense. Finally, after twenty-nine years of marriage, they both agreed it was time to divorce and see what else life might offer them. Their only child, Kaitlyn, was now twenty-five years old and living on her own. They were glad that "she would not be affected by this" and agreed to give the news together to their daughter. "Neither of us was prepared for her reaction," remembers Helen. "We figured that she would be upset, but knowing how unhappy we both have been, she would agree that it was for the best. Boy, were we in for a surprise."

Kaitlyn threw a fit. She cried and hollered. She yelled at her parents for trying to ruin her life. She begged them to reconsider. It was an awful time for the entire family.

Kaitlyn's reaction makes her sound like a self-centered, immature child, but in the family structure, she *is* the child, and the news of the divorce and the fear it caused her sent her retreating to childish maneuvers. Her parents figured that because she was an adult now, they could sit down and address the issue as adults. But this approach ignores the fact that Kaitlyn will always be their child and will have feelings and fears connected to that role. In addition, Kaitlyn's severe reaction might have been in response to the fact that she had been out of the family home for six years. She did not know what was going on between her parents, and so she was not prepared for an announcement of such finality. The most obvious cause of this explosive reaction in this family is the lack of open communication, which apparently had gone on for years. This is a good time for Kaitlyn and her mother and father to begin to talk about their feelings, their needs, and their hopes for the future.

There is no correct way to break this news to your adult children, and there are no hard rules about how the family should proceed through the divorce process. All divorce circumstances are unique. In one family, divorce may be quite common and not a big deal. In another family, this may be the first divorce in the family's documented history, and it will be very difficult for everyone. Some divorces are quite civil; others are very brutal. Some follow years of abuse and heartache; others seem to die out without a sound.

But whatever your circumstance, you'll find that often an adult child's view of who he is and his place in the world is intimately bound to his parents' marriage and the nature of his family. This image can be severely shaken by divorce. That's why it's so important to let your adult children openly discuss their feelings about this change in the family situation. Open communication is really all you have that can make the situation better.

WHY TALK ABOUT YOUR DIVORCE

Kim's friend, Mara, called her late one Sunday night ready to offer a sympathetic ear. "My mom just told me about your parents," she said. "I'm so sorry. Do you want to talk about it?"

"What are you talking about?" asked Kim. "What's the matter with my parents?"

"You know," Mara hesitated. "About the divorce."

"What divorce!!??" screamed Kim. "I don't know anything about a divorce."

"Oh, I'm so sorry," Mara backed off. "I guess my mother has her facts messed up. Somebody told her that your parents were getting divorced, but if that were so, I guess you'd know. Right?"

Wrong. The truth was that Kim's parents were getting a divorce but had not told her because they were afraid the news would hurt her. Because the time had never seemed quite right, they kept putting it off until finally someone else did the job for them.

Connie and Frank agreed that there was no reason to tell their adult children about their decision to divorce. "We agreed," said Connie, "that this was between us and really none of the kids' business. We didn't want them making a big deal out of this or trying to make us feel guilty. When the whole thing is over, when Frank moves out and there's no turning back, then we'll tell them. But this is hard enough on both of us as it is. We don't want them to make it even harder."

Debbie and Jim told their three children about their decision to divorce and then retreated into silence. "After the initial announcement," remembers their daughter Cindy, "they never told us a thing about what was going on. If we asked for any details, they'd both say something like, 'We're taking care of it.' I think they were trying to protect us, but instead they made things very stressful and frustrating."

In these three families, the decisions that were made about how and when to communicate to adult children about the parents' divorce all assumed that now that the children are adults, they can be separated from the divorce process. This is a major communication mistake for everyone. Of the many, many reasons to talk to your adult children about your divorce, keep the following in mind:

- When you decide to get a divorce, you should talk to your adult children because that decision directly affects their lives in many ways, and there are many opportunities for misunderstandings, hurt feelings, and broken relationships if your divorce is cloaked in a veil of secrecy.

- You should talk to your adult children to offer them reassurance. They are adults and do have their own lives now, but they are also your children. Your divorce may stir up many old emotions, fears, and insecurities from the past. They need to be able to talk to you about these feelings to reduce the potential for harm that can be caused when parents separate and the children are in the dark.

- Keeping a steady flow of open communication during this stressful time will help all family members better deal with the changes and confusion inherent in any divorce.

- Your divorce is a life event for the entire family. There is no way to shield your children from what's happening in your life. You can't decide to shut them out to protect them or your own privacy. You can't expect life to go on as usual for your children; their parents are divorcing, and that fact will affect them directly.

- Talking about your divorce provides your adult children with a growth opportunity. The way you handle this difficult circumstance will be a model for them about how to handle other life transitions. When you talk honestly and willingly, you show them that even in difficult times, the family can remain close and talk things over. In fact, you'll find that when family communication continues even in tough times, it often happens that they grow closer together and learn valuable life lessons.

Not talking about your divorce is not an option if you'd like a healthy, honest relationship with your children.

WHEN TO TALK ABOUT YOUR DIVORCE

Meredith's parents invited her out to dinner at a restaurant that had long been a family favorite. They talked and laughed and caught up on the news of their lives. Then over dessert, Meredith's mother leaned over and said, "Honey, Daddy and I brought you out to dinner because we have something to tell you. We've decided to get a divorce." Meredith stared at both of them in silence. Then she grabbed her purse and rushed out of the restaurant and drove herself home. She hasn't spoken to either of her parents since that night several weeks ago, and she spends most of her nights alone in her apartment crying. She can't believe that her parents were acting so friendly and laughing through their whole dinner together and then tell her they were divorcing. How can that be?

The reason for Meredith's struggle with the news of her parents' divorce probably has more to do with the surprise element than the actual fact. One might think that adult children are bound to be aware of problems in their parents' marriage, living out of the home they should be able to have a more objective view, and many have even been the sounding board over the years for marital problems. So they can hardly be shocked when the marriage finally falls apart. But apparently many adult children are surprised at the news. Authors Noelle Fintushel and Nancy Hillard conducted a survey asking adult children how they felt on hearing the news of their parents' decision to divorce. Fully 45 percent of respondents said that their parents' divorce came as a total surprise. According to these authors, this figure corresponds to other research on the subject as well.

If you are thinking that your adult child won't be shaken by the news because "he's got to suspect that it's coming" or because "he's old enough now to hear the truth," think again. You may need to give him a little more warning before you break the news. A far better scenario for Meredith would have been one in which her parents were more honest with her about their marriage all along. The majority of divorces don't happen overnight. They are usually the result of years of small disappointments, transgressions, and incompatibilities. Certainly, many parents try to hide their troubles from young children. But it is better to let your adult children see the process of a failing relationship than to allow them to be hit with the pile of rubble at the end.

Without going into any details, you should talk to your adult children about your feelings during the decision-making process. When you begin the move away from your spouse, you might start to talk about feeling "let down in my marriage" or even "fed up with being emotionally alone." Give your kids a glimpse at your life so the final decision won't be so shocking. Ongoing honest communication makes the announcement of a divorce decision an expected next step rather than a sudden announcement.

The surprise divorce announcement is also difficult to handle on a more psychological level. Divorce is a tragic loss, very much like death. For an adult child, a parental divorce is the death of many life fantasies. Even in a volatile relationship, the adult child often lives under the assumption that "soon" her parents will work things out and be happy. Divorce brings an end to this hope, and so the event is often grieved by the adult child in ways similar to the grief following a death: denial, isolation, anger, bargaining, depression, and finally acceptance. This grieving process after a divorce is similar to the one after a death in another way also. Just as it is much more difficult to move through the grieving process after a sudden, unexpected death, it is more difficult to process the grief of a sudden, unexpected divorce. If your adult children are blindsided by an abrupt announcement, you can expect them to have many more problems dealing with this news than if they had been allowed to have a glimpse of the process as it was unfolding.

Whether you have prepared your children for your decision to divorce or have sprung it on them out of the blue, the subject is not something for a one-time, sit-down conversation. It is your life. It is ongoing, and so your conversations about it will also be part of a process of change and growth. When you first discuss the issue, it's not necessary to map out every detail. There will be plenty of time to talk about holiday arrangements and questions about the children's inheritance. Divorce is now part of your life; therefore, it should be one of the subjects you talk to your adult children about throughout the process of separation and rebirth.

WHAT YOU SHOULD TALK ABOUT

The details of your conversations with your children will be dictated by your personal circumstance. But there are some general guidelines that can help both you and your children get the most out of these conversations. When you talk to your children, be very aware of the dialogue suggestions in the following areas:

- Lurid details
- Pointing the finger of blame
- Sending mixed messages
- Inappropriate guilt
- Negative or unexpressed feelings
- Choosing sides
- An egocentric reaction
- Silence
- Communication mistakes

The Lurid Details. "Honey," began Jessica's mother, "There's something I have to tell you. Your father and I have decided to get a divorce. I know this is hard for you to hear, but I think you're old enough to understand. The truth is, we haven't had good sex in over twenty years. At first, we went to a sex counselor, and we tried all kinds of new positions and things, but it just didn't work. Then your father started cheating on me to get his kicks with younger women. It's not a good idea for us to stay together anymore. Are you okay with this?"

No matter what Jessica said to her mother, she probably was not okay with this. In those few minutes, Jessica had to absorb more than she could emotionally handle. She had just learned that her parents had been unhappy for years, that they were breaking up, and on top of that, she learned intimate details of their sex life. This is too much for a child of any age to take in. No matter how old your adult children are, they are still your children. So when you talk about your divorce to your children, don't give them the lurid details; they don't want them or need them.

Instead of saying, "Your father and I are no longer sexually compatible."
You might say, "Your father and I have decided it's best to divorce."

Instead of saying, "Your mother had an affair fifteen years ago, and I have never been able to forgive her for that."
You might say, "Your mother and I have been unhappy together for a long time."

Instead of saying, "Your father has been in therapy for a personality disorder that sometimes makes him physically abusive to me."
You might say, "Your father and I simply cannot live together anymore."

If your child insists, "But why?!"
You might say, "Because of things that have happened in our marriage that are personal and private and not open for general discussion."

Pointing the Finger of Blame. Brandon's dad wanted his son to understand why he was divorcing his mother after twenty-six years of marriage. "No one could live with your mother. You've seen how demanding she is. She always has to be in control of everything. And she's so busy with all her friends that she's never home with me anymore. She gives me no love or affection, and I just can't live like this anymore."

Like Brandon's dad, you might feel the need to point a finger of blame at your spouse when talking to your kids about the divorce. It's natural to want them to side with you and to give you their sympathy. But look at this from your kids' point of view. How can Brandon respond? If he agrees with his father, he will be betraying his mother. If he disagrees with his father, he will be looking for an argument. Pointing a finger of blame when talking to your adult kids about your divorce is always a bad idea.

Try to remember this advice: if what you're tempted to say is harmful to your spouse or if it's no more than dumping on the other person so you can feel better, you should not say it. Of course, this can be very hard to do, especially if your adult child tries to blame you and you know it's not your fault. If your adult child says, "How can you do this to Mom when she needs you?" and you know that you have done everything you could to help your wife deal with her alcoholism, it's natural to want to set the record straight, but that's not what will help your child. Yes, this is hard to do, but it is what's absolutely best.

Instead of saying, "This is not my fault. If your mother would choose me over the bottle, this wouldn't be happening!"
You might say, "This is a decision I have made that I believe is for the best. You should talk to your mother about her role in this."

Instead of talking about your spouse, talk about *you* and *your* feelings. This will give you plenty to talk about without disparaging your child's other parent.

Instead of saying, "Your dad is driving me crazy."
You might say, "I'm not very happy."

Instead of saying, "Your mother has never been a good wife."
You might say, "I want to move forward with my life in a good direction."

If they say, "Is it true that Dad's been cheating on you?"
Instead of saying, "He sure has been. He's a dog who deserves to be raked over the coals, and that's what I'm going to do to him."

You might say, "That's something you'll have to ask your father about."

If they say, "It's all over town that she's cheating on you. I don't blame you for divorcing her."
You might say, "Trusting in a relationship after that trust has been broken is very difficult, and, yes, that is one of our issues, but there are many more as well."

Sending Mixed Messages. Some parents know that they shouldn't share the intimate details of the marital troubles with their children, but still they can't resist trying to blame their spouse through innuendo or hints.

Instead of saying, "I'm not going to burden you with the details, but your mother has done some awful things."
You might say, "Your mother and I agree that this will be best for both of us."
You might say, "I've decided that this is something I need to do."

Inappropriate Guilt. We all know that when parents of young children divorce, the children commonly think it's their fault. All books about divorce are quick to advise divorcing parents to make sure they tell their children that they had nothing to do with the breakup. This advice is good even when your children are adults.

Don't be surprised if your adult child cries out, "This is all my fault!" It's a rather natural reaction of some children. But although you can clearly see that your child has nothing to do with your marital problems, don't brush the idea off. If your child feels that way, he needs the opportunity to talk it out.

Instead of saying, "Don't be silly. This has nothing to do with you."
You might say, "Tell me why you feel that way."

The answer might be an incident that has some direct bearing on your problem, such as the time he innocently mentioned that he saw his dad having lunch with a female friend (and it turned out to be the last straw on a long string of infidelities). Or it might be something inconsequential from long ago that you don't even remember, like the time you argued with your spouse over your child's haircut. In any case, your adult child needs to get those feelings out and hear you say that he or she had nothing to do with your decision to divorce.

It often happens that parents divorce when their youngest child has left the house, either to work or to go to college. This too can cause guilt feelings on the child's part. The first question from this youngest child is usually, "Did you stay together because of me?" (with the implied message that they're getting divorced because that child has finally moved out of the house, on top of the implied message that the parents had lived a very unhappy life because of that adult child). This kind of question can be answered only with the truth.

Instead of saying, "Of course not, honey. The timing is just a coincidence."
You might say, "It was a decision that your father and I chose to make. That's what we wanted to do. Now, it's not an issue."

Negative or Unexpressed Feelings. Don't underestimate the strong feelings your adult children may be struggling with during and after your divorce. When their world falls apart, the shock, disbelief, fear, disorientation, and anger it causes can be overwhelming. Your adult child will probably have a complex mix of emotions to deal with during your divorce process. Many of your conversations should be about these feelings. Of course, you too are struggling with your own mix of feelings, but because you are the parent in this relationship, you should not unburden yourself on your child. The best thing you can do at this point is practice empathetic listening skills. Put yourself in her place, and listen from her point of view. You don't have to have all the answers; you don't have to feel obliged to make her feel better or to make the hurt go away. You just have to listen and use encouraging remarks like, "Why do you think you feel that way?" or, "How did you come to that conclusion?" or, "Tell me more." Talking out loud helps us all sort out our feelings and adjust to difficult situations. Give your child the freedom to talk while you listen.

Instead of saying, "I thought you were a mature adult. This shouldn't be so hard for you to accept."
You might say, "Tell me how this makes you feel."

Instead of saying, "Oh, don't be angry. This has nothing to do with you."
You might say, "Why do you think you feel so angry?"

Instead of saying, "Why are you acting so sad? This wasn't your marriage."
You might say, "You seem so sad. What are you thinking about?"

Instead of saying, "Don't let this ruin your day. Don't even think about it."
You might say, "I know you will have a lot of strong feelings about this. Any time you want to talk, I'm hear to listen."

Choosing Sides. At some point in the divorce proceedings, you may get the feeling that your adult child has taken sides against you.

Don't just stew over it; this is something you can have a conversation about. But rather than giving your interpretation of your child's behavior, just note the behavior and state how it makes you feel.

Instead of saying, "I think you're taking your dad's side."
You might say, "I've noticed that you're spending your free time with your dad, and you haven't been to see me in quite a while. I'm feeling that you're angry with me. I'm wondering if there's something we need to talk about."

An Egocentric Reaction. Adult children will have lots of questions that may seem self-centered, but are just natural reactions to a change that will affect them directly. They will wonder how this is going to affect them. How will this affect them financially? How is this going to affect them emotionally? How is this going to affect their time? What will happen on holidays? Whether they feel free to verbalize these "self-centered" questions or not, encourage your children to ask you about anything they're wondering about. The fact is that you probably won't have all the answers yet yourself, but it's still good for your children to get their worries out and know that they are issues you'll eventually deal with.

If they say, "Well, what are we going to do on holidays? There's not enough time in one day to visit Tim's family and then go to two different places to visit both of you!"
You might say, "I don't know how all the details will work out, but I do know that we're going to make it work out okay for everybody. We will still be a close family."

If they say, "How is this going to change things for me?"
You might say, "I'm not really sure yet. Of course, this change will make things different for us, but we will still be a family and we will be happy."

Silence. Thirty-seven-year-old Ken remembers how hard it was to deal with his mother's silence during her divorce proceedings. "My mother was so ashamed that my father was divorcing her that she hid in the house for months. She didn't want to see anyone, or face any of her friends, or talk to me. I think she somehow felt the divorce was a reflection on her ability to be a good wife, the only role she had ever played in life. So when her marriage fell apart, she was horrified. I just wish she would let me talk to her. But she refuses to be part of any conversation that has the word *divorce* in it."

Like Ken's mother, some people who divorce after many years of marriage are so embarrassed or ashamed of what they perceive as a failure that they don't want anyone to talk about it. In this case, the adult children are left to worry and wonder what's going on. They feel left out and hurt because they get the implied or stated message that this is a shameful family secret, and they aren't free to talk about their own feelings to anyone. This is a no-win situation for everyone.

If you are having a difficult time facing this life event and have retreated into silence, you are making the process far more difficult for yourself and for everyone around you than it needs to be. It's okay to talk about what has happened to your family, and it's okay for them to talk to you about it. In order to heal and to move on with life, your children need to be able to talk to you. Don't shut them out.

Common Communication Mistakes. No one can tell you exactly how to talk to your adult children about something as personal as your divorce. Only you know the state of your relationship; only you know your family history and the children's personalities. But there are some general guidelines you should keep in mind that will help you have discussions that are healthy and helpful rather than hurt-ful and potentially damaging to your relationship. Always avoid putting your adult child into any of the following roles:

• *The Adviser.* Some divorcing parents look to their grown children for advice. In most life circumstances, there is nothing at all wrong with this, but in the case of divorce, it is a mistake. If your child is asked to help you decide what to do in this circumstance, you are asking him to take some responsibility for how things proceed, and he risks feeling like your accomplice against the other parent.

Don't say, "Do you think I should contest the divorce?"
Don't say, "Should I ask for alimony?"
Don't say, "How do you think your mother will feel if I move in with my girlfriend?"
Don't say, "Where can I find a good lawyer?"

• *The Sounding Board.* The polar opposite of the parents who won't talk about the divorce at all are the parents who talk too much. Some divorcing parents use their adult children as a sound-ing board. They call every day to talk about the ongoing battle: what he said, what she did, what his lawyer said, what my lawyer said, and on and on.

Don't say, "Wait until you hear what your mother did now."
Don't say, "You won't believe this one!"
Don't say, "I don't understand these lawyers. They expect me to agree to . . ."
Don't say, "I'm so angry at your father. He's so unfair. Listen to this!"

• *The Ally.* Some divorcing parents use their children as an ally. They plead their case so the adult child will take sides against the other parent. They reveal every indiscretion, every weakness, every cruelty of the other parent in the hope of gaining the child's love and loyalty.

Don't say, "Your father is a liar!"
Don't say, "Your mother is making this so difficult."
Don't say, "Your father has no idea how difficult this is for me."
Don't say, "I hope you never become like your mother."

- *The Go-Between*. Some divorcing parents use their children as a go-between. They decide that they are not going to talk to their spouse, so they use their children to relay messages.

Don't say, "You tell your father . . . "
Don't say, "Call your mother up right now and tell her . . ."
Don't say, "I can't talk to your father about money right now, but would you bring up the subject? Ask him if he is going to keep the company stocks or cash them in."

- *A Crutch*. During a divorce, it is not uncommon for one parent to become dependent on his or her adult children. With the marriage partner no longer there to lean on, this parent might look to her children to provide emotional support and companionship.

Don't say, "I'm going to be counting on you to help me through this."
Don't say, "I'm going to need your support and understanding."
Don't say, "Even though your father left me, I know you'll always be here for me."
Don't say, "I don't know what I'd do without you to lean on."

- *The Confidant*. Some divorcing parents use their children as confidants. They confide intimate details of the case; they pour out their heart looking for sympathy; they cry and complain. They rely on their adult children to give them comfort and understanding.

If your only source of support and advice is your adult child, both of you are in an unhealthy situation. You need to find someone else you can trust and talk to. Most experts agree that in this situation, the help of a trained therapist is a good idea. A therapist is covered by the rules of confidentiality, and the right one can give you solid, valid direction as well as an empathetic ear. A person making a life-changing decision does need someone to talk to, someone to bounce things off of, someone to confide in. But this person should not be your adult child. Your child cannot take on the role of your confidant. The burden of giving advice to a divorcing parent or of listening to intimate details of a parent's life is just too heavy for any child to live with.

IN THE END

Divorce at any age is a major life event. It forces family members to make major adjustments in their practical everyday lives and their emotional lives. It challenges what was believed about the past, it changes the present, and it makes the future uncertain. That's a lot for any family to deal with, but with open communication, the family can meet the challenge and come out in the end with a closer, more mature, and enduring relationship.

EXPERT HELP

This chapter was written with the expert help of therapist and psychologist Patricia E. Wicks, Ph.D., of Omaha, Nebraska. She was formerly a professor at Creighton University and has been in private practice since 1985. She is board certified as a Diplomate Fellow Prescribing Psychologist and has extensive training and experience working with couples, families, adolescents, and children.

Your Adult Child's Divorce

"If you can offer yourself as a resource without taking control of the situation you will give your adult children a priceless gift during this difficult time."

L. Mickey Fenzel, associate professor of psychology, Loyola College, Maryland

Yvette knew her son Paul and his wife weren't the happiest couple around. They argued a lot; they complained often about each other; and when they weren't arguing, they lived in stony silence. Over the past year, Yvette noticed that when Paul brought the two children to visit his parents on family holidays, his wife was conspicuously missing. "So I can't say I was really surprised when Paul said he had moved out of his house," says Yvette, "but I just felt so awful for him and the kids, and his wife too. I wanted to get them together and talk this out and make them see how really lucky they were and help them find a way to work this out. But my husband says it's none of our business, so I have to keep my mouth shut and watch Paul ruin his whole life. I just can't stand it, but I don't know what role I can play without butting in where I don't belong and where I'm not wanted."

Yvette's mixed feelings are very typical of what many parents experience when they learn that their adult children are going through a divorce. (According to the National Center for Health Statistics, there are approximately 1 million divorces a year. Considering that two sets of families are involved in every divorce, that's

185

a lot of people struggling with this issue.) Most parents want to help, but they don't want to interfere. They want to take on the protective role of parenting, but they want to respect their child's adulthood at the same time. There is no question that it is very difficult to step back and watch lives fall apart, hearts break, and grandchildren cry. So what can you do? What can you say?

So much of what you can say to your adult child who is involved in a divorce depends on the history that you and that child have had. If the adult child is used to the parent taking control, he may allow that to happen and put you in charge. But most family therapists feel that adult children do not welcome uninvited parental meddling when they're in the process of a divorce and usually resent the implication that they can't handle this themselves.

What you say also depends largely on personal circumstances such as the needs of the grandchildren, or financial status, and the kind of support system your child has built. How much help does she need? How much support does she have through friends and other family members? All these factors will play a part in helping you determine your own role during this difficult time. Exactly what you will say and what you will talk about will be a private matter in your family.

In this chapter, you will find some general guidelines for engaging in helpful conversations on a variety of subjects commonly related to divorce. But you'll see that the most powerful communication tool you can use when talking about any divorce-related subject is active listening skills. When you put yourself in this supportive role, you don't have to have all the answers, and you don't have to solve the problems. You give your child a great gift by simply allowing him to talk out loud and express feelings while you respect his privacy.

WHY TALK ABOUT YOUR ADULT CHILD'S DIVORCE

There are right and wrong reasons to talk to adult children who are going through a divorce. Before you begin a conversation on this subject with your child, stop to think *why* you want to talk.

Be cautious if you want to talk to your adult children because you feel the need to be "helpful," impose your values, or gain information.

- *Being a "helpful" parent.* Jack didn't waste one minute of time when he heard that his daughter was separating from her husband. He immediately called his attorney to arrange a meeting and then started to fix up her old room. "Wendy, you come home right now," he told her. "You won't have to worry about a thing. I'll take care of you, and I'll make sure that you come out of this with everything that creep has. I'm going to take you over to your bank in the morning so we can withdraw your money, and then we'll sell your stock so he doesn't get any of it."

Jack jumped into action to help his daughter. He quickly fell back into the role of protective father and was ready to control the situation so his little girl didn't get hurt (or lose any money). There are many parents like Jack who feel a need to jump into the parental role when they see their children as being in need. These are the parents who will hire the attorney, run the necessary papers back and forth, make the telephone calls, and generally direct the show. But talking to a grown adult as if he or she was still a little child is a mistake, even when times are tough.

- *Imposing values.* "What is the matter with you?" shouted Harriet at her thirty-six-year-old son. "You think you can just walk out on your wife and daughters? Is that how you were raised? You think you can run away from responsibility? You think you can take wedding vows and just turn and run as soon as you don't feel 'happy' anymore? Well, let me tell you that your father and I have been through some tough times, but we hung on to our marriage. That's not something you just throw away."

Harriet wanted her son to know how she felt about divorce and responsibility. She was very upset that his actions reflected badly on his upbringing—and she told him so. Many parents have strong opinions about divorce, and they feel a need to explain and clarify the family view. In many families, the breakup of a marriage comes with cultural, religious, and personal feelings, beliefs, and taboos. Some parents come on very strong in their united effort to convince their adult children that what they're doing is wrong. This is especially likely to happen in families where divorce is rare or religious beliefs forbid it. In these cases, the parents have an opinion on this subject that they want their child to respect, whether they agree with it or not.

There's nothing wrong with expressing your opinion and your family beliefs, but you can't demand that your adult children agree with them. You are no longer in charge of their moral upbringing. In the end, they, not you, must live with themselves and the decisions they make.

• *Gaining information.* When your adult child tells you that he is getting a divorce, a natural response is, "Why?" Many of the conversations that follow this announcement will focus on the details. As you'll see later in this chapter, however, there is a difference between listening to what your child wants to tell you and digging for personal details that may not be your business to know.

It is a thin line you walk when you try to "help" your adult child through a divorce, and so you should be cautious about what you say and why you say it. But go right ahead and talk all you want if you plan to give support. These conversations are not pity parties or angry tirades against the offending spouse. They don't cast blame or look for retribution. They are wonderful opportunities for you to say,

"How can I be here for you?"
"I'm hear to listen if you need to talk."
"Would you like to talk about it?"

WHEN TO TALK ABOUT
YOUR ADULT CHILD'S DIVORCE

The telephone call was not completely unexpected because Jean had known for a while that her daughter wasn't happy in her marriage. "Mom?" her daughter began. "I just wanted you to know that Tom and I have separated. We have some problems to work out, so I'm staying with my friend for a while. I'll call you next week when I have a better idea of what's going to happen."

"Next week!" yelled Jean. "Are you kidding? I can't wait all week wondering what's going on. Come over here right now, and tell me everything."

Any parent would want to talk to a child in crisis right away. There's a natural instinct to jump in to soothe and solve. But when an adult child is facing a personal crisis, you have to respect her wishes and her time schedule. Your child will let you know when it's time to talk about the divorce. He will ask your advice. She will come to cry on your shoulder. He will bring up the subject. She will ask you to look over some legal papers. These are times when you know your child is open to your thoughts. These are the times it's reasonable to bring up your own concerns and questions.

However, if your child does not come to you and does not seem to want to talk about the divorce, you need to respect that preference. You can't make an adult tell you what's going on, what happened, and why he or she is doing this. But you can keep an open door that lets your child know that if he wants to talk, you'd be glad to listen. After that, all you can do is follow his lead.

WHAT YOU SHOULD TALK ABOUT

Your child will tell you what she wants to talk about. You'll know what to talk about simply by following her lead. When the time is right, this section gives you some dialogue dos and don'ts that will help you navigate this new terrain, which is full of unexpected ditches that can give you a tumble if you aren't alert. It will look at these general topics:

- The details
- Feelings
- Blame
- The in-law
- Advice
- Possessions
- Moving back home

The Details. How much of the details about the marital problems that brought on the divorce should you know? Only as much as your adult children freely offer to tell you. Each person has a unique degree of protected space that no one else can enter. Your child may or may not feel comfortable sharing intimate details with you. Her right as an adult to privacy has to be respected. If you get nothing but silence, don't get angry; back off, and let her know you'll be glad to listen if she should ever want to talk.

Instead of saying, "Tell me everything. I can't help you if I don't know what's going on."
You might say, "Would you like to talk about what happened?"

Instead of saying, "Is he cheating on you? I've had a feeling that he's been up to no good."
You might say, "If you want to talk about it, I'm here."

Instead of saying, "Have you been drinking too much again? I've warned you that that would ruin your marriage."
You might say, "Whatever caused this split in your marriage is your own business. But I want you to know that whatever it is, I'm your father, and I love you. If you need my help, I'll always be here for you."

Instead of saying, "What were you thinking! Why would you have an affair when you have such a wonderful husband at home?"
You might say, "We've all made mistakes in life. This is one that is going to hurt you, but I'm here to help you, not judge you."

Feelings. During the divorce process, both you and your divorcing adult child will experience complex and sometimes overwhelming feelings that can mirror the stages of grief suffered after the death of a loved one. Before you both reach the stage of acceptance, you may each experience denial and isolation, anger, or depression. But the conversations you have with your adult child about these feelings should focus on his or her feelings, not your own. You have to be secure enough not to let your own emotional reaction to this situation get in the way. From his point of view, this divorce is about him, not you. If you dump your own emotional upset on your child, he will learn not to trust you with his problems. If he learns that what he tells you makes you unbearably sad, or dangerously angry, or even depressed, he will stop talking to you. If you react to the details of the marital upset by injecting how this makes *you* feel, you'll alienate your child by taking the focus off him when he is looking for support.

When you turn your attention to your adult child's feelings, try to identify which stage of the grief process she is at and try to meet her there. If she is angry, let her be angry and talk about that anger. You can't rush her through this process. Don't try to get her to focus on solutions before she has dealt with the difficult emotions and is ready to address more problem-focused coping.

When your child opens up and talks about her feelings, your goal should be to give her room to talk and think out loud. This can be very helpful for someone who needs to sort things out mentally and needs to hear the feelings put into words. Remember that you don't have to solve the problems, make the pain go away, calm the anger, or perk up her spirits. Your most valuable contribution to the conversation is your ability to sit back and listen and add occasional encouraging remarks that help her to continue talking.

Instead of saying, "What am I going to do? I don't know if I can handle this."
You might say, "This must be very difficult for *you*."

Instead of saying, "I'm so upset I haven't slept in a week. I just can't think straight, and I cry all the time."
You might say, "How are *you* feeling?"

Instead of saying, "If I were you, I'd be furious."
You might say, "How do *you* feel about that?"

During this difficult time, you too need to talk about your feelings to someone you can trust and you feel comfortable with (just don't let that person be your child). Find another source of support, such as a spouse, friend, clergy, or another family member. You might also consider talking to a therapist who is trained in family counseling and can help you work through these sometimes overwhelming feelings.

Blame. The need to find someone to blame for the breakup of a marriage is human. Because you will be hearing only one side of the story, your family may all blame your child's spouse. Or if it is your child who has a serious problem with drugs, alcohol, adultery, gambling, or domestic abuse, you may find it hard to avoid blaming him. But divorce is rarely one person's fault, and pointing the finger of blame is rarely helpful to the situation. In your conversations with your child, try to focus on feelings and future actions. Avoid conversations that focus on blame.

Instead of saying, "Her parents are to blame for all this. If they didn't meddle so much, you two would have been fine."
You might say, "What do her parents have to say about your separation?"

Instead of saying, "He is a monster. It's no wonder you want to leave him."
You might say, "How do you feel about him?"

Instead of saying, "I think all those friends of hers at work were a bad influence. They were all single and always wanted her to go out partying."
You might say, "What do you think you'll do next?"

If you feel your child is to blame for the marriage problems because he has problems with domestic abuse, alcohol, drugs, or gambling, these are serious issues that require special handling, not blame, ridicule, or criticism. Because these issues pose the potential for harm, it is best to address these needs first, separate from the divorce issue. Be sure to read the chapters on each of these problem areas for professional intervention suggestions and guidelines.

Don't say, "I should have known you would mess up."
Don't say, "You don't seem to do anything well."
Don't say, "I don't blame your wife for leaving you."
Don't say, "You're hopeless."

You also don't have to blame yourself for your adult child's marital problems. You will not help anyone if you start looking back over your family life to find the roots of this problem.

Don't say, "If your father and I had been happier and hadn't fought in front of you kids, this wouldn't be happening to you."
Don't say, "If I hadn't gone back to work when you were little, I don't think you'd be having these relationship problems now."
Don't say, "If your mother and I had stayed together instead of divorcing when you were young, you would have been able to have a better marriage of your own."
Don't say, "If I had stepped in sooner when I saw you were having marital problems, I could have helped you avoid this."
Don't say, "If I had stayed out of your marriage and not interfered so much, this wouldn't have happened. This is all my fault."

The In-Law. When your adult child announces that he or she is getting a divorce, you are faced with the loss of a family member. Your child's spouse was your in-law and is now going to be excluded from your life. This may be devastating news for you if you were very fond of this person. Or this may be the best news you've heard all year if this was someone you never liked. Whatever your feelings about your soon-to-be ex-in-law, be very careful what you say to your adult child.

If you want to keep in touch with your ex-in-law for personal reasons (beyond making arrangements for visitation with your grandchildren), be patient. In the storm of the immediate divorce, it's probably not a good time to go visiting. Your child will take this as a betrayal and lack of loyalty. Wait until things calm down, and the divorce is final. Then you can pursue an adult friendship if you like that doesn't put you in "enemy" territory.

Instead of saying, "You know I've always thought of Joe as my own son. What am I supposed to do now. Never see him again!?"
You might say, "Where is Joe living now?"

If you never liked your child's spouse, this isn't a good time to say so. If you say or imply, "I told you so," you are asking your child to accept blame for making a bad decision at a time when he's looking to you for support. This can damage your own relationship. Even when your child is saying awful things about this person, it's best to bite your tongue. You add fuel to an already hot fire when you put down the spouse (and put yourself in an awkward position if they should reconcile and you have let out all your negative feelings that you had so thoughtfully hidden during the marriage).

Instead of adding to the litany of hateful things about the spouse, it's best to reflect back your child's feelings without adding your own.

If your adult child says, "I hate him. He's so cruel and thoughtless."
Instead of saying, "I never thought he was good for you."
You might say, "I can appreciate how upset you must be."

If your adult child says, "She's a terrible mother. I don't want to leave the kids alone with her."

Instead of saying, "I remember the time she brought Danny over here with no socks on! I knew right then that she didn't care what happened to those kids."

You might say, "That is a serious matter. Have you thought about what you plan to do about it?"

If your adult child says, "I'll show him. He's never going to see his kids again."

You might say, "That's something you'll have to think about when you're not so angry. It sounds as if you plan to punish the children because of what he's done."

If your adult child says, "I should never have married him."

Instead of saying, "I told you so."

You might say, "I can understand why you feel that way now, but at the time you loved him."

Advice. Naturally, you'll want to offer advice to help your adult children through this difficult time, but how much and what type of advice you give depends on your child. You have to be able to judge how open your child is to help. She may be still trying to sort out feelings and isn't ready yet to find a good lawyer. He may be hoping that there will be a reconciliation and isn't able even to think about getting his finances in order. From one day to the next, it may be hard to figure out what your child wants from you because he may seem to be saying, "Help me—but don't tell me what to do."

As your adult children work their way through the process of separation and divorce, you can best help by being available and nonjudgmental. This will make you a safe person to talk to. Unless your children directly ask for advice, it's usually best to hold back.

You can help by asking leading questions that encourage them to think and analyze the situation for themselves.

Instead of saying, "I think you should . . ."
You might say, "Do you know what you're going to do next?"
You might say, "Why are you taking that step at this time?"
You might say, "Do you know anyone you can talk to to get some guidance on this?"

There are a lot of practical matters your adult child will have to deal with during the process of divorce. There are legal, financial, housing, and child rearing considerations, to name just a few. These will all be topics of discussion, but it's important to let your child lead the conversation and keep yourself in the supportive role rather than the controlling one. Offer yourself as a resource without taking charge.

Instead of saying, "I know a lawyer I'll call right now to get you started."
You might say, "Have you thought about hiring a lawyer? I know a good one I can recommend if you'd like."
You might say, "Would you like some help finding a good lawyer?"

Instead of saying, "Call your financial adviser and bank manager right now, and do whatever you have to do to make sure she doesn't wipe out your accounts."
You might say, "Have you and Susie talked about how you'll take care of financial matters?"

Instead of saying, "You make sure that she understands that I want to see my grandchildren every Saturday."
You might say, "When you're feeling better and things have settled down a bit, I would like to talk to you about making arrangements so I can see my grandchildren."

Possessions. At some point in the divorce process, your adult child and spouse will divide up the family property and assets. The decisions that will be made will be confidential matters between the attorneys and the divorcing couple. Your child may choose to tell you the details, or he may not. Either way, you may have some questions you'd like to ask, particularly about items that belong to you or your family, or that you paid for or helped finance—perhaps an heirloom ring that was given to the new bride, a set of your grandmother's sterling silverware, a power tool bench, a new car, or even the house they live in.

Timing is important here. You'll want to talk about this issue before the matter is legally settled, but you don't need to bring it up in the middle of an emotional discussion shortly after the decision to divorce is made. If your daughter is crying because her soon-to-be-former husband has canceled her credit cards, that's not the best time to add, "Well, you tell him that we want our lawnmower back." In a calm moment, after the rush of emotions has settled, tell your child that there are a few property issues you'd like to talk about.

Instead of saying, "You tell him that we want back the fifteen thousand dollars we gave him to buy that car! And we want Grandpa's pocket watch back. And we want you to have the bedroom set that we gave you for a wedding present."

You might say, "Here is a list of the things that we have paid for or that belong to our family that we would like to see returned to you. Look it over, and let us know if you agree, and then please give it to your lawyer so he knows about these things when he's negotiating the divorce agreement."

Moving Back Home. The doorbell rang at three o'clock in the morning. Through groggy eyes, Melinda saw her daughter standing in the darkened doorway with the baby in her arms and tears streaming down her face. "I can't live with him anymore," she cried to her mother. "I've never told you this, but he has a temper, and when he comes home late and drunk, he hits me. I'm leaving him." Now wide awake, Melinda led her daughter to her old bedroom and helped her get the baby settled. There was no discussion about where they would live. Of course, it would be right here, at home.

Moving back home after the marriage breaks up is one option that many adult children choose—some out of necessity, others out of choice. But experts feel that ideally, it is better if adult children who are divorcing do not return to their childhood home. This is the place where they too easily assume the role of dependent child and lose the ability to stay in charge; moving back home does not encourage them to move to the next step of their lives as mature adults. It may be true that moving home has its drawbacks, but often financial and other circumstances make the move a necessity at first.

Some parents welcome their separated children (and grandchildren) with open arms. Others are distressed that their own lives are going to be drastically affected by the return of their child and grandchildren. In either case, the subject needs to be talked about so that misunderstandings don't make a difficult time even tougher. If your child assumes he will move back home and you assume he wouldn't dare, that's going to cause trouble in your relationship. Talking things out is the only way to avoid this trouble.

If your adult child does move in, you'll need to talk about the details after the emotional upset of the situation calms down. You'll need to talk about when and how long and what financial arrangements need to be made, among others. The chapter called "Moving Out," starting on page 109, provides some guidelines for talking about living arrangements that will give both of you what you need.

IN THE END

Talking about your child's divorce is an ongoing process. You're not going to have a one-time, sit-down long discussion, and that will be it. If you and your child have a good relationship and he or she feels comfortable talking to you during this difficult time, you will have many opportunities to lend support. There will be a time and a place for all your discussions. Be patient, be a good listener, and remember that your child is an adult who was mature enough to handle an independent life during the marriage and can do it again if given the chance.

EXPERT HELP

This chapter was written with the expert help of L. Mickey Fenzel, Ph.D., associate professor of psychology at Loyola College, Maryland. He is also a psychotherapist with a private practice in Towson, Maryland, and works with adolescents, adults, and families. He has done research and presented workshops on divorce and divorce recovery.

PART THREE

Problem Areas

Extended Dependency

"If you find that you are 'protecting' your child from all the hard things in life (like paying bills, getting a job, cooking meals, and so on), you may have created a codependent relationship that isn't good for either of you."
  Barbara Ensor, clinical psychologist

Total independence in adulthood is a myth. No one is completely independent. Even adults need others, and throughout a lifetime, a person's family should always be a source of support and aid. But in healthy family relationships, this reliance is mutual. We give to each other. We help each other. We give and take on a balanced scale. If your adult children are doing all the taking, if they are still playing the role of child and looking to you to make decisions for them, provide financially for them, and do their laundry and fix their flat tires, this is an unhealthy dependency that needs to be recognized and talked about.

This extended dependency occurs in many families when there is a blurring of the line between adolescence and adulthood. The so-called adult child is not making a move to take the leap from childhood to adulthood. When this happens the parents who thought they would now be retired from the active parent role and have their home, their time, and their finances to themselves, find themselves stuck in the parent role and often don't know how to get out of it anymore than the adult child knows how to move on and grow up.

If you are worried about your adult child's extended dependence, you are not alone. This generation, in particular, is having difficulty breaking free emotionally from the family and find themselves standing stuck in the doorway to maturity. Sociologists suggest a variety of reasons for this situation: permissive or overly controlling parents, a fluctuating job market, a sense of entitlement that clashes with reality, a spoiled childhood, and a strong economy that enabled parents to give their children everything they want. Whatever the exact reason, the result is extended dependency that can take many different forms.

Twenty-five-year-old John is still living at home. He sleeps all day and practices with his rock band all night. He hasn't yet had a paying job, but he insists that soon his band will be getting a recording contract. His parents don't want to criticize him or sound as if they don't have faith in his talent, so they patiently wait for John to grow up.

Margaret is finishing her fifth year of college, and still there is no sign that she will be graduating soon. She has changed her major several times and seems always to fall short of degree requirements. Her parents have taken out extra loans to cover this unexpected cost, but they are wondering when she will "find herself" so they can stop supporting her.

James graduated from a nationally recognized university. He took a good-paying job for six months, but then quit to travel around the country for a while. Now he is back home with no car, no money, and no job. He is hanging out with his old friends, begging his parents to borrow the car, and having arguments with them over their requests to do some chores. "It's just like it was when he was a teenager!" cries his mother.

Thirty-year-old Kara is married and has a young child, but she hasn't cut free from her parents yet. She calls them every day with a problem or dilemma she "needs" them to solve. She asks their advice before she makes any decision, and she defers to their judgment over her husband's. Her parents are happy she respects their opinion, but are starting to worry that this may cause problems in her marriage.

Whatever your story, the fact is that your adult child is acting like a small child, and it's bothering you (otherwise you would not be reading this chapter). It's probably not bothering your adult child. Many adult children don't seem to mind letting their parents make decisions for them, and they are very comfortable having their lifestyle financially subsidized. That's why it's up to you to find a way to talk about this situation if you ever want it to end.

As you look at your adult children's situation and try to determine if you need to talk to them about the subject of extended dependency, you have to make judgments about what they can or cannot do for themselves. If your daughter is a single mother who is trying to juggle ten things at once and she asks you to pick up her son at preschool once in awhile, this is not cause for concern. The reality is that she has a legitimate need for your help. But if you are being asked to do things that the adult child can and should certainly do for himself or herself, you may be feeding extended dependency by the way you respond.

This chapter will help you look more closely at why your adult child may be still hanging on to your apron strings and what you can say to help him cut himself loose.

WHY TALK ABOUT EXTENDED DEPENDENCY

We all need to talk to our overly dependent adult children because silence condones the behavior and allows it to continue unchecked. This is not good for them or for you. A few general reasons to have dialogues that promote independent living include talking:

- For practical reasons
- To change a love-me-do-for-me attitude
- For the sake of your relationship
- To break old habits
- To let go

For Practical Reasons. One realistic reason to talk about the subject of dependency is the fact that you are not going to be around forever. The older you get, the more restrictions you may have on your own financial resources, physical health, and mental acuity. You cannot plan to keep doing everything for your kids forever.

You may also need your adult children to cut the strings because you can't carry them any longer. You might have younger children who need your time and attention. You may not have the finances to continue supporting another adult indefinitely. You may want to move on to another stage of your own life that does not include active parenting. For very practical reasons, your adult children must learn to provide for their own needs and wants.

To Change a Love-Me-Do-for-Me Attitude. Your adult child may be confusing love with "what have you done for me lately?" Some adult children seem to have an attitude that says, "If you love me, you'll lend me money," or, "If you love me, you'll let me live here rent free," or, "If you love me, you'll watch my kids, do my laundry, and cook supper before I get home from work." If you think your grown kids may have this kind of attitude, you'll need to have a good talk to straighten them out. They need to learn that love isn't a one-sided, give-to-me kind of emotion. On an adult level, we all need to recognize the needs of others. If your grown children haven't learned that yet, you'll need to tell them.

For the Sake of Your Relationship.   If you don't talk to your adult children about extended dependency, your relationship with them will deteriorate. You cannot continue to play parent to an adult without becoming resentful and angry. You may feel that your adult children visit and call only when they need something. You may be tired of running interference to keep them out of trouble. You may be worn out being the maid and cook to a grown person. It is very annoying to be asked to take responsibility for someone whom you have no control over and no leverage. When you've finally had enough and you explode, your adult children will have no idea what's wrong.

If you have always picked up after your adult child, he will wonder why you are complaining now. When your child was a teenager, did you always clean up after his messes? Make his bed? Put his laundry in the hamper? Wipe his crumbs off the table? Did you blow your top once in a while when you got tired of cleaning up after him? The same thing is happening now. You're taking on responsibilities that are not yours. This is not good for an adult relationship, and you need to speak up and say so, or nothing will ever change. If you continue to clean up afterward, you end up feeling used, and at the same time you steal your child's right to learn to be grown up and independent. Both of you will end up feeling resentful.

To Break Old Habits.   Sometimes parents cause extended dependency by the way they talk to their adult children. They talk to them as if they were still children who need mommy and daddy to solve their problems. They ridicule or criticize every independent move the adult children try to take, and soon they have created an immature, dependent adult child. To change this kind of parent-child dynamic takes some hard work. You'll need to break old habits, bite your tongue a lot, and give your adult children large doses of encouragement, even when you feel they are making mistakes. This is certainly not easy to do, but it is the primary solution to giving your grown kids the self-confidence they need to be independent individuals.

To Let Go. One of the nice things about having a dependent adult child is the feeling that we are still needed. Despite the annoyance of having a child who won't grow up, there's no doubt that on some level, it's comforting to hold onto the parent role for as long as we can. Talking to our adult children about their extended dependency forces us to let go and forces them to face adulthood.

When we let go, we give them the freedom to take on adult responsibilities (without feeling guilty when they fall short), make their own decisions (that may not be the ones we'd make), struggle (even when we could make things easier for them), be accepted for who they are (not who we thought they should be), make mistakes (even though we could have told them so), and experience life for themselves (not through our parental filter).

WHEN TO TALK ABOUT EXTENDED DEPENDENCY

You should talk about the subject of extended dependency when you realize that your adult children are too often asking you to do things that they should be doing for themselves. But before you have a sit-down talk about growing up, it's a good idea to get a clearer picture of why they are being so dependent. The next time they want you to take over their adult responsibility, ask them, "Why do you think it's better that I do this instead of you?" Their answers will guide you in the conversation that follows.

When you ask this question, you might find that your child has a reason that has nothing to do with extended dependency. Asking you to balance a checkbook, for example, may be just an excuse to come over and visit and check up on how you're doing without having to say so. Asking you to come and fix a flat tire out on the highway may be your daughter's way of dealing with her fear of having to meet road service strangers in the dark. There may be reasons for what seems like dependency that you haven't thought of, so ask.

On the other hand, you might find out that your adult children want to be taken care of because they lack self-confidence. If they say something like, "I'll mess it up" or, "I can't do it as well as you can," you'll know that you need to begin to talk to them in ways that boost their self-esteem and give them the confidence to make decisions and try things without your help.

Another common reason for extended dependency is a fear of failure. If your adult child says, "I'm not good enough to apply for that job," or, "I really don't want to try doing that myself; I need your help," he might be afraid to fly alone.

You might also find that your adult children rely on you because it's just easier than doing for themselves. Knowing that will assure you that it's time to talk about growing up.

WHAT YOU SHOULD TALK ABOUT

The subjects of conversation about extended dependency are unique to each family situation. Your child may be living at home and be financially dependent, while another family may be struggling with the adult child who has moved out physically but is still tightly involved emotionally. The scenarios are endless, but the general principles are the same. When you talk to your adult child about extended dependency, it's best to talk to her as an adult, about one specific issue (not her entire life and times and problems), and with understanding, but also with determination to help her take the necessary daily steps that lead toward maturity and independence.

Breaking the Ice

At first, you may feel uncomfortable broaching the subject of dependency. It's often the subject that's like the eight-hundred-pound gorilla sitting in the living room that no one talks about; you all know it's there, but no one wants to be the first to acknowledge it. If that's the case in your house, take some time to break the ice by talking about other people first, venturing into the topic slowly, and taking time to explain your feelings and point of view.

Talk About Other People. Lots of other families live with dependent adult children. Talk about *them*, and see what your adult child has to say. This conversation will give you insight into her feelings about adults who hang on to their parents too long.

You might say, "Aunt Sally was telling me about her friend who is very upset because her twenty-seven-year-old son just doesn't seem to want to grow up. He likes eating at their house. He likes his mother to do his laundry, and he often asks his parents for money. What do you think a parent should do in that kind of situation?"

You might say, "I was reading an article in a magazine about adult kids who don't seem to want to grow up. It had all kinds of examples about people in their twenties, thirties, and even forties and fifties who acted more like children than adults. What do you think causes that?"

You might say, "I ran into Mrs. Smith in the store today. She was telling me that her son still hasn't graduated from college after six years. How can that be?"

Go Slow. It's not necessary to throw your adult kids into deep water to teach them how to swim. After you've done your child's laundry for years, it's tough to refuse suddenly. If your child is in the habit of using you, relying on you, or letting you make his decisions, it may take a gradual weaning process to get him on his own two feet.

Instead of saying, "No, do it yourself from now on."
You might say, "Bring it over, and we'll do it together."
You might say, "Bring it over, and I'll show you how to do it. It's not hard, and I'll be around if you run into trouble."
You might say, "I'm really tight on time today. Come over, and put your clothes in the machine. I'll put them in the dryer, but when you come back, you can fold them." (Then be ready to admire the job, even if some whites get mixed in with the dark colors!)

Instead of saying, "Grow up, will you?"
You might say, "I know you can do this."
You might say, "I don't know if I've given you enough credit for what you are capable of doing. I want you to know that I am proud of you, I do trust in your decision-making abilities, even though it may not sound like it sometimes. In the future, I'm going to try to back off and let you make your own decisions."

Explain Yourself. Before you go on strike, talk to your adult children, and tell them why you feel they need to do these things for themselves. This isn't a debatable point: adults need to be able to take care of themselves. This isn't a reason for argument: you have a right to say no to anyone who asks you a favor. But because you've been saying yes for so long, you should explain to avoid hurt feelings and misunderstandings.

Don't let this discussion evolve into an argument. While expressing love and confidence, use a tone of voice that is calm and empathetic. Then admit that you're concerned and feel that things need to change.

Instead of saying, "From now on, you pay all your own bills."
You might say, "I'm concerned that you're not making more of an effort to pay your own bills. As an adult, it's your responsibility to make sure you don't spend more than you earn. So I want you to know that I love you, but I'm not going to pay any of your bills anymore."

Addressing Specific Issues
There are many circumstances in which young adults may try to shrug off their responsibilities. Each one deserves attention. The suggestions that follow will give you an idea of how you can communicate your love while at the same time cutting the cord. The following suggestions focus on these situations:

- Building self-confidence
- Facing a fear of failure
- Transferring responsibility

Building Self-Confidence. In high school, Jack was overwhelmed by the college application process. Every time he mentioned a possible school or major, his parents would say, "You don't want to go there," or, "I don't think that's best for you." Ultimately, Jack couldn't decide where he wanted to go or what he wanted to do. So he sat week after week and stared at all the forms but never filled them out. Finally, his parents stepped in. They sorted out the applications, picked the ones that seemed best to them, filled in the requested information, wrote the essay, and mailed them.

When two of the four colleges accepted Jack, he couldn't choose one over the other, so his parents picked the one they thought would be better for him. In the middle of his sophomore year, he dropped out of school and returned home. He didn't know what he wanted to do, so his parents asked a family friend to hire him as an assistant manager of a local store. Soon Jack was promoted to manager and wanted to move into his own apartment. After scanning the classified ads for available apartments, Jack gave up. He had no idea what he wanted, so his mother found him a one-bedroom apartment just around the corner.

Now Jack's parents spend much of their time at Jack's apartment fixing his plumbing problems, hanging his curtains, and doing other odd jobs for him. But they're getting a little tired of this. "When," they wonder, "is Jack going to grow up and do things for himself?" It never dawned on them that by making decisions for Jack and by taking charge, they were making him feel incapable of doing anything for himself.

The kind of emotional dependency that Jack has on his parents begins early in parent-child relationships. For a variety of reasons, some children grow to believe that they can't function without the help of their parents. They often have been protected from mistakes and failures. Their parents baited their fishing hooks, threaded their needles, and completed their school projects. Their parents have always wanted "only the best" for their children and taught them to believe that "mother [or father] knows best." This leaves the adult children feeling that their own judgment is not as good as their parents'. Now they need parental approval and cannot make their own decisions. Even as adults, the parents constantly protect them from mistakes, difficulties, and hardships, and so they see their parents as the rescuers, the protectors, and they are the child, dependent and helpless. This is an unhealthy relationship that is difficult to untangle once the child has reached adulthood and is a major cause of extended dependency.

If you see that this kind of dependency has developed in your family, it's time to make an effort to learn to trust that your adult children will make the right decisions for themselves. This is not easy to do, especially if the parent has had a controlling relationship in the past.

• *Have you been a controlling parent?* If you are still telling your twenty- or thirty-year-old how to dress, what to eat, and where to live, you are trying to retain your control over her life and contributing to her extended dependency. Ask yourself when the last time was that you offered words of praise or expressed support by saying, "I know you'll do the best"? Have you encouraged independence by saying, "You're doing a good job"? This may not be easy for you to do, especially if you feel your adult child is immature and needs your help to make decisions, but if you don't try, neither you nor your child will age well.

If your adult child is thinking of changing jobs, buying a house, getting married, or making some other major decision, don't automatically jump in with a negative comment. Hold back and listen. Let her think it through by talking out loud. If the decision is one that will not harm her physically, then give her room to try. If you feel the decision would be a mistake, then your child will find that out for herself. That's how we all learn the best lessons: by giving life a try and learning from the experience. When you talk about these kinds of life circumstances, build self-confidence by offering praise or by expressing confidence in their ability to make good decisions. With words and actions, you need to say, "I trust you to be an adult." Send signals of acceptance that say, "You are a good person, a valued person. You have the ability to make good decisions."

Instead of saying, "I think you're crazy to try this."
You might say, "I trust you. Go ahead."

Instead of saying, "You shouldn't wear that style dress."
You might say, "That's pretty material, and it's a good color for you."

Instead of saying, "When are you going to stop eating junk food?"
You might say, "I meant to ask you if you'd like my recipe for chili. I remember you always loved that."

Instead of saying, "You should ask for a raise at work."
You might say, "How's work going? Any new projects lately?"

• *Does your adult child always do what you tell him to do?* If your adult child is very obedient and does what you tell him to do, you're in an unhealthy relationship. Mature adults have to be able to think for themselves, take their own calculated risks, and learn from the outcome. You can't continue to run his life forever. If you try, you'll end up with an overly dependent adult child who is afraid of taking life's risks and afraid of making any decision without your help. Adults who are overly dependent on their parents may feel, "If I do this without my parents' help, I'll do it wrong." This is a self-esteem problem that needs to be recognized and countered with lots of encouraging conversations.

If your adult child says, "I want to remodel the kitchen."
Instead of saying, "Don't waste your money. Your kitchen looks just fine."
You might say, "I know you've always disliked that kitchen. I'll bet your creative eye could do a really nice job in there."

If your adult child says, "I want to buy a townhouse on Cedar Street."
Instead of saying, "The condos on Main Street are much better. Go over there and take a look."
You might say, "Good idea."

If your adult child says, "Should I buy a convertible or a truck?"
Instead of saying, "Don't be crazy. Buy an SUV; it's safer and more practical."
You might say, "Buy whichever one you think is best for you."

• *Do you value differences?* If your children do not like your style of dress or music, this does not mean they are immature and not ready for independence. It means they are maturing into adults who live in their own world, not your world. When your child rents a loft that you hate because it looks like a basketball court, you encourage independence by keeping your criticism to yourself and congratulating your child on finding such open space to live in.

You must also value the differences between your adult children and the adult children of your friends and relatives. You will continue to squash self-confidence if you compare your adult child to other adult children. It is not motivating to hear about other people the same age who have good jobs, are living independent lives, and are fully on their own. It is discouraging, deflating, and one more reason to retreat to the safety of the child role.

Don't say, "When your brother was your age, he already was married and owned his own house. What's the matter with you?"
Don't say, "Your cousin Eileen was just promoted. And Aunt Helen says she is going to buy a condo by the beach for a summer home. You don't even have a job."
Don't say, "All your friends have grown up and moved away. Why are you still here?"

Instead say, "Tell me about your plans. What do you hope to be doing in two years?"

Instead say, "This job gives you a good chance for advancement. I think in a short time you'll be doing very well for yourself. I know you can do well there."

Instead say, "You have to find your own way, and I know you can do it. I have confidence in you."

Facing a Fear of Failure. Kim graduated first in her high school class. Her teachers praised her. Her parents bragged about her. And her friends envied her. She then graduated at the top of her college class and ran with high hopes into the world of fashion design, where she had dreams of making a name for herself. After six months, when no one would take her design ideas seriously or use them in upcoming shows, she quit and moved back home. She said she needed time to think about what she wanted in life—and then spent the next year watching daytime soap operas. What happened to all that promise? To her ambition? To her thirst for independence?

Many young adult children come into maturity with high expectations. They think they will burst on the adult scene and make an instant mark on the world. When their high expectations hit smack up against reality and they find that only entry-level jobs and cheap studio apartments are within their grasp, and that they are no more special than the next person, some pull back and retreat into the security of being a child again. In this role, the expectations are lower, they're safe from failure, and the responsibility for achieving is delayed.

This is especially likely to be the case for those who were high achievers and school intellects. These young people built their lives around a sense of specialness that for a while allowed them to avoid reality and its challenges and the possibility of rejection that lurks around every new corner. Now, to maintain that special status, they must cling as much as possible to the role of child instead of becoming a vulnerable, open-to-mistakes, one-of-the-crowd adult.

If your adult child was a high achiever as a child and seems to be stuck in a life rut right now, you can help him move forward by recognizing his fear and being sensitive to the expectations you express.

Don't say, "You've always been good at everything you do. There's no reason you won't be the best at this job."
Don't say, "Everyone had such high hopes for you. You had everything going for you. What happened?"
Don't say, "I thought you'd be a millionaire by now; you had so much potential."

Instead say, "Give it a try. If it doesn't work out, there's no harm done."
Instead say, "I trust you to do your best. Whatever happens, happens."
Instead say, "Don't be afraid to try new things. That's the only way you can grow as an adult."
Instead say, "If you fail at something, it's not the end of the world. Your family and friends will still love you, and you'll always have the opportunity to try again."

Transferring Responsibility. Martha was very proud of her daughter, Ceil. At twenty-seven, Ceil had a good job, her own apartment, and lots of friends. With such a busy life, Martha was glad to help Ceil do the daily chores that she just didn't have time for. Ceil dropped off her laundry on the weekends for her mom to wash, dry, and fold. Martha was also glad to do Ceil's ironing and run her suits to the dry cleaners. Martha cooked single-serving meals and wrapped them up for Ceil to eat during the week. When Ceil was working late, her mom would run over to her apartment to take in the mail, turn on the lights, and walk the dog. Ceil often said she didn't know what she would do without her mother. An outsider can see more objectively that if her mother backed off, Ceil might be forced to grow up and do the things that adults have to do for themselves.

Wouldn't you love it if someone came into your life right now who would make your difficult decisions for you? Who would do things for you without asking anything in return? Who would give you money and a good meal anytime you asked? Anyone would love that. So if you take on responsibilities that belong to your adult child, don't expect him or her to ask you soon to please stop. If your adult child is overly dependent on you, evaluate if you're letting him do that by accepting the responsibility for things that he should be doing himself.

Ask yourself if your child has ever had to sacrifice today to gain something tomorrow. Has he ever had to do without or plan ahead? Has she ever had to put aside personal desires to fulfill a responsibility? Without these experiences, your child will come to believe that life should be easy. If you take over all the difficult daily tasks, he won't understand why he should ever have to struggle for anything.

If you find that you are protecting your child from all the hard things in life (paying bills, getting a job, cooking meals, and so on), you have created a codependent relationship that isn't good for either of you. People who are in a codependent relationship inappropriately take responsibility for the other person's actions and decisions. In this kind of relationship, if your daughter doesn't pay her rent, you feel the need to write out a check so she won't get evicted. In this kind of relationship, she won't learn the consequences of not paying debts. Why should she save money for her rent if she knows you'll bail her out? If your thirty-year-old son wants to buy a house but won't commit until you look it over to make sure he's making a good decision, he has learned to avoid taking responsibility for his own decisions by pushing the final word off on you.

To break a codependent relationship, you'll need to work hard to separate your life from your child's. If he comes home and tells you he just lost four thousand dollars at the racetrack, you have no need to reach for your wallet. All that's necessary is a simple response of acknowledgment—something like, "Oh, that's really too bad." You are not responsible for another person's actions. When you take this responsibility, you enable your child to continue being dependent with no consequence, and you show a fundamental lack of faith in her ability to make a good decision (*good* in the sense that you think it is right and best).

Once you can accept in your heart that your child is an adult who needs to act like a responsible person and that you don't need to fix his problems or protect him from life, you'll find it much easier to back off and let him grow. You'll realize that you are no longer obligated to take care of him. You'll be able to see your offspring as an adult who needs to make his own decisions and live with the consequences.

Your adult children may be avoiding adult responsibilities for an endless list of reasons that may include fear of failure, laziness, low family expectations, need for attention, or fear of independence. Whatever the reason, you can begin to transfer responsibility back to your child where it belongs. Try using this standard three-statement formula:

1. Acknowledge that you understand your child's point of view.
2. Explain your feelings, and state your position firmly and without apology.
3. When appropriate, offer to help problem-solve a solution that does not involve you.

If you stick to this formula, you'll figuratively be pushing your baby birds out of the nest whether they like it or not because you know that it's necessary and in their best interest in the long run.

If they say, "Could you call my boss [girlfriend, client, someone else] and say that I can't make it to our meeting today?"
Instead of saying, "What do you want me to say?" Or, "Forget it. I'm not doing that anymore."
You might say, "I know it's hard for you to break an appointment. But I don't feel it's my place to take on that responsibility. I will not call for you. I have no doubt that you can stand up for yourself and make that call."

If they say, "Dad, could you loan me another hundred dollars?"
Instead of saying, "Sure. Times must be tough for you." Or, "No way until you pay me back what you already owe me."
You might say, "I know you're short on money, but I'm feeling disappointed that you have not repaid me for the last several loans I've given you. As an adult, I think it's important that you learn how to manage your own money and that you pay back money that you borrow. If you'd like, I'd be glad to help you figure out how to meet your expenses this month without taking a loan."

If they say, "Mom, I'm going on a short vacation next week, and so the kids will stay with you. Okay?"

Instead of saying, "Sure honey. What days will you be gone?" Or, "No. I'm tired of watching your kids."

You might say, "I'm glad to hear that you planned a vacation. But I feel that you ask me to watch your children far too often. I'm not available next week. How else can you handle this?"

When you hand the responsibility for life back to your children, don't expect them to think this is a great idea. Dependency is a very real emotional state that is not easily or quickly altered. When you first refuse to take responsibility for her actions, your daughter will probably be shocked and then enraged. She may make excuses ("It's not my fault I got fired. My boss never liked me"); she may try to make you feel guilty ("Fine. I'll get evicted, and it'll be your fault. Is that what you want?"); she may try to connect your love with her needs ("Sure you say you love me, but then you won't even help me"); she may even say terrible things to hurt you ("You're so useless. If you won't even help your own daughter, what good are you?"). This is a painful experience for all family members. But a dose of tough love is needed here. Do not argue. Do not defend yourself. You are right, and you're doing what's best for your adult child in the long run.

Here's how you might respond when your child uses excuses, guilt, love, or hurtful insults to remain dependent.

• *Excuses.* If your child responds with an excuse, you can acknowledge that that might be true, but it doesn't change the fact that she will have to face the consequences. If you accept the excuse as a reason for avoiding adulthood, you teach your adult child that things that happen "are not my fault." You or someone or something else own the problem, not her.

If they say, "My boss doesn't appreciate how hard I work. There's no way I can live on what he pays me."

Don't say, "That's so unfair. No wonder your credit card bill is so high."

Instead, you might say, "Yes, it is hard to earn a living today, but adults have to find a way to spend no more than they earn."

You might say, "If you don't think the situation is fair, what can you do to change it?"

You might say, "What do you plan to do if you can't pay your bills?"

• *Guilt.* If you child tries to make you feel guilty, don't take the bait! Remind yourself over and over that parents do not owe their adult children a peaceful, untroubled life. Your adult children have to learn that hardships are a part of living; they are not your fault. They also need to know that whatever happened in their childhood and whatever mistakes you may have made as a parent are all in the past. They need to get over it and move on with life.

If they say, "Why did you make me major in business? I hate business, and now I can't get a job I like."

You might say, "I did encourage you to consider business, but then, not now, was the time to say you didn't like it. What can you do now to handle this problem?"

If they say, "You and Dad had such a bad relationship, how can you expect me to make a commitment to anyone?"

You might say, "My relationship with Dad is an issue for us to deal with. Your relationship problems are an issue for *you* to deal with. Don't get the two mixed up."

If they say, "If they repossess my car, it'll be your fault."

You might say, "No. Your car is your responsibility."

• *Love.* Love is not a one-sided kind of emotion. Mature, adult love is give and take. So if your adult child is doing all the taking, he needs to learn how to grow up and shoulder his share of the relationship. Remember that saying, "I love you, I care about you" is not the same as saying, "I will pay your bills, I will iron your shirts, and I will give you money."

If they say, "How can you say you love me if you won't do this for me?"
You might say, "I do love you. But if you think that people who love you should take over your adult responsibilities, we need to talk about how love between mature adults works."

If they say, "You don't love me!"
You might say, "Adult love is built on mutual respect and caring. Right now, you're expecting to be cared for without any plans to give anything back. That's not love; that's an unhealthy dependency."

• *Hurtful remarks.* These are hard to handle. If your adult child hurls insults at you, your natural inclination may be to defend yourself and turn the insults back on him. This can have only one outcome: you'll both end up angry and emotionally drained. Instead, do all you can to remain calm and refuse to join in the battle. In fact, sometimes saying nothing is best. Look at your child to show you are listening, but say nothing rather than something that will make the situation escalate or that you will regret later.

If they say, "All you care about is yourself."
You might say, "I disagree, but you're entitled to your opinion."

If they say, "You're a selfish, stingy person."
You might say, "I disagree, but you're entitled to your opinion."

If they say, "I will never treat my children the way you're treating me. You're very cruel hearted."
You might say, "How you raise your children will be your business."

IN THE END

Although it's true that a parent is always a parent and the job never ends completely, it's also true that the job changes over the years. Now your job is to exert influence that helps the adult child be independent, not dependent. The key to doing this is in conversations that show your adult children that your relationship has changed. Let them know that you see them as adults. Talk to them that way. Interact with them that way. As you continue to expect adult behavior from them and make it clear that you're no longer accepting excuses, they will begin to see themselves as adults and find that they enjoy the feeling of independence.

EXPERT HELP

This chapter was written with the expert help of Barbara Ensor, Ph.D., a psychologist in an independent practice in Baltimore, Maryland. She specializes in family and individual therapy.

Financial Ties

"As parents, we want to provide for our children financially, but sometimes it's better if they learn the hard way. Personal experience with some financial hardship can teach character and responsibility for one's own actions."

Robert K. Doyle, chair of the Personal Financial Planning Committee, Florida Institute of CPAs

Before she left for college, nineteen-year-old Karen and her parents made a financial arrangement that they all thought was fair. Her parents agreed to pay all her college expenses: tuition, room, board, books, and fees. Karen agreed to get a part-time job to pay for all the other incidental costs of living: clothing, recreation, and the occasional noninstitutional meal. Now, in her sophomore year, Karen is $2,740 in debt on her credit cards and wants her parents to help her protect her credit record.

Twenty-seven-year-old Tim is unemployed, *again*. This is the fourth job he has lost within the past two years. He is well educated, has the ability to do very well in his chosen field, and seems to want to be successful, but he says he just can't find a job that is fulfilling. Once again, he wants his parents to "loan" him some money so he can pay his bills until he finds a job.

Thirty-two-year-old Jane and her husband have found the house of their dreams; however, it is $20,000 more than they can afford. They've both asked their parents to chip in some money for the down payment with assurances that they can then handle the monthly mortgage.

Forty-two-year-old Ben owes his parents fifteen thousand dollars on a loan they gave him ten years ago when he was struggling to establish his own business. Yesterday, he bought himself a sixty-five thousand dollar sports car, and his parents are furious. How could he spend that kind of money on a luxury item when he hasn't yet paid back his loan?

As our children age, so do their financial situations, decisions, and problems. Should we bail them out? Should we continue to support their mistakes? Should we cut the financial strings? There are no hard and fast answers to these questions. How you financially support your grown children is a personal decision. How you help them learn how to save, invest, and budget will depend in large part on your individual family dynamics. Some families are very open about their personal finances; others are secretive. But in either case, you should be aware that the decisions we make and the things we say to our children about financial issues are often dictated by our own needs as parents. Do we need our adult children to be dependent on us? Or do we want them to be responsible for themselves and become financially independent? This chapter is written under the assumption that you would prefer the latter. It will help you find the words you need to support your children with love while you get them on the right track financially.

WHY TALK ABOUT FINANCIAL ISSUES

Financial security and independence are the result of mature self-sufficiency. It is natural to want this for our children. But according to the Administrative Office of the U.S. Courts, each year more than a million adults in this country fail to meet this goal and file for bankruptcy. In the year 2000, for example, 1,262,102 bankruptcy filings were recorded. Of these, 97 percent were nonbusiness, personal filings—individuals falling into financial ruin. This is why somebody needs to talk to adult children who are having difficulty keeping their financial affairs in order before they become one of these statistics.

If your young adult child is dependent on you for financial help, you might be tempted to assume that she will automatically cut the financial ties as she matures. But experts say that financial independence is not something that everyone learns without parental guidance. We teach our kids about many financial issues throughout life: how to earn an allowance, how to save, how to budget, how to avoid being ripped off. Whether we offered detailed lessons or taught through example and conversations, our children learned certain attitudes about money and how to save and spend it. These lessons don't end the day they become legal adults, especially with grown kids who are still dependent on their parents for financial support. These adult children may have a good reason for hanging on to the family purse strings. They may be in college and unable to earn a living wage. They may be at an entry-level position that promises future security but won't pay the rent right now. They may be unemployed and in need of temporary support. In all these cases and thousands of others, grown children look to their parents for financial help. The question of whether you should give it has no short, easy answer. It depends on many factors discussed in this chapter, but the lines of communication should always be left open.

If we don't talk to our adult children about the financial issues that affect the quality of their lives, we leave them exposed to the school of hard knocks. How are they supposed to know how to invest? How to budget for a household? How to protect their credit rating? Sure, everyone makes some mistakes along the way and learns from them, but if we've learned financial lessons that we can pass on to our kids that will help them avoid bankruptcy, eviction, or worse, we should pass this knowledge on and hope they listen. Just as it's not necessary to let our young children burn their hand to learn the lesson about staying away from a hot stove, it's not necessary to watch our adult children fall into financial ruin to teach them the lesson of budgeting and saving. If they repeatedly refuse to heed our advice and learn these lessons, then certainly it might be necessary to step back and allow them to burn that hand on the fire of experience.

WHEN TO TALK ABOUT FINANCIAL ISSUES

When Kent graduated from college, he was very open with his parents about the job offers he was receiving and how much each one paid. He talked with his mother and father about the pros and cons of each one, about the benefits offered, about the pension plans and stock options. His parents gave their opinion and tried to help him make the best choice. But two years later, when a headhunter came calling and enticed Kent to move to a new company, his parents were surprised that he didn't mention anything about the offered salary and benefits. Something had changed about Kent's attitude toward his parents' involvement with his finances. Should they ask him?

If Kent isn't offering the information, he's not asking his parents to help him financially, and he's not about to lose his house to foreclosure, his parents should respect his right as a mature and financially stable adult to keep the details of his paycheck to himself. This is a right we grant to our friends and colleagues and is one that we should extend to our children. If they are financially secure, we should not probe.

However, there may be times when some financial advice may be welcomed. If, for example, your son initiates a conversation about the stock market, this is a good time to talk about your own views on sound investing. Or, if your broker passes on some valuable information to you, you might want to share that with your adult children. Or, if your son or daughter is thinking of buying a house and starts talking about the cost of mortgages, points, and closing fees, this is an invitation to you to join in the conversation. In these circumstances, the advice isn't intrusive or overbearing. It is simply the sharing of financial information, adult to adult.

At other times, it may be absolutely necessary to have a long talk with your adult children about financial issues. When they show a pattern of financial irresponsibility, you might be able to help them get on track. When they are about to jump into a venture that will put them over their heads in debt, you can be the voice of reason or concern (which they have the right to ignore if they choose). When they are overly dependent on you for financial support, you have the right (and some may say an obligation) to guide them away from you and toward financial independence.

There are many times in the course of your adult child's life when the subject of finances may be on the table. The challenge for you is to know when to get involved and when to hold back.

WHAT YOU SHOULD TALK ABOUT

The details of your conversations with your adult children about their financial lives are as unique and many as your children. This section will give you a foundation on which to build those conversations. It will suggest the words that will help you begin to guide your children to financial independence, make them feel a sense of responsibility, and make wise financial decisions.

Breaking the Ice

Personal finance is not necessarily a subject that must be discussed in serious sit-down, face-to-face style. It is something that you can talk about in general terms in any casual conversation as easily as you can talk about the weather. If you are thinking about talking to your adult children about their financial habits or difficulties, you might first break the ice on the subject by striking up conversations in which you can easily talk about finances in a neutral, nonthreatening way. Talk about yourself, your friends and neighbors, and information in the news to get the subject going.

Talk About Yourself. You can teach lessons about financial responsibility without giving a lecture when you talk about your own financial experiences. In casual conversations, you can recall your mistakes and their consequences and the lessons learned. You can reminisce about the early days in your career when you were struggling to put aside enough money to buy a house and raise a family. You might mention the loan your parents gave you and your determination to pay it back as quickly as possible. If you worked a second or third job, talk about it. Explain the sacrifices you made and the rewards you reaped. If you found yourself in financial trouble at some point, talk about it. Let your children know that you too have struggled to be financially independent.

You might say, "I remember once I wanted this red car I saw in the used car lot down on Seventh Street. I asked my dad to loan me seven hundred dollars for the down payment. He wouldn't hand over the money, but he did offer to hire me to work in his store at night to earn some extra money. At two dollars an hour, it took a long time to earn the money I needed, and by that time the car was gone. But I did end up with some money in my savings account that helped me pay the rent and security deposit on a new apartment your mom and I wanted to move into."

You might say, "I remember being so poor during college that when my friends went out to a bar on the weekends, I would tag along and drink water all evening. Once I asked my parents to give me more spending money, and they did. I took the whole fifty dollars and immediately spent it on a pair of brown boots. Talk about being dressed up with no place to go!"

You can also broach the subject of your children's financial situation by first talking about yourself and then turning the conversation around.

You might say, "My financial adviser told me the other day that although the stock market is taking a dive lately, my money is in pretty secure funds. Do you have a financial adviser?"

You might say, "I've been having a hard time lately keeping my credit card balance down. How do you do it?"

You might say, "I decided to buy new furniture for the living room, and I'm trying to decide if I should wait until I save up the money or if I should just charge it. What would you do?"

Talk About Your Friends and Neighbors. Friends and neighbors give you plenty of objective circumstances to talk about. It's common knowledge that people in every walk of life run into financial trouble sometimes. Everyone has to make financial decisions that affect the rest of their lives. And sometimes even your own family members make mistakes that others can learn from. There's no need to let the conversation drift into gossip. Stick to the facts, state the situation, and then draw your conclusions.

You might say, "The Johnsons who live in the green house on the corner just moved out because the bank foreclosed on the mortgage. The bank won't do that without warning, and they'll usually try to work out some kind of payment schedule to avoid taking the house. I wonder what could have happened to cause such a drastic move?"

You might say, "Did I tell you that the Smiths moved to another state? Apparently, they were really struggling financially and found that real estate and the cost of living is so much less expensive farther south, so they decided to make the move. It's difficult for a lot of people in this area to make ends meet."

You might say, "I have sad news about Uncle Jed. You know he's a big gambler? Well, it seems he gambled away all his assets, and now he's filing for bankruptcy. Can you believe that he let gambling ruin him financially?"

You might say, "I feel badly for your cousin, Beth. She wants to go to college, but her parents just can't afford it. You know how Aunt Ann and Uncle Bill always spent every dime they had on the biggest and the best of everything. Well, now they have no savings to fall back on. I know you always thought Beth was lucky because she got everything she wanted, but now you can see why it's important to pass up some of those luxury items and put money away in savings."

Talk About the News. The newspaper, TV, and radio are filled each day with financial news and information. This makes it easy to strike up a conversation about the stock market, credit card sales, bankruptcy, and the like. You might also look out for stories about people who have made good or bad financial decisions.

You might say, "I read today that there's a good chance that the social security system is going to fall apart by the time I retire. That's not a major surprise. That's why your father and I have been contributing to an individual retirement account—that is, an IRA—for years. Have you started an IRA?"

You might say, "Last night's news did a segment on credit card debt. I was amazed to find out how much the average American charges each year and how many cards some people have. Do you think most of your generation spends more than they earn?"

Addressing Specific Issues
There are many financial issues that you may need to talk about to your adult children. The topics offered in this section will give you an idea of the way these issues can be discussed and how you can help without indulging or meddling. The topics are:

- Charge cards and credit rating
- Cutting financial ties
- Teaching financial responsibility
- Investing and saving
- Estate planning

Charge Cards and Credit Rating. Safeguarding a credit rating is a paramount concern for young adults. They have no real credit history yet, and so what they do right from the start will affect their ability to borrow money for a future business, housing, car loans, credit loans, and so on. Once a credit history is damaged, it is very difficult to fix; in fact, it takes about seven years for the record to be cleared. How will your grown kids know this if you don't tell them? Do they know this when they line up for registration on the first day of college and a credit card vendor offers them a card even though they have no money and no job? Of course not; it's assumed by the card company and by the unemployed student that the parents will take care of the bills. This is something to talk about before the card is used.

If your adult child doesn't make enough money to pay the cost and interest of charged items, speak up before the charging begins to avoid any misunderstandings later.

You might say, "I know you're an adult now and can make financial decisions on your own, but I just want to tell you right up front that I will not be able to help you if you get into debt with that card. This is your responsibility, so it would be a good idea to think twice before you charge anything."

When it's too late for this warning and your adult child shows up at your doorstep asking for help to pay off a credit card debt, you have an important decision to make. Will you chip in to help save his credit record? What you say to your adult child in this situation will depend on what you feel about his or her sense of financial responsibility. If you feel that this is a one-time mistake that has taught your child a good lesson about overspending, you might be more willing to help out.

You might say, "I will help you pay this bill because a ruined credit record will haunt you for years and I don't want that to happen to you. But I want you to know that I will do this only once, and I want you to pay me back. You have seen what happens when you spend more than you earn; after I pay this debt, all your future credit bills will be your responsibility."

If your child has a history of irresponsibility with money and has asked you to bail her out before, then the conversation will take a different turn. You are no longer responsible legally, psychologically, or emotionally for the debts of your child. Some children do not understand this unless they are told in no uncertain terms.

You might say, "No. This time you have to take responsibility for your own debts. You charged those items; you have to pay for them. If this damages your credit history, that will certainly make it harder for you to borrow money in the future, but that's what happens to people who spend more money than they make and can't pay the bills."

This is difficult to say to our kids at any age. But if your goal is to build financial responsibility and independence, you cannot keep putting your hand in your pocket every time their creditors come knocking.

Cutting Financial Ties. Thirty-two-year-old Dana told her parents that she wanted to go back to college for an advanced degree. They were proud to hear her map out her plans and glad that she seemed motivated to improve her career status. But they were stunned when she asked them to loan her fifteen hundred dollars for the first semester. They had already loaned Dana three thousand dollars to start up her own cottage industry. They had loaned her two thousand dollars for the down payment on her car. And they had given her untold amounts of money through the years when she was "a little short this month." It was now looking as if she just expected them to hand over this tuition money.

If your adult children develop a habit of depending on you for financial help and this dependence is keeping them from becoming financially responsible, it's time for tough love solutions.

It's very difficult to say no when children of any age beg for help, but if your children are physically and mentally able to provide for themselves financially, some financial experts believe you have a parental and moral obligation to help them do that.

Cutting the financial umbilical cord needs to be swift (although not necessarily painless). If your child has shown a pattern of financial dependence or entitlement, it's time to stand firm. When your child returns yet again for a handout, you can very calmly say, "I am not going to loan you any more money. I think it's very important to your life as an adult that you learn to take care of yourself. Now it's time to start."

Obviously, any adult child who has grown accustomed to relying on parental money will not take this news well. Some may be angry enough to throw hurtful accusations your way. The hardest to deflect is the one that says, "How can you say you love me if you won't help me?" If this happens, keep in mind that loving your children has never been easy. When they were little, it wasn't easy to get them to eat good foods or get to bed on time. It wasn't easy to discipline disobedience or teach them the consequences of their actions. But because we love our children and want them to grow to be physically, mentally, and emotionally healthy and strong, we did things they didn't like.

The same is true in adulthood. Money and love are not the same thing. You do not show love by giving in to your child's cries for more and more money. You show love by refusing to keep them financially dependent on you. You don't show love when you hand over the money. You show love by helping them find a way to earn and save their own money. Financial lessons that give adult children a sense of responsibility and independence are far more valuable to the quality of the life they will live than any dollar amount you can offer. You will never teach your child the value of hard work and money if you keep reaching into your own pocket when they fall short or overspend.

Your kids won't see it that way. They'll say (or think), "What's the big deal? You can afford it." Knowing this, it can be hard to say no to them because it feels selfish. But remember that they are adults now, and your finances are separate from theirs. You do not owe them a living; that is something mature people earn for themselves.

If you simply can't afford to pull your adult children out of every financial hole they dig, you have to say so and make it clear that you're not willing to trade your financial security for theirs. Then offer some other form of support so they know you're not turning your back on them.

You might say, "I can't help you. I have budgeted my money to make sure that I can pay all my bills every month. If I hand this money over to you, I will end up short myself. Why don't we sit down and find a way to help you budget and save, so you can get this bill paid on a reasonable schedule and then live within your means in the future?"

Some financially secure parents don't know how to say no to their kids so they use "can't afford it" as an excuse to turn their kids down. They say, "I wish I could help you out of this jam, but I just don't have the money to do it." That answer makes it easier to say no, but it causes its own problems. If you say you can't afford to help your kids get out of financial trouble, you compromise your right to spend your own money without guilt. If you can't afford to help your daughter avoid eviction, how can you go on a nice vacation? How can you buy a new stereo system? How can you buy any luxury item with your grown children standing on the sidelines knowing you lied about your ability to help them? In the long run, it's better to be honest about why you have decided to cut the financial strings.

Let your children know that because you love them, you feel it's your obligation to help them grow into financially independent adults and that you know that will never happen if you keep handing them money.

You might say, "Yes, I can afford to pay this debt for you, but you could afford it too if you learn to manage money. I have worked hard for my money; I have saved and budgeted so that I am now financially secure, and I'd like to see you do the same thing."

Teaching Financial Responsibility. If you decide that you do want to help your children out of their financial difficulties, but you also want to teach them how to manage money responsibility, there is a solution that lies halfway between saying no and handing over the money: you can require them to demonstrate financial responsibility before you hand over the money.

You might say, "When you show me that you can earn and save five thousand dollars, I will give you another five thousand dollars. But not until then."

Or, you might want your adult children to show you that they can manage money better before you give them any more. They can demonstrate responsibility by reducing the debt on their credit cards. They can put off expensive luxury items until they have the money in hand to buy them, resist buying the most expensive car on the lot, and learn not to spend $100,000 a year when they make $75,000.

You might say, "I will be glad to help you financially when you can show me that you have learned to live within your means. When you cut up your credit card and pay five hundred dollars toward the balance, then I'll be glad to share the money I have with you."

You also teach financial responsibility by attaching strings to any bailout. Experts say that if you give your grown children money, you have the right to insist on certain conditions. You might require your child to cut up the credit card. And even if you can easily afford to hand over the money, you should insist on a reasonable repayment schedule. You might also charge interest to discourage repeat borrowing. A grown child who repeatedly turns to his or her parents for financial support needs to learn that even if Mom and Dad once again hand over the money, there will be consequences.

You might say, "I will help you pay this bill, but I want to do this grown-up to grown-up. You're not a little kid anymore, and so you know that borrowing money requires responsible action on the part of the borrower. I want you to repay me three hundred dollars a month payable on the fifteenth of each month. If the payment is late, there will be a 10 percent late fee added on to the balance. Do you think you can do that? If you agree to these terms in writing, I'll be glad to write out a check for the amount you're asking for."

Beware of the excuses you make for your child. Once you decide to cut financial ties and teach financial responsibility, be careful that you don't find yourself giving in to their continued begging. It's easy to rationalize why you should help them. You might reason, "It's so hard for kids today. The job market is bad. Things are so much more expensive these days. Rents are out of this world. This is a tough economy."

These excuses are good reasons to help responsible young adults get on their feet, but they do not explain why a grown child needs to rely on his parents for financial help again and again and again.

You might say, "I know times are tough, but they're tough for everyone out there trying to make ends meet. Just like everyone else, you have to find a way to make your income match your expenses. I'd be glad to baby-sit your kids if you find you need to take on a night-time or weekend job."

Investing and Saving. How can I talk to my adult child about saving? Isn't he too old for these lessons? Financial investment managers hear these questions all the time. Yes, it's a good idea to teach lessons about saving when your children are young, but putting aside half of their allowance each week is not quite the same as learning how to make that money grow and provide for later years. If you or a financial adviser can sit down and talk to your adult children about things like compound interest, they will have a better understanding of some basic financial matters.

You might say, "Did you know that if an eighteen-year-old person puts two thousand dollars a year into an individual retirement account for ten years and then stops all contributions but lets that money sit there, by the age of sixty-five, that twenty thousand dollars will have grown into nearly $1 million?"

Many young adults figure they'll start serious saving when they move up their career ladder and have more income. But by that time, they may have developed spending habits they can't break and the ability to earn on interest is diminished.

You might say, "If another person begins saving at the age of thirty-five by putting two thousand dollars a year into an IRA, after thirty years of making this annual contribution, this person will not have nearly as much money saved as the person who started at age eighteen."

The exact figures depend on a number of variables, but you can get a financial adviser to make up an impressive bar or line graph to illustrate what will happen to money saved today when it is invested carefully. You can be sympathetic to your kids' reluctance to sacrifice now for security tomorrow, but these kinds of facts give them a good reason to pass up that new stereo and put the money into a secure fund.

Estate Planning. Some parents are very open with their adult children about their personal finances; others do not discuss their financial status at all. Regardless of how you feel about this issue, there are some things adult children need to know about your estate so they will be able to carry out your wishes after your death and avoid unnecessary probate problems.

Every one of your children should know what to expect on your death. They should know where your important papers are kept, where you bank, the name of your investment broker, and the person you want to be the executor of your will.

You might say, "Although I don't expect to die any time soon, I do want you to know some of my basic financial information so it will be easy for you to locate my papers and accounts."

You might also talk to your adult children about the terms of your will. If all your assets will be divided equally among them, tell them so. If an unpaid loan you gave to your eldest son is to be deducted from his share of the inheritance, make sure he knows that. If you are putting your money into a trust, your children should be aware of this. If you have made stipulations that control the purse strings from the grave (because, for example, you know your children do not have the financial maturity to handle a large lump sum), you need to talk about this too.

You might say, "I want you to know that I have made a stipulation in my will that you will be the beneficiary of all my assets, but you will not be given that money in one lump sum. Through my bank executor, you will receive ten thousand dollars each year. Of course, I don't expect to die any day soon, but I just want you to know so you can make your own long-term financial plans."

You should tell your adult children who has power of attorney for you if there should come a time when you cannot make important decisions for yourself. An important aspect of financial planning is designating a durable power of attorney, that is, the person who is legally permitted to make legal and financial decisions on the behalf of another even when that person is incapacitated. Without a previously designated power of attorney, the family must go through an expensive court process to be granted that power of attorney once the parent becomes mentally or physically incapacitated. If you want one of your children to have power of attorney, this is something you should discuss.

You might say, "Because I think you've grown into a very responsible person, I was hoping that you would agree to have power of attorney over my legal and financial matters if I were to become incapacitated or die. I don't want to scare you or worry you that anything is wrong with me. I just want to have this matter legally taken care of while I am in good health so that I don't have to worry about it in the future."

Look to the Experts
If you know your kids aren't likely to take financial advice from you, try to get them together with an objective, third-party professional who can give them the guidance they need. You can't make your adult children listen to professional advice, but you can open the door and then leave the follow-up up to them.

You might say, "I have a friend who is a financial adviser. He has helped me tremendously with my investment decisions. Would you like to talk to him? He has some unique insights about how to save and budget and make your money work for you. Would you like his number?"

IN THE END

They say that love and money are the two hardest subjects to talk about. Put the two together in a parent-child dynamic, and the difficulty is naturally compounded. You can ease the difficulty if you talk to your adult children openly and often about general financial subjects. Then when something personal and important comes up, you'll be able to put all the facts on the table matter-of-factly and guide your children to greater financial responsibility and independence.

EXPERT HELP

This chapter was prepared with the expert help of Robert K. Doyle, CPA, PFS. Doyle is a principal of Spoor, Doyle & Associates in St. Petersburg, Florida, where he manages the Personal Financial Planning Practice (PFP). He is a licensed certified public accountant, a personal financial specialist, a registered investment adviser, and the chairman of the Personal Financial Planning Committee of the Florida Institute of CPAs. Doyle also serves as a member of the PFP Executive Committee of the American Institute of Certified Public Accountants.

Substance Abuse

"You have to learn a language that the substance abuser can understand. When the family members are looking at the situation, they see the drug as the problem. But to the addict, the drug is the solution, and *you* are the problem if you're getting in the way of having that drug. So when you each talk about 'the problem,' you're talking about completely different things."

Jeff Jay, president, Terry McGovern Foundation

You are not alone. The Web site lovefirst.net tells us that one out of three people is living with or related to someone with an alcohol or other drug problem. Although we see their problem, they cannot. When we offer help, they refuse. When we talk to them, they blame us or someone else. It begins to feel hopeless, but it is not. The first step toward treatment and recovery is through honest, loving conversation—a conversation that is very different from the ones you have had on this subject in the past.

This chapter will teach you a new way of looking at a substance abuse problem and give you the words you need to talk to your adult children about your concerns, your feelings, and your love. And it will help you bring your addicted child to treatment and recovery.

WHY TALK ABOUT SUBSTANCE ABUSE

If you suspect or know that your adult child has a problem with alcohol or other drugs, you know that this is your problem too. You

247

cannot turn away, ignore, or deny what substance abuse is doing to this person you love and care for.

But if in the past your conversations have turned into angry shouting matches and you have a collection of broken promises too many to count, you may be ready to give up. You may have decided that there is nothing more you can do because "he just won't listen to me." Besides, some people believe that you can't help an addict until he or she has hit rock bottom and asks for help. While it's true that the addict must be willing to accept help, a recent survey of recovering addicts found that 70 percent found help after a friend, family member, employer, or coworker intervened.

You should not give up, but you might need to change your approach. Now is the time to talk without anger, blame, ridicule, or judgment. Now is the time to lead your child to treatment and recovery with words of encouragement and love.

WHEN TO TALK ABOUT SUBSTANCE ABUSE

Ben's fiftieth birthday party brought him great joy. He looked around the family dinner table and was proud and thankful for his wife, his four children, their spouses, and his grandchildren. Life had been very good to him and he was at peace—with one exception. Ben's youngest daughter, Clara, seemed to have a drinking problem. Tonight again, she was drunk, loud, and quick to pick arguments. This had been going on at every family gathering for over a year, and Ben decided that tonight he was going to step in and talk to his daughter.

While waiting for the birthday cake, Ben called Clara aside into his bedroom and asked her to sit down. He told his daughter that he was very disappointed with the way she was abusing alcohol. "I've been quiet about this, hoping you'd straighten up by yourself," Ben said. "But this is just getting worse and worse. I want you to promise me that you'll stop drinking before you lose your job and end up sick."

"Get off my back. You don't know what you're talking about, so how 'bout you just shut up!" yelled Clara as she walked out of the room, grabbed her coat, and slammed the front door behind her.

The entire family froze in silent embarrassment. Suddenly, no one was in the mood to sing "Happy Birthday" as Ben's wife walked out of the kitchen at that moment with the cake ablaze with its festive candles.

Ben's intentions were good, but his timing was terrible. Conversations like these are often a disaster because they take place at a time when the person in need is under the influence of the drug and least likely to listen. When you talk to your adult child about substance abuse, he or she has to be sober, straight, and clearheaded. This means that the conversation may have to take place first thing in the morning, or whenever else it is that you can catch him or her straight.

It's also most effective if you talk immediately after some kind of crisis. If you talk when all seems to be going well, your words of concern or worry are ignored as parental meddling. But when your adult child is feeling the after-burn of trouble (maybe being fired from a job, or being thrown out by a spouse, or being arrested for driving while intoxicated), that's a good time to sit down and talk. She will be much more open to accepting help at this time. As the severity of the crisis goes up, the readiness to accept help also goes up.

You should also talk to your adult child about a substance abuse problem when you decide that you will no longer support the addiction. If you have been enabling the abuser by paying debts, making excuses, or ignoring the problem, have a sit-down conversation when you're ready to stop. (See "Talk About What You Are Going to Do and Not Going to Do" later in this chapter.)

WHAT YOU SHOULD TALK ABOUT

In all your conversations about substance abuse, focus on your feelings and treatment options. There is absolutely no reason to hash over all the terrible things that have happened because of the abuse problem. Be focused on treatment, be positive, and be firm.

This section will give you information that will help you:

- Be prepared
- Have one-on-one conversations
- Have a structured family intervention

Be Prepared. Unless you're in an emergency situation in which your child's life is in imminent danger, don't talk about this problem until you've put a lot of time into preparing for your conversation. It's almost impossible to sit down and have a spontaneous conversation about substance abuse that leads to treatment and recovery. Before you talk, think, research, and get ready. Reading a chapter like this is a good start; reading other books, exploring Web sites, and talking to counselors are also recommended preparatory steps.

You should also know exactly what you want your adult child to do when you finish having the conversation. Know in advance where he can go for help immediately. Find a treatment center, talk to the counselors, and get the details on admission. Even if your child is facing a court date for drunken driving and agrees to get help after the two of you talk, he'll probably change his mind by the time you figure out where to go for that help.

Instead of saying, "Do you promise to get help for your alcohol problem?"
You should be ready to say, "Will you come with me right now to the Alcohol and Drug Rehabilitation Center and sign yourself in and follow the program to completion? I've looked into this center. I've talked with the doctors there. And they're ready to take you in and help you if you call them right now."

You should also have a fallback position ready. If you want your child to begin an inpatient program and he says that he absolutely won't, you can then offer the compromise of an outpatient program that you also have investigated. Often, the person will feel so good about having another choice she'll take the fallback option.

Have One-on-One Conversations. "What is the matter with you?" screamed Rose at her thirty-eight-year-old son, Jason. "You promised you'd give up drugs. You swore on the life of your child. And you just go and do it again. I don't understand how you could be willing to give up so much. I don't blame Nora for throwing you out. When are you going to face your problem and grow up? We've all had it with you. Do you understand?"

What Jason understands is very different from what Rose intends. He understands that he's no good. He understands that he's alone. He understands that he's weak and has no hope of ever being drug free. He has had this "conversation" with his mother before.

She has argued, pleaded, threatened, and cried. With honest intentions, he has made promises—and then broke them all. Everyone, including Jason, is ready to agree that there is just no hope.

If you find yourself having conversations like this one with your adult child, it's time to back off and change your approach. Start fresh, and reconsider the way you talk and the words you use. From now on, you're going to reframe the problem around the medical issue, not the person. You're going to talk without blaming, bargaining, pleading, or threatening. You will not use judgmental language. This is going to be hard because you will get frustrated and fed up and fall back into old habits of talking. But consistently positive and affirming conversations are the only hope you have of helping your child seek treatment.

From now on, think about your child's addiction as a medical problem—one that is no different from any other medical problem. How would you talk to your adult child if he had a terrible toothache and wouldn't go to a dentist? Although you would be frustrated at his stubbornness, you would probably be concerned, loving, and firm in your insistence that he needs help. Do the same for your child's addition problem. It is a medical issue, not a sign of moral weakness or laziness. It is a physical problem that needs medical attention. You will not lead your child to seek treatment by calling him names or alienating him from the family. You will break through that wall of denial when you show that you are persistent and constant in your love and concern.

Instead of saying, "How can you let your life just fall apart like this?" *You might say,* "I've taken some time to learn about chemical dependency, and I've learned that this is a critical medical and health issue. That's how we need to deal with this."

Instead of saying, "Grow up!"
You might say, "This problem isn't your fault, and it isn't my fault. It's no one's fault. It's a medical problem that needs medical attention."

Instead of saying, "I can't stand your lies anymore."
You might say, "I understand now that when you say you'll take care of this problem by yourself, it's like saying you'll take care of a toothache by yourself. You really can't. I'm here to help you get the professional help you need to take care of this medical problem."

Instead of saying, "Unless you promise to stop drinking, I don't want to see you anymore."
You might say, "I know now that when you promise you'll stop drinking, that's a promise you can't possibly keep. That's like a person who gets migraines promising that she won't get headaches anymore. I understand that without help, you can't keep those promises."

Instead of saying, "What kind of a man are you? How can you let your wife and kids down like this?"
You might say, "Your wife and kids want you to get better. They want you to be healthy. I'd like to help you get the medical help you need to do that."

You'll notice that many of these suggested dialogue starters are "I" statements. This puts the focus on your feelings rather than on your child. This helps keep your child from taking a defensive position and shutting you out. Never hesitate to say things such as, "I am concerned," or, "I care about you so much." But be careful. Don't let your "I" statements place blame:

Instead of saying, "I see that you're out of control with your alcohol use."
You might say, "I see that the alcohol has turned on you."

This is closer to the truth when it comes to addiction because an addicted person cannot be expected to be in control of the problem.

Instead of saying, "I'm so angry about this."
You might say, "I'm concerned about your health."

This Time Is Different.   At one time or another, you have probably tried all these supportive statements that avoid blame and judgment. You might be thinking, "I've done that, and it didn't work." The key difference here is that in the past when the supportive statements didn't get immediate results, you probably eventually reverted back to the angry and blaming statements. In this new approach, you must become like a broken record. No matter how often your adult child falls back into the grip of addiction, you must continue to use supportive talk only. Keep reminding yourself how you would talk to your adult child who had an untreated medical problem or whose treatment regimen failed. You would be encouraging and hopeful. Do the same for your child who is grappling with the illness of addiction.

You might say, "I'm here for you, and I will help you get the help you need when you're ready. You can always turn to me."

This reaction is very powerful because it preserves the relationship rather than continues old family arguments. This changes the way the abuser views the problem and its possible solution.

Talk About What You Are Going to Do and Not Going to Do.
The telephone rang around dinnertime. When Meg answered, she immediately recognized her daughter's drunken, slurred voice.

"Mom," Kathy said, "I'm in a lot of trouble. I'm being evicted from my apartment because I haven't paid the rent for the last three months. Could you please loan me some money? I swear I'll pay you back. I've just hit a little bit of a bad time right now." Meg had heard this before: "Mom, could you help me with my car payment?" "Mom, could you loan me some money for groceries?" Meg was sure her daughter had an alcohol problem that caused her to miss work and maybe had even caused her to be fired. "I have no one else to turn to Mom. Please?" begged Kathy. "I'll give you a loan," said Meg, "but I want you to swear to me that you'll stop drinking. Do you promise?" "Yes, sure," said Meg. "Thanks a lot. I love you."

Like Kathy, all substance abusers need enablers—people in their lives who make it easier for them to stay addicted. These are well-meaning friends and family members who unwittingly help the disease to progress. The enablers may be the source of money or the things that money can buy, like food and shelter. They may be the source of alibis or services such as legal help. Or they may simply ignore the problem.

If you have been an enabler, now is the time to change and use the crises caused by substance abuse as opportunities. Your child is more likely to accept medical help when he's hurting; don't be too quick to ease the pain. Do not give or lend money for the addiction or to cover debts caused by the addiction. For example, if the rent money has been spent at the bar, don't block the natural consequences of that action. Otherwise, it is really you who are buying the next drink. Instead, direct her toward treatment:

You might say, "I'm willing to help, but I'm only willing to help you in the right way. I have witnessed how alcohol has turned against you, and I'd like to assist you in getting help for that problem. I'm willing to do whatever it takes to get you the right kind of help."

Your adult child is not going to say, "Oh, good! I was hoping you'd say that."

He or she is going to say, "If you just pay my rent, I'll be just fine. If you lend me the money, I promise I'll get this under control. You're right. I have to do something about this, and I will."

Don't argue this point or get lassoed into going along with this plan. Once a chemical dependency has developed, the addict can't handle this independently. Just repeat your position, and state your prepared action plan. Be calm and persistent.

You might say, "I love you. I'm willing to help you, but I'm only willing to help you in the right way. If you check into a treatment center today and make a commitment to me that you're going to follow the program, I will take care of your rent problem."

You might say, "I love you. I care about you. But I'm not going to help you live like this. I will not lie for you any more. I'm not going to make up stories to cover for you any more."

You might say, "I realize that when I paid your car payment for you last month, all I was really doing was subsidizing your drug and alcohol use. And as much as I love you, I'm just not going to do that any more."

Get Support for Yourself. Giving up your role as an enabler is not easy. It's much easier to fix the problem by paying the rent. It's easier to relieve the immediate tension by lying to spouses and bosses. Enabling is easy; this is hard. This makes you feel awful, and you will need help from others who have been in this position. Become involved in a program of recovery. Al-Anon, Nar-Anon, and Families Anonymous are invaluable resources (see the Resources section at the end of this chapter). It is often too difficult to stop the enabling process without help and support from those who have been down this road. Join a group, and draw on their experience, strength, and hope.

Dealing with Failure. After your heart-to-heart talk and your commitment to become a helper but not an enabler, you will naturally have high hopes that something good will happen. But if it doesn't, you may feel like a failure and you may feel more anger toward your child. But try not to lose heart. You *have* made a difference. It takes time for your loving response to sink in; it's rarely immediate. You really have done something positive: you have changed the dynamics of your relationship with the abuser. Before, you were an angry and judgmental enabler. Now you are a loving helper. But you will probably be tested many times before your child believes that you really have changed. That's why it's important to follow through. If you say you're not paying the rent, don't pay it. If you say you're not lying to her spouse anymore, don't do it. If your child falls off the wagon, say, "I love you."

This "love first" approach is a good first step toward helping your adult child. Sadly, the success rate of one-on-one conversations is quite low. But even if your child does not turn her life around after all your efforts, your conversations and offers of help still have value because they set the groundwork necessary to move on to a group intervention, which can have a strong and positive impact.

Have a Structured Family Intervention. If you're not getting any results from your one-on-one conversations it's time to step up your efforts to the next level: a structured family intervention. Intervention is the most effective technique families can use to help a loved one suffering from chemical dependency—alcoholism or other drug addiction. It is also the most ignored. But just as

CPR is often the first lifesaving step in helping a heart attack victim, intervention is the most powerful step that a family can take to initiate the recovery process.

In a structured family intervention, members of the substance abuser's family and close friends come together to meet with the abuser and map out an agreeable plan for treatment and recovery while always preserving the dignity of the alcoholic. Ultimately, he must agree to accept help. Your role is to help break his denial, so that he can make the best choice.

Intervention requires new ways of communicating. Forget everything you've been told about intervention, and begin anew. Learn for yourself, and then ask other family members to learn. Those who are willing to try the intervention can prepare themselves by reading about how interventions work. You might suggest (or even supply) the books and other resources recommended in the Resources section at the end of this chapter. Once everyone is educated, make a family decision about intervention. If you decide to move ahead, planning and preparation are your keys to success. Take no shortcuts.

Before you can all sit down together and talk to the substance abuser, you need to talk to each of these people to make sure that they understand the rules. This is not a time for anyone to talk with a critical, judgmental, angry, or blaming attitude. You have to communicate to these people how to talk about this issue in a supportive and loving way. Those who cannot should not be part of the intervention.

It's impossible to give a full education on the process of an intervention in a single chapter, but the following steps leading up to the intervention should give you a good idea of how the process works. It should help you plan how to get organized, what to say, and how you will proceed.

The following checklist is adopted from the Love First program created by Debra and Jeff Jay. It will give you an idea of how an intervention should be planned, but you should do more reading and research before you schedule your own intervention.

- Bring together three to eight people who are important to the alcoholic and are willing to learn how to help.
- Set up a planning meeting to discuss moving forward with the intervention.
- Choose a team chairperson.
- Discuss the importance of not alerting the alcoholic to the intervention plans.
- List ways you've tried to help the alcoholic that may have enabled the addiction.
- Put in writing all the negative consequences caused by the addiction problem.
- Write a one- to two-page letter to the alcoholic.
- Read your letters to each other, editing out anger, blame, and judgment.
- Identify financial resources for covering treatment costs.
- Choose a treatment center, answer its preintake questions, and make an appointment for admission.
- Set a date, time, and place for the intervention.
- Create a plan likely to guarantee the alcoholic's presence at the intervention.
- Identify objections the alcoholic may use to avoid or postpone treatment, and then formulate your answers.
- Determine who should drive the alcoholic from the intervention to treatment.
- Rehearse the intervention.
- Find a discreet place to park your cars.

- Plan to arrive at the intervention location thirty minutes before the alcoholic is expected to be there.
- If the intervention is taking place at the alcoholic's home, arrive as a group.
- After the intervention, call the admissions staff, and let them know whether the alcoholic has agreed to treatment.

When the intervention is well planned and conducted properly, about 85 percent of substance abusers will accept help *that day*. But there is a small window of opportunity here where the addict's wall of denial breaks down and he or she is able to say, "Yes, I agree, I want help." You have to be prepared with all the facts about where to go before the mood and commitment change.

You can hire a professional interventionist if you feel uncomfortable with the idea of an intervention, or if you don't have time to prepare, or if the people in your family are unable or unwilling to participate. To find an interventionist in your town, call a local alcohol and drug treatment center. If none is available locally, call a nationally recognized treatment center. Hanley-Hazelden Center and the Betty Ford Center maintain a list of interventionists who work nationwide. You can also look under "alcoholism" in the telephone book. When contacting an interventionist outside your town, ask if he or she offers telephone conferencing calls for initial family consultations.

IN THE END

Finding the right words that will save your adult child from the destructive influence of alcohol or other drugs is a difficult quest. Ultimately, you may not be able to say or do anything to change their course. This is not a reflection on the quality of your parenting skills; it is a testament to the power of addictive substances to steal the heart and soul of our loved ones. In the end, all you can do is try your best, offer your love, and be there to support your child. He must do the rest.

RESOURCES

Al-Anon
1600 Corporate Landing Pkwy.
Virginia Beach, VA 23454
(757) 563-1600; wso@al-anon.org; www.al-anon.alateen.org

This fellowship organization helps families and friends of alcoholics recover from the effects of living with the problem drinking of a relative or friend.

Alcoholics Anonymous
Grand Central Station
P.O. Box 459
New York, NY 10163
(212) 870-3400; www.alcoholics-anonymous.org

Alcoholics Anonymous is a fellowship of people who share their experience, strength, and hope so they may solve their common problem and help others recover from alcoholism.

Cocaine Anonymous
3740 Overland Ave., Suite C
Los Angeles, CA 90034
(310) 559-5833
National referral line: (800) 347-8998; Cocaineanonymous.org

Cocaine Anonymous is a fellowship of, by, and for cocaine addicts seeking recovery.

Families Anonymous
P.O. Box 3475
Culver City, CA 90231-3475
Hot line: (800) 736-9805; famanon@FamiliesAnonymous.org;
www.familiesanonymous.org

Families Anonymous is a twelve-step recovery and support fellowship for family members and friends concerned about a loved one's current, suspected, or past use of drugs, alcohol, or related behavior problems.

Nar-Anon
P.O. Box 2562
Palos Verdes Peninsula, CA 90274
(310) 547-5800

This is a support group for family and friends of addicts based on a twelve-step recovery program.

Narcotics Anonymous
P.O. Box 9999
Van Nuys, CA 91409
(818) 773-9999; www.na.org

This is a nonprofit fellowship of men and women for whom drugs has become a major problem. It is also for recovering addicts who meet regularly to help each other stay clean.

National Clearinghouse for Alcohol and Drug Information
11426-28 Rockville Pike, Suite 200
Rockville, MD 20852
(800) 729-6686; www.health.org

This is a resource for current information and materials concerning alcohol and substance abuse prevention, intervention, and treatment.

National Institute on Alcohol Abuse and Alcoholism
6000 Executive Boulevard—Willco Building
Bethesda, MD 20892-7003
www.niaaa.nih.gov/

National Institute on Drug Abuse
6001 Executive Blvd., Room 5213
Bethesda, MD 20892
(301) 443-1124; www.drugabuse.gov

The mission of the National Institute on Drug Abuse is to support and conduct research across a broad range of disciplines and to ensure the rapid and effective dissemination and use of the results of that research to significantly improve drug abuse and addiction prevention, treatment, and policy.

Partnership for a Drug-Free America
405 Lexington Ave., Suite 1601
New York, NY 10174
(212) 922-1560; www.drugfreeamerica.org

Web Resources

alcoholanddrugabuse.com

This site is filled with information, resources, articles, support groups, stories, and Web links pertaining to substance abuse.

Hazelden Transitions Bookplace
www.htbookplace.org

This site offers a wide selection of books, audiotapes, and videotapes on substance abuse, addiction, prevention, and recovery.

www.amazon.com, www.barnesandnobel.com, or other on-line bookstores

Use the search term "alcoholism intervention" to find available books.

www.cybersober.com

Using the technology of MapQuest, CyberSober.com generates maps and driving instructions to 133,000 Alcoholics Anonymous, Al-Anon, and other twelve-step meetings. Other recovery-related information and on-line meetings are available. A membership fee is required to use these services.

EXPERT CONSULTANTS

Jeff Jay is president of the Terry McGovern Foundation in Washington, D.C. He is a professional interventionist, author, and trainer. His work has appeared on CNN and has been written about in *Parade Magazine* and the *Washington Post*. He is a graduate of the University of Minnesota and a certified addictions professional.

Debra Erickson Jay is a professional interventionist, trainer, and author who specializes in older adult intervention. Her next book focuses on older adults and chemical dependency. She is a former clinician at Hanley-Hazelden Center and a graduate of Ohio State University.

Jeff and Debra Jay are the authors of *Love First: A New Approach to Intervention for Alcoholism and Drug Addiction* (Hazelden, 2000). It can be ordered through their Web site at www.lovefirst.net.

Depression

"One of the most common myths about depression is that talking about it can make a person more prone to experiencing it. This will not happen. No one will become depressed because a loved one says, 'Watch out for signs of depression.'"

Alen J. Salerian, medical director,
Washington Psychiatric Center outpatient clinic

Sarah knew her thirty-two-year-old daughter, Stephanie, had been feeling a bit low lately, but she had no idea just how low until they sat down one day over a cup of tea. "I just don't know if I can keep going," Stephanie said. "I'm so disappointed with the way things have turned out. I thought that by now I would be more successful in my career and have a wonderful husband, but here I am divorced and stuck in a go-nowhere job. I don't think my health is so great either; I have no appetite, and I keep getting these awful headaches. Every day is just as bad as the day before."

Sarah couldn't believe her ears. Stephanie was a successful investment adviser, and Sarah thought she had adjusted very well to her divorce. "How long have you been feeling this way?" Sarah asked. "Oh, I don't know," replied Sarah. "About six months or so, I guess. Now I just don't feel like getting out of bed in the morning. Life stinks." Sarah didn't know what to say next. Why was Stephanie saying these things? How could she cheer her up? Was there anything she could do?

Sarah is not alone in her worries about her daughter. Depression affects more than 17 million Americans of all ages and races. Whether due to biological, environment, or psychological reasons, the numbers of those with depression increase with each generation. Typically, the first episode occurs between the ages of twenty-five and forty-four. Sometimes a stressful life event triggers depression. Sometimes it seems to occur spontaneously, with no identifiable specific cause. Depression may occur as repeated episodes over a lifetime, with periods free of depression in between, or it may be a chronic condition, requiring ongoing treatment over a lifetime. But whatever the trigger or rate of occurrence is, depression is much more than grieving or a bout of "the blues," and it's something you should talk to your adult children about.

This chapter discusses the medical illness of depression, and it sets out guidelines to help you know when your adult children are most at risk. It will also help you talk to them about this disease that they may be too embarrassed or unaware of to talk about.

WHY TALK ABOUT DEPRESSION

Forty-seven-year-old Robert had been feeling down for so long that no one in his family could remember the last time they had seen him smile. "What a shame," says his wife, Edie. "Rob has such a wonderful laugh—real loud and hearty. He could make everyone in the room feel good. But now he makes all of us feel tense and sad. He comes home and yells at one of the kids for something. Then he pours himself a drink and plops himself down in front of the TV. Some nights he'll have dinner with us, but most often he just sits in the living room until he falls asleep. He may or may not make it to bed. Then the next day, he starts all over again. If I try to talk to him about the way he acts, he gets angry and tells me to mind my own business. How much longer can we all go on living like this?"

Edie's description of her husband's life gives us a glimpse at what it's like to live with a severely depressed person. The quality of life is greatly diminished for the depressed person, as well as for everyone close to that person. And as Edie found out, it's not always easy to talk about depression because some people don't have all the facts about this disease. There are many who still hold firmly to these common myths:

- Depression is not a disease; it is an emotional condition caused by personal weakness.
- Depressed people cry all day.
- There is no cure for depression other than a strong will to "get over it."

These myths give you good reasons to talk to your adult children about depression if you suspect they are at risk. You can give them the facts that make it easier for them to seek help. Among the many good reasons to talk to your children about depression, you'll find these at the top of the list:

- Depression is a treatable disease. More than 80 percent of people who receive treatment experience significant improvement.
- Depression is much more than a feeling of sadness. The symptoms can also include nervousness, anxiety, sleep problems, loss of appetite, and physical aches and pains without identifiable cause.
- Depression can be more isolating and socially debilitating than any other chronic illness.
- Depression can be deadly. Untreated depression is the most common cause of suicide in the United States.

- Depression negatively affects all members of the family. The sadness, irritability, nervousness, and anxiety associated with it can be contagious. Other members of the family often find it very difficult to live with a depressed person and soon lose patience and compassion.
- Untreated depression can have a profound effect on physical health by exacerbating all other medical illnesses. It can increase cognitive impairment and intensify pain and other medical symptoms. It can also cause a person to neglect necessary medical care.

All of these reasons boil down to one underlying fact: unless you talk about the disease of depression to your adult children when you see they are at risk, the problem is unlikely to be diagnosed and treated, and the consequences can be severe.

WHEN TO TALK ABOUT DEPRESSION

Beth had changed a lot in the past year. Usually an outgoing person, Beth now wanted to be alone, and she had completely stopped going out socially at all months ago. She was very quiet but never really complained. She had lost weight but didn't seem to notice or care. "When I look back now," says her husband through his tears, "I can see all the classic signs of depression, but I guess I figured she was just going through a bad time and she'd snap out of it. She used to say things like, 'I wish I were dead,' but I never took that seriously. We all feel like that sometimes. If only I could go back and talk to her and really listen to her, maybe things would be different today."

Sadly, it's too late. Beth killed herself by taking an overdose of prescription pain pills before her husband realized how serious her "sadness" really was.

Some people feel that depression is a sensitive subject that's hard to talk about. But as Beth's husband found out, it's even harder to talk about the consequences of untreated depression. In addition to the times when your adult children may broach the subject of depression to you, this section will explain why you should talk about the possibility of depression when:

- You suspect your adult children are at risk
- Your adult children are suffering through a time of loss
- You see the telltale signs and symptoms of depression

Talk When You Suspect Your Adult Children Are at Risk. You should talk to your adult children about depression if they fit any of these risk factors commonly associated with depression:

- *Having a family history of depression.* It has recently been recognized that there is a very strong biological, familial component in most depressions. It is almost as genetic as eye and skin color. If you have a family history of depression, this is a subject you must talk about with your adult children. We all know it's important to pass on information about family medical history to our children, but unfortunately, in some families (often due to family or cultural biases), the fact of a family tendency toward depression is buried and left unspoken. So when a person does become depressed, the problem is aggravated by feelings of personal failure and the "Why me and no one else?" question.

If there is a family history of depression in your family, don't wait until you see signs of depression in your adult children to talk about it. Just as you would forewarn them about the need to be aware of a family history of heart disease or cancer so they can take preventive measures and be alert to signs and symptoms, you should do the same with depression.

- *Being female*. According to the American Medical Association, in the United States, a woman is about twice as likely as a man to be diagnosed with depression. Doctors do not fully understand why they treat more depressed women than men, but there are several theories. Some believe that woman are more susceptible to depression because their bodies experience a constant ebb and flow of hormones during the monthly menstrual cycle. Times of particularly great hormonal change in women are pregnancy, the time immediately after giving birth, and menopause. For many women, these milestones are marked by depressive illness.

- *Being alone*. The rates of major depression are highest among the unhappily married, separated, and divorced.

- *Having a chronic illness or caring for someone who does*. The physical and emotional stress of chronic illness is known to trigger depression in vulnerable individuals.

Talk When You Know Your Adult Child Is Suffering Through a Time of Loss. Life events can cause strong feelings of loss: loss of youth, loss of a career, loss of good health, loss of marriage through divorce, and so on. These losses create a fertile ground for those susceptible to depression. You should be aware of your adult child's feelings during these times of loss and be attentive to signs of depression. Also, be aware that these losses shouldn't be used as an excuse for ignoring depression. Saying, "Getting a divorce has been very difficult for Dan. It's understandable that he is depressed," and then doing nothing is like saying, "His blood sugar is very high, so it's understandable that he has diabetes," and doing nothing about that either. Both are medical illnesses that can and should be treated.

Losses from the past can also surface to cause depression in adulthood. The loss of a parent or significant loved one before the age of eleven may make a person more prone to depression as an adult. People who have gone through other catastrophic losses, survived disasters, or participated in combat during war are also at risk. Losses and other painful experiences themselves probably do not cause the depression, but they may result in a lifelong vulnerability or accentuate a genetic vulnerability.

Talk When You See the Telltale Signs and Symptoms of Depression. A doctor makes a diagnosis of major depression based on certain standard criteria outlined in the *Diagnostic and Statistical Manual of Mental Disorders* (DSM-IV). According to this manual, you should suspect depression if you see at least five of the following symptoms persist nearly every day for at least two weeks and they represent a change from the way the individual has felt or functioned in the past:

1. Depressed mood (feeling sad or empty or seeming sad or tearful)
2. Greatly diminished interest or pleasure in all or almost all activities
3. Significant weight gain or loss without dieting or increased or decreased appetite
4. Sleeping much more or much less than usual
5. Slowing down or speeding up of activity that is observable by others
6. Fatigue or loss of energy
7. Feelings of worthlessness or excessive or inappropriate guilt
8. Diminished ability to think or concentrate, or indecisiveness
9. Recurrent thoughts of death (not just fear of dying), recurrent suicidal thoughts without a specific plan, or a suicide attempt or specific plan for committing suicide

These signs and symptoms give you reason to talk to your adult children about the possibility of depression. But don't jump on this diagnosis without professional medical help; these same signs and symptoms can be the result of physical illness (such as hypothyroidism, diabetes, or heart disease) or abuse of alcohol or drugs.

Many of these symptoms can also be caused by the medications your children may be taking. Many medications that slow the body systems or change body chemistry can cause depression. And in other cases, medications can cause reactions that mimic the symptoms of depression. Medications associated with depressive symptoms include some nonsteroidal anti-inflammatory drugs (used to treat the pain of osteoarthritis, rheumatoid arthritis, and other joint diseases), anabolic steroids (used to treat anemia and advanced breast cancer and abused as performance-enhancing drugs by some athletes), anticonvulsants (such as phenobarbital, used to treat seizures), antihistamines, antihypertensives and cardiac drugs, anti-Parkinson agents, benzodiazepines (used to treat anxiety), corticosteroids (used to treat arthritis, asthma, and cancer, among other conditions), and hormones (like oral contraceptives or hormone replacement therapy). Changing the medication or even the dosage can offer quick remedy.

WHAT YOU SHOULD TALK ABOUT

Talking to your adult children about the signs of depression is sensitive business. Depending on your relationship and the kind of communication you have established over the years, you may or may not get them to open up and talk about their feelings and ask for help. But at the very least, you can talk to them about these three things: your own observations, your concerns, and your desire to help.

Breaking the Ice

When you decide to talk to your adult children about depression, remember that to some people the word *depression* has a stigma attached to it. They believe it is something that crazy people get or not something that strong, independent people get. They may even see depression as a moral failing and have a strong sense that if they would only pull themselves up by the bootstraps, they could overcome this.

For these reasons, when you broach the subject of depression, keep the following advice in mind:

• *Be compassionate.* In theory, of course, you will speak compassionately with a person who is depressed. In practice, it is much harder. A depressed person may not return your telephone calls, may grunt one-syllable answers or talk for hours about pain and problems, may have no interest in doing anything, or may act completely self-absorbed. This is a recipe for anger rather than compassion, but it's important to keep calm. Remind yourself that your adult child has a disease, and her actions are not totally voluntary. Although your efforts may not appear to be appreciated, experts say that social support during times of depression is very important.

• *Be accepting.* It's natural to try to cheer up a depressed person. But when you point out all the good things in life and try to convince a depressed person that he or she really has nothing to be sad about, you tend to trivialize those deep feelings and push the person away. Instead, listen and accept your child's emotions and perceptions as real.

• *Be empathetic.* Don't argue when your child says something that sounds ridiculous to you, like, "I have nothing to live for. Nobody cares about me." Instead, you might say that you understand how hopeless and disappointing life can be at times. Help her express these feelings of despair without being judgmental.

- *Be patient.* Depression is a process that takes time to develop, time to cause alarm, time to understand, and time to resolve. Let your child know that you offer your support no matter how long it takes and that you will always be there when he wants to talk.

- *Choose your words carefully.* When you talk about depression, keep these don'ts in mind:

Don't say, "You're so unhappy because you have a lousy job. Get out of it."

Even if this kind of observation is true, it's not helpful. It puts the blame for the pain of depression on the person. Suppose you have a child who falls off the playground slide and breaks his leg. While the child lies on the ground frightened and in pain, you don't need to point the finger of blame and say, "Your leg is broken because you were reckless." This is the time to offer comfort. Later, when the pain has eased, you can give a lesson on playground safety. It is never a good idea to give advice when someone is hurting, even if your observation is correct. It is offensive to the person in pain.

Don't say, "Cheer up. Things are not so bad."

This demoralizes the person. It's the same as telling someone with a toothache, "Why don't you cheer up and forget about your toothache." If you're the one with the toothache, you won't appreciate or value that advice. You need medical care, not a philosophical lecture. The same is true of someone suffering depression.

Don't say, "Why don't you get out and enjoy life instead of staying in your house all the time?"

This strongly implies that the depression is that person's fault and that she is not doing what she should do to get over it. But the fact is that the brain of a depressed person is not pumping enough neurotransmitter chemicals like serotonin, norepinephrine, and dopamine. If the production of these chemicals is compromised, a person will not feel better no matter how often he gets out of the house.

Addressing Specific Issues

The details of a conversation about depression will depend on your child's willingness to talk about his feelings and physical symptoms. The following section offers some conversation starters on topics commonly related to depression:

- Talk about the facts.
- Talk about the difference between depression and sadness.
- Talk about the symptoms of depression.
- Watch for signs of substance abuse.
- Talk about thoughts of suicide.
- Talk about treatment options.

Talk About the Facts. Depression is a physical disease caused by an imbalance of brain chemicals responsible for transmitting messages about mood and behavior. When these chemicals no longer function effectively, depression may be the result.

You might say, "You don't seem to be yourself anymore. I've noticed that you haven't been keeping up the house, and you've mentioned that you've gotten behind on your bills. I'm wondering if maybe you should talk to your doctor about these things. I've read that several medical conditions like anemia and thyroid disease can affect energy level and make it difficult to do daily activities. I've also read that often a change in the production of certain brain chemicals can cause depression and affect the way we feel and act. With the right prescription medication, these imbalances can be corrected. Maybe you should talk to your doctor about this. What do you think?"

Talk About the Difference Between Depression and Sadness. We all go through periods of feeling sad and frustrated with life experiences, but depression is different. Sadness is usually attached to a specific life event like a loss of a loved one or a financial failure. But depression (sometimes called major depression, major depressive disorder, or clinical depression to distinguish it from ordinary sadness) often does not have a clear cause, and when there is a cause, it persists long after.

It can be very difficult to identify the line that separates sadness from depression. The symptoms of normal grief are not entirely different from those of depression; it is a matter of degree. Although normal grief causes things like appetite and sleep changes, depression may show itself in extremes of behavior: not eating at all or eating too much, not sleeping at all or sleeping too much, complete withdrawal or talking incessantly, being extremely hostile or totally apathetic. If these extremes interfere with a person's life at home, in the workplace, or in social situations and continue for a prolonged time (more than two weeks), it's time to talk about depression and what to do about it.

You might say, "I know it's normal to feel sad occasionally, but I'm worried that your feelings of sadness are lasting such a long time. And I've also noticed that you haven't been eating much lately and don't go out with your friends very often. There's a difference between being sad and having a medical problem that can make you feel this way. Why don't you call your doctor for a checkup this week?"

Talk About the Symptoms of Depression. It's never normal to be depressed. Talk to your adult children if you see any of these typical signs of depression:

- *Unexplained changes in emotional health.* These include feelings of:

  - Emptiness—not sad, not angry, not happy, just empty.
  - Hopelessness—the feeling that there is nothing better in the future. "It doesn't matter; I won't be around much longer anyway."
  - Remorse—getting stuck in the past where things should have been different and life could have been better.
  - Guilt—depression-caused fatigue and listlessness that result in things not getting get done, promises being broken, and appointments being canceled. When this happens, some people feel a strong sense of guilt that translates into, "I'm not good. I don't deserve such a loving family. I always let everybody down."

You might say, "I've noticed that you don't seem to be enjoying life as much as you used to, and I wanted to talk to you about that. What do you think about the way you've been feeling lately?"

- *Unexplained changes in physical health.* Emotional changes are an important clue to the onset of depression, but they are not the only symptoms. In fact, physical changes related to depression may occur before the emotional ones. Typically, watch for unexplained pain, headaches, decreased energy, stomach problems, insomnia or hypersomnia, loss or increase in appetite.

You might say: "I'm worried about you. You've been complaining of so many medical problems that just won't go away. Have you thought about making an appointment with your doctor?"

- *Unexplained changes in cognitive health*. Depression often causes mental cloudiness and confusion. It can show itself as memory loss, language inhibition, difficulty with concentration, diminished learning capacity, and even delusions and hallucinations.

You might say, "I know you're concerned about problems with forgetfulness and memory. Have you made an appointment with your doctor? These symptoms can be caused by medical conditions that can be easily treated."

- *Unexplained behavioral changes*. Depression affects not only how a person feels but how he or she acts as well. Depressed people may withdraw from socializing. They often lose interest in activities they previously loved. They may become irritable and cranky. They may complain about physical ailments that have no observable cause.

You might say, "You used to enjoy visiting with us on Sundays, and I can tell that you really don't anymore. It seems that you feel annoyed all the time, and we're worried about that. I'm wondering if there might be something physically wrong going on that you should get checked out. Would you call your doctor this week and set up a medical exam and some blood tests?"

Watch for Signs of Substance Abuse. Alcohol and drug abuse can be tightly woven into the problem of depression. They can both mask the symptoms of depression and cause them. People who are vulnerable to depression may use alcohol or medication to alter their mood. Consciously or unconsciously, they may use these substances to self-medicate the symptoms of depression. Unfortunately, the physical, social, and psychological problems associated with substance abuse give them more reason to be depressed and bring them further down into the hole of hopelessness, isolation, and sadness. They then feel the need to use more alcohol or medication to pull themselves back up. It's a vicious cycle. If your adult children are abusing alcohol or medication, be sure to read the preceding chapter, "Substance Abuse," and consider that this abuse may be connected to underlying depression.

Talk About Thoughts of Suicide. Thirty thousand people commit suicide every year. This amounts to the number of deaths that would occur if a 747 airline crashed every week. Because these deaths don't happen all at once, they don't catch our attention as the national tragedy they are. But if you have reason to think your adult child may be thinking about suicide, you cannot ignore the issue. Ninety percent of people who commit suicide tell someone about their plans; most are not taken seriously.

Given these frightening statistics, you should not be afraid to talk to your adult children about suicide if they've been dropping hints like, "I'm no use to anyone. I'd be better off dead." Bringing up the subject will not cause someone to become suicidal or push him to carry out his threats. Talking about this subject shows that you take his feelings seriously.

However, don't give a lecture on the value of life to remind the person of all the good things worth living for. Of course, there is a tendency to say, "These should be the best years of your life. Why are you feeling so sad?" When you lecture like this, you imply very strongly that a person has total control over depression. That is not the case. Depression is a biological illness much like diabetes, heart disease, or stroke. Although there are ways we can control our

own mood, we cannot control the course of depression just by willing it away. If you remind your child that he should be happy, he will
feel a greater sense of shame and failure than he is already feeling.

If you suspect your child is suicidal, don't get emotional and
excited. Try to be very matter-of-fact. The best way to know if your
child is thinking of suicide is to ask. Talking about suicidal feelings and plans can actually decrease the risk. Ask direct, caring
questions.

You might say, "Have you thought about dying?"

You might say, "Do you ever think about hurting yourself?"

You might say, "How would you do it? When would you do it? Where
would you do it?"

Talking about these thoughts gives a person an opportunity to
talk through strong fears and negative emotions and in the process
help him feel less alone.

It is often difficult to talk to your own son or daughter about
suicide. They may not be able to talk about the depth of their feelings to you; they may worry that their pain will upset you; they may
on some level hold you responsible for their depression. For these
and many other complex family dynamics reasons, if your child is at
risk for suicide, you should enlist the help of a professional like the
family practitioner, a psychiatrist, or someone at a crisis hot line. If
the situation is severe, bring your child to a hospital emergency
department or call 911.

Talk About Treatment Options. Mild depression may respond well
to at-home therapies. Support from family and friends, opportunities for social activities, exercise, and long talks often help individuals with otherwise good coping skills. But in many cases, depression

does not respond to self-help remedies. In these cases, a thorough physical and mental medical evaluation is necessary. Usually the best place to start an evaluation of depression is with the primary health care provider. Your children are probably comfortable with this person and are more likely to make an appointment and talk freely about their symptoms than they would be if they arrange an evaluation with a psychiatrist or psychologist right off the bat (although a referral to one of these specialists may come later).

It's usually not best for you to take charge and make the appointment for your child. Unless there is reason to suspect the possibility of suicide, it is better to form a partnership with your child that allows you to help and guide while she maintains her dignity and independence.

Emphasize that the first step is an educational opportunity, not treatment.

Instead of saying, "I think you should get psychological treatment." *You might say,* "I'm not an expert, but I've noticed that you've been very sad for quite a while. It might be helpful for you to talk to an expert in this area and find out if there is a problem that needs treatment."
You might say, "What do you think? Do you want to see your doctor about these symptoms? Would you like me to give him a call?"

Although the physician will explain the treatment options if depression is diagnosed, before meeting with the doctor, your adult child may be worried about what will happen. If this is the case, you can explain that there are generally three treatment options:

• *Medication.* Medications for depression alter the action of brain chemicals to improve mood, sleep, appetite, energy levels, and concentration.

- *Psychotherapy*. Talking with a trained therapist can effectively treat some types of depression. Short-term therapies (usually twelve to twenty sessions) focus on the specific symptoms of depression. In addition, some benefit may be gained from cognitive therapy, which aims to help a person recognize and change negative thinking patterns that contribute to depression. Interpersonal therapy focuses on dealing more effectively with other people in the belief that improving relationships can sometimes reduce depressive symptoms.

- *Biological treatments*. Electroconvulsive therapy is an effective treatment that is used in cases of extreme depression. This is an option a mental health professional may recommend when rapid improvement is necessary (to prevent suicide, for example) or when medications have failed. During treatment, anesthesia and muscle relaxant medications protect the person from physical harm or pain. Improved procedures make this treatment much safer than in previous years when the idea of "shock therapy" was very frightening.

IN THE END

Talking to your children about their struggle with depression is a great gift of love, but you have to accept your own limitations when you do this. You can't solve your child's depression. You can't make it go away. You can't even tell them how to make it stop. The most helpful thing you can do for your adult children suffering depression is to offer tolerance, understanding, and compassion. And then direct them to the medical professionals who can help.

RESOURCES

American Psychiatric Association
1400 K St., N.W.
Washington, DC 20005
(202) 682-6220; www.psych.org

American Psychological Association
750 First St., N.E.
Washington, DC 20002
(202) 336-5500; www.apa.org

National Alliance for the Mentally Ill
2101 Wilson Blvd., Suite 302
Arlington, VA 22201
(703) 524-7600; www.naimi.org

National Foundation for Depressive Illness
P.O. Box 2257
New York, NY 10016
(212) 268-4260; www.depression.org

National Institutes of Mental Health
6001 Executive Blvd.
Bethesda, MD 20892
Public inquiries: (301) 443-4513;
nimhinfo@nih.gov; www.nimh.nih.gov

National Mental Health Association
1021 Prince St.
Alexandria, VA 23314
(800) 969-6642; www.nmha.org

EXPERT CONSULTANT

This chapter was written with the expert help of Alen J. Salerian, a renowned psychiatrist serving as medical director of the Washington Psychiatric Center outpatient clinic, Washington, D.C. He is a senior consultant to the FBI and maintains a private practice with numerous government leaders, foreign leaders, foreign royalty, and other prominent Washingtonians as patients. He specializes in depression, behavioral disorders, sexuality issues, relationships, and fear and death.

Physical Domestic Abuse

"If you care about someone, you can't watch that person walk into a dangerous situation or struggle with a circumstance that is harmful. You speak up. But how you talk about the subject of abuse will make all the difference in the outcome."

Noelle C. Nelson, clinical psychologist

Marsha and Pete had joined their daughter, Keri, and her husband at a local restaurant to celebrate the young couple's first wedding anniversary. Since the wedding, Keri rarely visited her parents and often canceled plans at the last minute, so Marsha was especially happy that they were finally together. But by the end of the evening, Marsha had the uneasy feeling that something was very wrong. It was nothing she could put her finger on exactly, but Keri seemed quiet and tense. When her husband complained that his food wasn't prepared the way he liked it, Keri nervously apologized. "I thought that was odd," remembers Marsha. "Her husband always seemed like such a nice guy. Why would he get so angry over the food, and why would Keri act as if it was her fault?" Later, Marsha kissed her daughter goodbye in the parking lot. As she walked off to her car, she turned around for a last look and wave and saw Keri's husband roughly push her into his car. "I can't believe that he would ever hit Keri, but I had a bad feeling about the way they were both acting." The next day, Marsha called Keri and asked if her husband was still angry. Keri quickly explained that he was under a lot of

287

pressure at work, and it was really no big deal. But Marsha still worried and wondered if she should talk about her concerns or keep quiet.

Across town in Anywhere, U.S.A., a shocked mother was sitting at the hospital bedside of her twenty-seven-year-old daughter who was struggling to survive. She had a fractured skull, a broken arm, three broken ribs, a split lip, and a knife wound that had barely missed a major artery. She kept going back over and over incidents in her daughter's relationship with her boyfriend that should have tipped her off that he was a batterer. She remembered the time her daughter argued with him on the telephone when she visited her parents without first getting his "permission." She remembered the time when her daughter planned to attend her father's company golf outing but canceled at the last minute because "Jesse really doesn't want me to go." She remembered little things like the jealousy that her daughter believed was a sign of real love. "Why didn't I talk to her about how I felt? Why didn't I warn her?" regretted her mother now.

These are the stories of two mothers whose daughters' intimate relationships put them in highly dangerous situations. One mother has the opportunity to help her daughter avoid further harm, and the other now has the opportunity to help her daughter get out and stay out of the harmful relationship. Finding the words to do this won't be very easy. Physical domestic abuse (also called battering) is a tough subject to talk about with anyone at any time. Talking to your own adult children about this subject that can seem "shameful" and "humiliating" can be especially difficult. As adults, your children will make their own decisions about whom they want to date and marry. They will probably not tell you about the person's bad temper, or possessive personality, or troublesome cruelty to animals. If you notice these and other worrisome signs on your own, you'll probably feel a strong need to point out the potential for danger—but at the same time fear that you may be meddling or overreacting. Should you say anything at all? Should you wait until your child mentions a problem herself? Should you throw caution to the wind and speak your mind?

This chapter will help you answer these questions. It explores how you might talk to your adult daughter early on when you first notice warning signs that the relationship could turn violent. These are tips for prevention. This is followed by a section that addresses how to talk to your adult daughter when you see the result of physical abuse in bruises, cuts, or broken bones.

The Bureau of Justice has determined that 95 percent of the victims of domestic violence are female. For that reason, this chapter will address talking to adult daughters who are potential or actual victims. However, if you feel your son is being physically abused in his relationship, the advice and suggested dialogues are equally appropriate for that circumstance as well.

WHY TALK ABOUT PHYSICAL DOMESTIC ABUSE

The main reason to talk to your daughter about physical abuse is that you love her and want to keep her safe from harm. But you may hesitate when you see warning signs because if you have never been battered yourself, you may think that domestic violence isn't something that happens to "nice" people. You may have misconceptions about the kind of person who would hurt a woman he loves. The fact is that battering cuts across racial and socioeconomic lines. It occurs in middle-class and upper-class homes, as well as in working-class and poor families. It happens to couples who are married, living together, or just dating. It affects people of all educational backgrounds. The following statistics should help you more clearly see that you have many very good reasons to talk to your daughter about physical domestic abuse:

- In the United States, a woman is more likely to be assaulted, injured, raped, or killed by a male partner than by any other type of assailant.
- An estimated 3 to 4 million American women are battered each year by their husbands or partners.
- The Federal Bureau of Investigation (FBI) reports that 30 percent of female homicide victims are killed by their husbands or boyfriends.
- National Crime Survey data show that once a woman is victimized by domestic violence, her risk of being victimized again is high. In the six months following an incident of domestic violence, approximately 32 percent of women are victimized again.
- More than 1 million abused women seek medical help for injuries caused by battering each year.
- The FBI estimates that only 10 percent of domestic assaults are reported.
- In the United States, three thousand women are killed each year by their husbands, lovers, or boyfriends.

These numbers give you very good reasons to talk to your adult daughter about physical domestic abuse.

WHEN TO TALK ABOUT PHYSICAL DOMESTIC ABUSE

Talking about domestic abuse doesn't have to be a hush-hush subject that comes up only as a desperate last resort. Instead, it can be a subject of general discussion in any household at any time. In fact, it is far better to talk about abuse in general when you have absolutely no reason to suspect anyone close to you is a victim than to wait until there is a need and you decide that someone should say something.

Talk about abuse as you would any other newsworthy topic. When you see a news report about a domestic violence incident, talk about that in casual conversation. When you hear the details of a criminal trial about a domestic homicide, talk about it. This is your opportunity to talk about the warning signs, the characteristics of an abusive personality, and the existence of safety plans when necessary (as explained later in this chapter). Getting this subject out in the open as something the two of you can calmly talk about also sends a message to your daughter: if she should ever become a victim herself, you are someone she can talk to about it.

Of course, you should also talk about physical domestic abuse when you see warning signs that indicate she may be in a dangerous situation. If she is aware of these signs, there are ways that she can prevent herself from becoming a victim.

And finally, you should talk about physical violence when you see the damage for yourself or when your daughter comes to you and tells you that she is being abused. In these cases, it's time for talk and action.

WHAT YOU SHOULD TALK ABOUT

If you speak to your daughter as a caring friend who is concerned, you have a chance to influence her decisions, actions, and ultimate well-being. But if you speak as a protective parent who knows what's best and takes charge and tells the adult child what to do, it's likely you'll make matters worse by putting your daughter in the defensive position of having to protect her batterer and save her own dignity and independence.

Breaking the Ice
When you broach the subject of domestic physical abuse, you have to choose your words carefully. To avoid shutting down the conversation when you talk to your daughter, keep these don'ts in mind:

Don't be self-righteous: "I would never let anyone treat me like that."
Don't be judgmental: "You're making a big mistake, and you're heading down a dangerous road."
Don't be critical: "You always hook up with the wrong guys."
Don't use blame: "You're asking for it if you don't do something to protect yourself."
Don't be dramatic: "I know what I'm talking about. This is the kind of guy who's going to blow your brains out one of these days."

When you talk about any issue involved in physical domestic abuse, speak with love, care, compassion, and respect for your daughter's adulthood. This is not the time to argue or debate.

Addressing Specific Issues
The circumstances and needs of women facing physical domestic violence are unique to each person. This chapter cannot tell you exactly what you should say to your daughter, predict precisely what information she needs, or even presume to know how you can best help her. But in the following sections, you will review some general situational conversation starters that will help you know where to begin and how to proceed. The important thing is that you talk to your daughter so she knows she is not in this alone and let her know you care and are nearby if she needs you. Conversations you might have may focus on:

- What to say to prevent physical abuse
- What to say if you see signs of physical abuse

- What to say if your daughter refuses to leave
- What to say if your daughter wants your help

What to Say to Prevent Physical Abuse. If you have a gut feeling that your daughter may be in an abusive relationship, share your observations. State what you've observed and how you feel; do this somewhat delicately because it's possible your adult child is not aware of the warning signs and has no idea that she is in a potentially dangerous situation. The basic message is this: *I love you. I see this, and it concerns me*. Make a neutral observation, and then leave it alone.

When you mention your concern, your daughter is likely to say something that translates into, "Oh, don't be ridiculous." Expect that. Your goal at this point is to bring up the subject in a neutral (not combative) manner as something for her to think about.

If your child says, "That's crazy!"
You might say, "I know it might seem that way to you. This is just something I've observed, and I wanted to mention it to you as something to think about. That's all."

To help your daughter avoid abusive relationships, you need to know the warning signs. Here are the most common to watch for:

- *An obsessive, whirlwind relationship*. If you see that someone is sweeping your daughter off her feet and monopolizing all her time, that he's someone who says, "I must be with you. I love you. Cancel your other plans and be with me," this is cause for concern. This person may also check up on your daughter, calling your house to see if she really is there. You may hear your daughter constantly apologizing to him for where she has been, whom she has been with, or what she has been doing. If your daughter apologizes to him for her activities and agrees to change her plans and follow his "orders," she shows this person that she is a potential victim.

You might say, "I've noticed that you are spending all your time with your new boyfriend, John. I understand that someone can have very strong feelings for someone right away, but I just want to encourage you to take your time and get to really know him. Some people who are very possessive have the potential to be abusive."

• *Isolation.* If someone is isolating your child from family and friends or if she is losing interest in things that used to be important to her, this is reason to worry. Some potential abusers need to have total control over their partners and can do this best when family and friends are not in the picture.

You might say, "I've noticed that you aren't seeing any of your old friends anymore, and you very rarely visit me. This concerns me because not only do I love you and like to see you occasionally, but also because that is one of the common signs of a possible abusive relationship in the making. It's important for you to maintain your family ties and your friendships. You should be very suspicious of the motives of someone who tries to keep you from seeing other people."

• *Jealousy.* Does your daughter's partner get angry if she smiles at a male friend? Does he like her to stay at home where she won't meet anyone new? Does he accuse her of flirting? Does he check her car mileage or ask his friends to watch her? Your daughter's partner may tell her that jealousy is a sign of love, but she needs to know that it is not. It's a sign of possessiveness and lack of trust.

You might say, "I'm bothered by the way that Kurt seems a bit jealous and possessive. Have you noticed that? Be careful that you don't let his jealousy change the way you live your life."

- *Verbal abuse.* You may hear subtle putdowns at first and then more direct insults. Your daughter's partner may degrade her and put down her accomplishments. This is a systematic way of weakening a person's sense of self-worth. Without a strong sense of self, your daughter will have difficulty recognizing an unhealthy relationship and asserting herself to get out of it.

You might say, "I don't like the way Matt called you stupid in front of all of us. I can only imagine how that made you feel. You should be careful about letting someone chip away at your self-esteem."

- *Dr. Jekyll and Mr. Hyde syndrome.* One of the primary characteristics of abusive individuals is the Dr. Jekyll and Mr. Hyde syndrome. If your daughter has hooked up with this personality, she'll find that he is everything she'd ever hoped for: kind, considerate, and thoughtful. Then in the blink of an eye, this person turns into a monster, and she won't have a clue what happened. She'll rack her brains trying to figure out what went wrong and how she can apologize and make it right. Life with this person is like walking through a minefield; you never know when there's going to be an explosion. These individuals don't get angry; they get enraged. They aren't disappointed; they pout for days. Their mood swings are totally unpredictable. This volatile behavior is very characteristic of abusers.

You might say, "I've noticed that Kent is sometimes moody. Have you noticed that? Does his mood swings take you off-guard? Be careful. Very often people who have the potential to be abusive act like that."

If your daughter won't listen to you and thinks the whole idea is nonsense, at that point all you can do is give her information that she can look into herself if she chooses.

You might say, "If you're interested in knowing more about these warning signs and the personality characteristics of batterers, there are organizations and Web sites that talk about this problem [see the Resources section at the end of this chapter]. I've written some down if you ever want to look it up." (And then just leave the paper behind without asking for any further discussion.)

What to Say When You See Signs of Physical Abuse. Battering is a leading cause of injury to women. Knowing this, you can't be blind to the fact that it could happen to your daughter. But silence and secrecy are the hallmarks of abuse, so you can't wait until you see for yourself an incident of physical battering. It's very unlikely to happen. You should be alert to signs that give you the sense that something is very wrong in the relationship.

These signs include all those mentioned earlier in this chapter, as well as telltale physical signs. Does your daughter have bruises, abrasions, or broken bones without reasonable explanation? Does she say, "Oh, I'm so clumsy; I tripped right over my own two feet." Or, "I don't know why I bruise so easily; the slightest bump, and I end up with a big bruise like this." Or do these physical signs appear more frequently than would be expected in a healthy person? If so, don't hesitate. There's nothing lost by bringing the subject up if your suspicions are wrong, but so very much to gain if your suspicions are correct.

When you talk to your daughter about your fears, keep these tips in mind:

- Ask direct questions about her situation, but gently. Give her time to talk. Ask again a few days later. Don't rush into providing solutions.

- Listen without judging. Often a battered woman believes her abuser's negative messages about herself. She may feel responsible, ashamed, inadequate, and afraid you will judge her.
- Explain that relationship abuse is a crime and that she can seek protection from the police or courts and help from a local domestic violence program.

Once you bring up the subject, your daughter may feel great relief that her secret is out, or she may coolly deny any problem, or she may respond with anger and even rage at the disclosure of her secret. Whatever her reaction is, stay calm and steadfast in your concern and willingness to talk about it any time she would like. Following are a few possible reactions and how you might deal with them.

Shame

If your child says, "I'm so embarrassed. I didn't want you to know about this."

You might say, "There's no reason to be embarrassed; this is not your fault."

You might say, "You are not the only person this has ever happened to. Unfortunately, many women face this problem."

You might say, "I care about you and want to help."

You might say, "Anything you say to me is strictly confidential. I promise I will tell no one."

Confusion About the Term Physical Abuse

If your child says, "He just pushes me around a little. He would never hit me."

You might say, "Just so you know, physical abuse is any kind of physical assault. That can be hitting, pushing, kicking, pulling hair, shoving, slapping, or any other kind of forced physical aggression."

Self-Blame
If your child says, "It's really my fault. I make him so mad."
You might say, "There is nothing you can do to another person that justifies battering. Physical violence in a relationship is never acceptable. It is *not* your fault."

Excuses
If your child says, "He's very tense because of his unemployment [poor health, addiction, childhood upbringing, or some other excuse]."
You might say, "Battering is not *caused* by anything. Violence is a choice made by one person to control another."

If your child says, "He was under a lot of pressure at work. He won't do it any more."
You might say, "There's something you should know about physical abuse. People who are experts in domestic violence say that it tends to get worse and become more frequent with time and that it rarely goes away on its own."

Alcohol or Drug Use
If your child says, "He does it only when he's drunk. It's not really his fault."
You might say, "Injuries to you are more likely to be more serious when he is using alcohol or other drugs. But alcohol and drug addiction do not cause violence. Stopping his drinking will not stop the violence."

What to Say If Your Daughter Refuses to Leave. Katherine knew her daughter's husband beat her quite regularly. It had been a long time since she was able to hide the bruises and abrasions. The cut and swollen lip, the black eye, and the bruised upper arms were now nothing new. Her daughter no longer told tales about falling down the stairs or tripping on a loose rug in the dark. The problem was out in the open, but still she stayed with him. After each new battering, Katherine again asked her to leave, and she again refused. "Why not come home with me just for a while?" her mother pleaded. "Please?" "No, Mom," insisted Kate. "He's really sorry this time. You should have heard him begging me for forgiveness. He was even crying. He's been so kind since this happened. He knows I've had it, and he's promised me that he'll never do it again. I have to give him that chance. He's really sorry."

Katherine couldn't believe her ears. She and Kate had had this exact same conversation a month ago. Doesn't her daughter remember how sorry her husband was back then? Doesn't she remember all the things he always promises her? What is the matter with her?

You too might be totally baffled if your daughter admits that she is a victim of battering but refuses to leave her partner. Unfortunately, this is not at all unusual. The reasons that victims stay with their abusers are so many and complex that your daughter herself may not be able to put a finger on exactly why she can't leave. It is probably due to a mix of situational and emotional factors:

Situational Factors
- Economic dependence
- Fear of greater physical danger to herself and her children if she attempts to leave
- Fear of emotional damage to the children
- Lack of alternative housing
- Lack of job skills
- Fear of involvement in court processes

Emotional Factors
- Fear of loneliness
- Insecurity over potential independence
- Guilt about the failed marriage
- A belief that her husband will change
- Ambivalence and fear over making a major life change

If you believe the violence is escalating and fear for your daughter's safety but she refuses to consider leaving, you might switch tactics if she has children in the house. Talk about the lasting negative effect of domestic violence on the children. Let her know the following facts compiled by the Strengthen Our Sisters Organization:

- Boys who witness domestic violence are more likely to batter their female partners as adults than boys raised in nonviolent homes.
- Of the children who witness domestic abuse, 60 percent of the boys eventually become batterers.
- Fifty percent of men who frequently assault their wives also frequently abuse their children.
- Children from violent homes have a higher risk of alcohol and drug abuse and juvenile delinquency.
- Children in homes where domestic violence occurs may experience cognitive or language problems, developmental delay, stress-related physical ailments (such as headaches, ulcers, and rashes), and hearing and speech problems.

If your daughter feels that her children are "too little" or "old enough" to be untouched by the violence, tell her that children of all ages are deeply affected by domestic violence. Infants exposed to violence may not develop the attachments to their caretakers that are critical to their development; in extreme cases, they may suffer from failure to thrive. Preschool children in violent homes may regress developmentally and suffer sleep disturbances, including nightmares. School-age children who witness violence exhibit a range of problem behaviors, including depression, anxiety, and violence toward peers. Adolescents who have grown up in violent homes are at risk for recreating the abusive relationships they have seen.

What to Say If Your Daughter Wants Your Help. Once you bring up the subject or once your daughter has had enough, she may be open to your help. But unless you're an expert on domestic violence, this probably isn't an area where you can rush in and solve the problem. The most helpful thing you can do is to listen without judgment and help your daughter get the help she needs from those who are trained to handle it. You can also help her take steps to keep herself safe.

You might say, "Relationship abuse is a crime, and just like any other crime, you can seek protection from the police or courts. You can also get help and information from a local domestic violence program. Call the National Domestic Violence Hotline at 1-800-799-SAFE for advice and referrals."

You might say, "I'd like to help you work out a safety plan."

If your daughter is in a violent relationship, one of the most important steps you can take is to help her make a safety plan for both home and the workplace. These plans suggest critical steps your daughter can take to increase her safety. Offer her the following plan recommended by the Family Violence Prevention Fund as a sample of what she can do to protect herself.

Workplace Safety Plan

- Save any threatening e-mails or voice-mail messages. You can use these to take legal action in the future if you choose to. If you already have a restraining order, the message can serve as evidence in court that the order was violated.
- Park close to the entrance of your building, and talk with security, the police, or a manager if you fear an assault at work.
- Have your calls screened, transfer harassing calls to security, or remove your name and number from automated telephone directories.
- Relocate your workspace to a more secure area.
- Obtain a restraining order, and make sure that it is current and on hand at all times. Include the workplace on the order. Provide a copy to the police, your supervisor, the human resource department, the reception area, the legal department, and security.
- Look into alternate hours or work locations.
- Review the safety of your child care arrangements, whether it is on-site child care at the company or off-site elsewhere. If you have a restraining order, it can usually be extended to the child care center.

Personal Safety Plan

- In case you have to flee, have the following available:
  Important papers such as birth certificates, social security cards, insurance information, school and health records, welfare and immigration documents, and divorce or other court documents.
  Credit cards, bank account number, and ATM cards.
  Some money.
  An extra set of keys.

Medications and prescriptions for them.

Telephone numbers and addresses for family, friends, doctors, lawyers, and community agencies.

Clothing and comfort items for you and the children.

- If you had the perpetrator evicted or are living alone, you may want to:

Change the locks on doors and windows.

Install a better security system: window bars, locks, better lighting, smoke detectors, and fire extinguishers.

Teach the children to call the police or family and friends if they are snatched.

Talk to the schools and child care providers about who has permission to pick up the children.

Find a lawyer knowledgeable about family violence to explore custody, visitation, and divorce provisions that protect you and your children.

Obtain a restraining order.

- If you are leaving your abuser, ask yourself the following questions:

How and when can you most safely leave? Where will you go?

Are you comfortable calling the police if you need them?

Who can you trust to tell that you are leaving?

How will you travel safely to and from work or school or to pick up children?

What community and legal resources will help you feel safer? Write down their addresses and telephone numbers, and keep them handy.

Do you know the telephone number of the local shelter?

What custody and visitation provisions will keep you and your children safe?

Is a restraining order a viable option?

- If you are staying with your batterer, think about:
  What works best to keep you safe in an emergency.
  People you can call in a crisis.
  If you would call the police if the violence starts again. Whether
    you can work out a signal with the children or the neigh-
    bors to call the police when you need help.
  Where you would go if you need to flee temporarily. Identify
    several places where you can go in a crisis. Write down the
    addresses and telephone numbers, and keep them with
    you.
  The escape routes if you need to flee your home.

IN THE END

Try not to get frustrated if your daughter stays with her abusive partner or goes back to him. Ending any relationship is a process that
takes time. It's even harder in a violent relationship. But don't give
up or resort to shouting and yelling. Let your daughter know you're
concerned, you're on her side, and you'll be there whenever she
needs your help.

RESOURCES

Help Hot Lines
National Domestic Violence Hotline
(200) 799-SAFE (7233)

National Family Violence Helpline
(800) 222-2000

Organizations
Center for the Prevention of Sexual and Domestic Violence
936 North Thirty-Fourth St., Suite 200
Seattle, WA 98013
(206) 634-1903; www.cpsdv.org

Family Violence Prevention Fund
383 Rhode Island St., Suite 304
San Francisco, CA 94103
(415) 252-8900; www.fvpf.org

National Coalition Against Domestic Violence
P.O. Box 18749
Denver, CO 80218
(303) 839-1852; www.ncadv.org

National Organization for Victim Assistance
1757 Park Road, N.W.
Washington, DC 20010
(202) 232-6682; www.try-nova.org

National Resource Center on Domestic Violence
6400 Flank Dr., Suite 1300
Harrisburg, PA 17112
(800) 537-2238

EXPERT CONSULTANTS

This chapter has been written with the expert help of two women who are very knowledgeable in this field of domestic violence.

Noelle C. Nelson, Ph.D., is a clinical psychologist. Her work as a therapist in Encino, California, and as a trial consultant has brought her in contact with many individuals caught in the pain of domestic violence. She is convinced of the need for a preventive approach that can stop domestic violence before it has a chance to develop. To help achieve that goal, she has written the book *Dangerous Relationships: How to Stop Domestic Violence Before It Stops You* (Insight Books, 1997). Visit her Web site: www.dr.noellenelson.com.

Esta Soler is the executive director of the Family Violence Prevention Fund, which works to end domestic violence and help women and children whose lives are devastated by abuse, because every person has the right to live in a home free of violence. Contact Ms. Soler at (415) 252-8900, or visit her Web site at www.fvpf.org.

Chapter Notes

Alternative Lifestyles
Caplan, M. *When Sons and Daughters Choose Alternative Lifestyles*. Prescott, Ariz.: Hohm Press, 1996.

Your Adult Child's Homosexuality
Just the Facts Coalition. "Just the Facts About Sexual Orientation." [http://pflag.org/schools.] Mar. 19, 2001.

Cohabitation: Yours and Theirs
Casper, L. M., Cohen, P. N., and Simmons, T. "How Does POSSLQ Measure Up? Historical Estimates of Cohabitation." Population Division Working Paper, No. 36. [www.census.gov/population.] May 1999.

Sibling Relationships
Dunn, J., and Kendrick, C. *Siblings: Love, Envy, and Understanding*. Cambridge, Mass.: Harvard University Press, 1982.

Leman, K. *The Birth Order Book: Why You Are the Way You Are*. Ada, Mich.: Fleming H. Revell Co., 1985.

Moving Out
Lugaila, T. "Marital Status and Living Arrangements. March 1998 (Update)." *Current Population Reports*, P20-514. Washington, D.C.: U.S. Census Bureau, Table 7.

Bombeck, E. "Grown Children Refuse to Leave Home Permanently." *Daily Camera* (Boulder, Colo.), Feb. 6, 1981, p. 13.

Your Divorce

Fintushel, N., and Hillard, N. *A Grief Out of Season: When Your Parents Divorce in Your Adult Years*. New York: Little, Brown, 1991.

Your Adult Child's Divorce

National Center for Health Statistics. "Fast Stats A to Z: Divorce." *Monthly Vital Statistics Report*, July 6, 1999. [http://www.cdc.gov/nchs/data/nvs47_21.pdf.]

Financial Ties

Administrative Office of the U.S. Courts. *Bankruptcy Filings Decrease in Fiscal Year 2000*. [www.uscourts.gov.] Nov. 21, 2000.

Substance Abuse

Jay, J., and Jay, D. "Love First: Intervention for Alcoholism and Drug Addiction." [http://lovefirst.net]. n.d.

Jay, J., and Jay, D. *Love First*. Center City, Minn.: Hazelden Foundation, 2000.

Depression

American Medical Association. *Essential Guide to Depression*. New York: Pocket Books, 1998.

American Psychiatric Association. *Diagnostic and Statistical Manual of Mental Disorders, DSM-IV-TR*. Washington, D.C.: American Psychiatric Association, 2000.

Physical Domestic Abuse

Nelson, N. *Dangerous Relationships*. New York: Plenum, 1997.

Strengthen Our Sisters, Inc. "Domestic Violence Statistics." [www.strengthenoursisters.org/statistics.] Feb. 28, 2001.

The Author

Theresa Foy DiGeronimo, from Hawthorne, New Jersey, is an adjunct professor of English at William Paterson University of New Jersey. She is also the author of *How to Talk to Your Senior Parents About Really Important Things* (Jossey-Bass, 2001) and, with Charles E. Schaefer, *How to Talk to Teens About Really Important Things* (Jossey-Bass, 1999) and *How to Talk to Your Kids About Really Important Things* (Jossey-Bass, 1999).

1-º7/06